systemd for Linux SysAdmins

All You Need to Know About the systemd Suite for Linux Users

David Both

Apress®

systemd for Linux SysAdmins: All You Need to Know About the systemd Suite for Linux Users

David Both
Raleigh, NC, USA

ISBN-13 (pbk): 979-8-8688-1327-6 ISBN-13 (electronic): 979-8-8688-1328-3
https://doi.org/10.1007/979-8-8688-1328-3

Copyright © 2025 by David Both

This work is subject to copyright. All rights are reserved by the Publisher, whether the whole or part of the material is concerned, specifically the rights of translation, reprinting, reuse of illustrations, recitation, broadcasting, reproduction on microfilms or in any other physical way, and transmission or information storage and retrieval, electronic adaptation, computer software, or by similar or dissimilar methodology now known or hereafter developed.

Trademarked names, logos, and images may appear in this book. Rather than use a trademark symbol with every occurrence of a trademarked name, logo, or image we use the names, logos, and images only in an editorial fashion and to the benefit of the trademark owner, with no intention of infringement of the trademark.

The use in this publication of trade names, trademarks, service marks, and similar terms, even if they are not identified as such, is not to be taken as an expression of opinion as to whether or not they are subject to proprietary rights.

While the advice and information in this book are believed to be true and accurate at the date of publication, neither the authors nor the editors nor the publisher can accept any legal responsibility for any errors or omissions that may be made. The publisher makes no warranty, express or implied, with respect to the material contained herein.

Managing Director, Apress Media LLC: Welmoed Spahr
Acquisitions Editor: James Robinson-Prior
Editorial Project Manager: Jacob Shmulewitz

Cover image designed by David Both

Distributed to the book trade worldwide by Springer Science+Business Media New York, 1 New York Plaza, New York, NY 10004. Phone 1-800-SPRINGER, fax (201) 348-4505, e-mail orders-ny@springer-sbm.com, or visit www.springeronline.com. Apress Media, LLC is a Delaware LLC and the sole member (owner) is Springer Science + Business Media Finance Inc (SSBM Finance Inc). SSBM Finance Inc is a **Delaware** corporation.

For information on translations, please e-mail booktranslations@springernature.com; for reprint, paperback, or audio rights, please e-mail bookpermissions@springernature.com.

Apress titles may be purchased in bulk for academic, corporate, or promotional use. eBook versions and licenses are also available for most titles. For more information, reference our Print and eBook Bulk Sales web page at http://www.apress.com/bulk-sales.

Any source code or other supplementary material referenced by the author in this book is available to readers on GitHub. For more detailed information, please visit https://www.apress.com/gp/services/source-code.

If disposing of this product, please recycle the paper

For Alice

Table of Contents

About the Author xv

About the Technical Reviewer xvii

Acknowledgments xix

Introduction xxi

Chapter 1: Learning to Love systemd 1

    Objectives 1

    Overview 2

    Linux Boot 2

    systemd Controversy 3

        Why I Prefer SystemV 4

        Why I Prefer systemd 5

        The Real Issue 5

        Replacing SystemV 6

    systemd Tasks 7

    More Data for the Admin 11

    systemd Standardizes Configuration 13

    Architecture 13

    systemd As PID 1 14

    Preparation 20

    Summary 21

    Exercises 22

TABLE OF CONTENTS

Chapter 2: Linux Boot and Startup 23
Objectives 23
Overview 24
Hardware Boot 25
    The Boot Sector 26
Linux Boot 28
    GRUB 28
    The GUID Partition Table 29
    The Kernel 33
Linux Startup 34
    systemd 36
Graphical Login 46
    Display Manager 47
    Window Manager 48
    How Do I Deal with All These Choices? 50
Console Login 57
    Virtual Consoles 59
How Logins Work 61
    CLI Login Screen 63
    GUI Login Screen 64
Summary 65
Exercises 66

Chapter 3: Understanding Linux Startup with systemd 67
Objectives 67
Overview 68
Exploring Linux Startup with systemd 68
Targets 73

TABLE OF CONTENTS

    Exploring the Current Target 76

    Switching to a Different Target 78

    Changing the Default Target 79

Summary 85

Exercises 85

Chapter 4: How to Manage Startup Using systemd 87

Objectives 87

Overview 88

Preparation 88

The Program 89

The Service Unit 90

    Creating the Service Unit 93

    Start the Service 96

    Reboot—Finally 104

    Changing the Sequence 106

    Ensure a Service Starts After the Network Is Running 111

Summary 114

Exercises 115

Chapter 5: Manage systemd Units with systemctl 117

Objectives 117

Overview 117

Preparation 118

systemd Suite 118

    Practical Structure 119

    systemctl 121

    Service Units 128

vii

TABLE OF CONTENTS

    Mounts the Old Way..133

    Creating a Mount Unit..139

Summary...142

Exercises...142

Chapter 6: Control Your Computer Time and Date with systemd......145

Objectives 145

Overview 146

Why Time Is Important to Computers 147

Multiple Times...147

NTP..148

    The NTP Server Hierarchy 149

    NTP Implementation Options 149

    NTP Client Configuration...151

    NTP Server Pools 153

Chrony..154

    Using chronyc from the Command Line 155

    Chronyc As an Interactive Tool..162

systemd-timesync 164

    Configure systemd-timesyncd...169

    Start timesyncd 171

    Set the Hardware Clock 172

    Do You Really Need RTC? 175

Summary...176

Exercises...177

TABLE OF CONTENTS

Chapter 7: Analyzing systemd Calendar and Time Spans 179

Objectives 179

Overview 180

Definitions 180

    Absolute Timestamp 180

    Accuracy 181

    Calendar Event 181

    Time Span 182

    Calendar Event Expressions 182

    Exploring systemd Time Syntax 183

Summary 193

Exercises 193

Chapter 8: Using systemd Timers 195

Objectives 195

Overview 195

System Maintenance Timers 196

Creating a Timer 202

Timer Accuracy 207

Timer Types 210

OnCalendar Event Expressions 212

Superfluous Timers 214

Summary 215

Exercises 216

ix

TABLE OF CONTENTS

Chapter 9: Using systemd Journals 219
Objectives 219
Overview 219
The Journal 221
The systemd Journal Service 224
Configuration 225
About that Binary Data Format… 226
The journalctl Command 229
    Commonly Used Options 238
    Other Interesting Options 240
    Journal Files 242
    Adding Your Own Journal Entries 243
Journal Storage Usage 244
    Journal File Rotation 246
Summary 253
Exercises 253

Chapter 10: Managing the Firewall with firewalld 255
Objectives 255
Introduction 256
    Ports 256
Firewall Rules 259
Firewall Tools 261
Block (Almost) Everything 262
Crunchy on the Outside 263
firewalld 263
    firewalld Zones 264
    Using --reload 288

x

TABLE OF CONTENTS

    Zone Files 289

    Panic Mode 293

    firewall-config GUI 295

nftables 295

Outbound Blocking 297

Fail2Ban 298

Cleanup 302

Summary 302

Exercises 303

Chapter 11: Resource Management with cgroups 305

Objectives 305

Introduction 305

Using cgroups for Process Management 306

Exploring the Cgroup Hierarchy 311

Managing cgroups with systemd 316

Summary 317

Exercises 318

Chapter 12: Using systemd-resolved Name Service 319

Objectives 319

Introduction 320

How a Name Search Works 320

resolv.conf 322

    Historical Usage 323

    Current Usage 324

Name Service Strategies 326

    The /etc/hosts File 326

xi

TABLE OF CONTENTS

    mDNS 329

    nss-DNS...337

    systemd-resolved.service 343

  Fedora Name Resolution Fails When Using systemd-resolved 345

    Determining the Problem 346

    Resolving the Problem...349

    Concluding Thoughts About nsswitch..355

  Summary..356

  Exercises..356

Chapter 13: Replacing rc.local in systemd 357

  Objectives 357

  Introduction..357

    Boot vs. Startup 358

  Local Startup..359

    Create the Executable File...359

    Create the systemd Service 361

    Enable the New Service 363

    Revise mystartup.sh 364

    Final Test 365

  A Temporary Option..367

  Cleanup 368

  Summary..368

  Exercises..368

Chapter 14: Getting More Out of the Journal 371

  Objectives 371

  Introduction..371

  Options to Narrow Search Results 372

TABLE OF CONTENTS

    A Troubleshooting Example 377

    Determining the Problem 377

    First Solution 380

    The Better Solution 383

Summary.. 385

Exercises... 386

Chapter 15: Analyzing systemd Startup and Configuration 387

Objectives 387

Overview 388

Linux Startup... 388

    Basic Analysis.. 389

    The Blame Game 390

    Critical Chain 391

    System State 396

    Analytic Graphs 399

    Conditionals.. 401

Listing Configuration Files 402

Unit File Verification 405

Security... 405

Summary.. 407

Exercises... 408

Chapter 16: Why I Support the systemd Plan to Take Over the World 409

Introduction... 409

More Data for the Admin 411

systemd Standardizes Configuration 416

Sometimes, the Pain 416

xiii

TABLE OF CONTENTS

Five Reasons SysAdmins Love systemd 417
- Boot Management 418
- Log Reviews 419
- Service Management 420
- Timers 422
- Targets 423
- Taking Control with systemd 423

Final Exercise 424

Appendix A: systemd Resources 425

Index 429

About the Author

David Both, SCSA, RHCT, RHCE, is an open source software and Linux advocate, trainer, writer, and speaker. He has been working with Linux and open source software since 1996 and has been working with computers for over 50 years. He is a strong proponent of and evangelist for the *"Linux Philosophy for System Administrators."*

He has taught RHCE classes for Red Hat and has worked at MCI Worldcom, Cisco, and the State of North Carolina. He has taught classes on Linux ranging from Lunch'n'Learns to full five-day courses.

David has written articles for magazines including *Linux Magazine*, *Linux Journal*, and *OS/2 Magazine* back when there was such a thing. David wrote for Opensource.com (OSDC) before it was closed by Red Hat. He now writes for Both.org while working with a core group of OSDC alumni to recreate the community that made OSDC so successful.

David has published eight previous books with Apress, including *The Linux Philosophy for SysAdmins*, August 2018; a three-volume self-study training course, *Using and Administering Linux – Zero to SysAdmin*, released in December 2019; and *Linux for Small Business Owners*, released in late 2022. The second edition of *Using and Administering Linux – Zero to SysAdmin* was released in 2023.

He has found some interesting and unusual ways of problem-solving, including sitting on one computer on which he was working.

About the Technical Reviewer

Seth Kenlon is a UNIX and Linux geek, open source enthusiast, and tabletop gamer. Between gigs in the film industry and the tech industry (not necessarily exclusive of one another), he designs games and hacks on Java and Lua. Visit gopher://ada.info-underground.net:70/1/klaatu or `http://seth.kenlon.com` for more information.

Acknowledgments

First, I need to say a special thanks to my awesome wife, Alice, who has been my head cheerleader. I could not have done this without you, my best friend, my sweetie.

I'd like to thank my editor, James Robinson-Prior, for seeing the need for this book. I'd also like to thank Shobana Srinivasan, Gryffin Winkler, and Jacob Shmulewitz for their efforts in making this book a reality.

I'd also like to thank all the people in production—the ones who take files full of words and produce the finished book in multiple formats. You always make my words look good.

Introduction

Explore the world of systemd, the modern but controversial replacement for init and SystemV init scripts. systemd can evoke a wide range of reactions from SysAdmins and others responsible for keeping Linux systems up and running.

　The fact that systemd is taking over so many system management tasks in modern Linux systems has engendered pushback and discord among some groups of developers and SysAdmins. Yet that wide reach of systemd is the very reason it's so popular with others.

　This book will help you to understand systemd's strengths and weaknesses and why there's no truth in the myth that systemd is a monolithic monstrosity. systemd is the mother of all processes and is also responsible for bringing the Linux host up to a state in which productive work can be done. You'll learn about the functions assumed by systemd, which is far more extensive than the old init program, and how it manages many aspects of a running Linux host, including

- Mounting filesystems
- Managing hardware
- Creating new systemd services and understanding existing ones
- Creating timers that trigger system maintenance events
- Starting and managing the system services that are required to have a productive Linux host

INTRODUCTION

- Using the systemd journal to access critical performance and problem-solving information
- Why the systemd plan to take over the world is actually a good thing

This book introduces you to systemd with an overview and exploration of the controversy surrounding it. We'll cover systemd's major components and how they can provide insight into Linux startup, as well as how to manage the tools and services required to operate and maintain a running Linux computer.

This book will help demystify systemd. You'll learn what it is, what it does, and how to use it to keep Linux systems up and running. You'll explore the major functional components of systemd with real-world examples to illustrate their typical usage. You'll also learn pragmatic workarounds, hints, and tricks to minimize the issues that systemd does have and ensure you have maximized your system's functionality and security.

You'll learn to manage each of the major functional components of systemd and learn from real-world examples to illustrate their typical usage by SysAdmins.

This book is intended for Linux system administrators (SysAdmins) who need to or are already in the process of switching from SystemV to systemd. It's also intended for SysAdmins with more systemd experience but who want to improve their knowledge and skills with systemd.

This book is not for anyone who is not a SysAdmin. If you're only interested in getting your work done and have no interest in what's happening under the covers, if you call upon others to fix your computer when something goes awry, this is not the book for you.

CHAPTER 1

Learning to Love systemd

Objectives

In this chapter, you will learn

- To differentiate the stages of the Linux boot process
- About the controversy surrounding SystemV vs. systemd
- To list the functions of systemd
- Why systemd is an improvement over SystemV startup and init services
- How the SystemV runlevels compare to systemd targets
- The functions of systemd during boot
- The functions of systemd while the system is up and running
- To list the dependencies of systemd targets
- To prepare for the experiments that start in Chapter 2

CHAPTER 1   LEARNING TO LOVE SYSTEMD

Overview

systemd—yes, all lowercase, even at the beginning of a sentence—is the modern replacement for init and SystemV init scripts. It is also much more.

Like most SysAdmins, when I think of the init program and SystemV, I think of Linux startup and shutdown and not really much else, such as managing services once they are up and running. Like init, systemd is the mother of all processes, and it is responsible for bringing the Linux host up to a state in which productive work can be done. Some of the functions assumed by systemd, which is far more extensive than the old init program, are to manage many aspects of a running Linux host, including mounting filesystems, managing hardware, handling timers, and starting and managing the system services that are required to have a productive Linux host.

This chapter provides a brief look at systemd, its features, and functions.

Linux Boot

The complete process that takes a Linux host from an off state to a running state is complex, but it is open and knowable. Before getting into the details, I'll give a quick overview from when the host hardware is turned on until the system is ready for a user to log in. Most of the time, "the boot process" is discussed as a single entity, but that is not accurate. There are, in fact, three major parts to the full boot and startup process:

- **Hardware boot**: UEFI[1] initializes the system hardware.

- **Linux boot**: Loads the Linux kernel and then systemd.

---

[1] UEFI is the Unified Extensible Firmware Interface. It's responsible for initializing the system hardware, locating and loading a boot record, and turning control over to the code in the boot record.

- **Linux startup**: systemd prepares the host for productive work.

The Linux startup sequence begins after the kernel has loaded either init or systemd, depending upon whether the distribution uses the SystemV or systemd startup, respectively. The init and systemd programs start and manage all the other processes and are both known as the "mother of all processes" on their respective systems.

It's important to separate the hardware (BIOS/UEFI) boot from the Linux boot from the Linux startup and to explicitly define the demarcation points between them. Understanding these differences and what part each plays in getting a Linux system to a state where it can be productive makes it possible to manage these processes and better determine where a problem is occurring during what most people refer to as "boot."

The startup process follows the three-step boot process and brings the Linux computer up to an operational state in which it is usable for productive work. The startup process begins when the kernel transfers control of the host to systemd.

systemd Controversy

systemd can evoke a wide range of reactions from SysAdmins and others responsible for keeping Linux systems up and running. The fact that systemd has taken over so many tasks in many Linux systems has engendered pushback and discord among certain groups of developers and SysAdmins.

SystemV and systemd are two different methods of performing the Linux startup sequence. Although most modern Linux distributions use the newer systemd for startup, shutdown, and process management, there are still some that do not. One reason is that some distribution maintainers and some SysAdmins prefer the older SystemV method over the newer systemd.

I think both have advantages.

CHAPTER 1   LEARNING TO LOVE SYSTEMD

Why I Prefer SystemV

I prefer SystemV because it is more traditional. Startup is accomplished using Bash scripts. After the kernel starts the init program, which is a compiled binary, the init program launches the rc.sysinit script, which performs many system initialization tasks. After rc.sysinit completes, init launches the /etc/rc.d/rc script, which in turn starts the various services defined by the SystemV start scripts in the /etc/rc.d/rcX.d, where "X" is the number of the runlevel being started.

Except for the init program itself, all these programs are plain text and easily readable scripts. It is possible to read through these scripts and learn exactly what is taking place during the entire startup process, but I don't think many SysAdmins actually do that. Each start script is numbered so that it starts its intended service in a specific sequence. Services are started serially, and only one service starts at a time.

systemd, developed by Red Hat's Lennart Poettering and Kay Sievers, is a complex system of large, compiled binary executables that are not understandable without access to the source code. It is open source, so "access to the source code" isn't hard, just less convenient. systemd appears to represent a significant refutation of multiple tenets of the Linux philosophy. As a binary, systemd is not directly open for the SysAdmin to view or make easy changes. systemd tries to do everything, such as managing running services while providing significantly more status information than SystemV. It also manages hardware, processes, and groups of processes, filesystem mounts, and much more. systemd is present in almost every aspect of the modern Linux host, making it the one-stop tool for system management. All of this is a clear violation of the tenets that programs should be small and that each program should do one thing and do it well.

Why I Prefer systemd

I prefer systemd as my startup mechanism because it starts as many services as possible in parallel, depending upon the current stage in the startup process. This speeds the overall startup and gets the host system to a login screen faster than SystemV. For example, my primary workstation has 32 CPUs at 3.5GHz and loads faster than some of my other systems with fewer CPUs but faster clock speeds.

systemd manages almost every aspect of a running Linux system. It can manage running services while providing significantly more status information than SystemV. It also manages hardware, processes and groups of processes, filesystem mounts, and much more. systemd is present in almost every aspect of the modern Linux operating system, making it the one-stop tool for system management.

The systemd tools are compiled binaries, but the code is open source. The tool suite is open because all the configuration files are ASCII text files. Startup configuration can be modified through various GUI and command-line tools, as well as adding or modifying various configuration files to suit the needs of the specific local computing environment.

The Real Issue

Did you think I couldn't like both startup systems? I do, and I can work with either one although I seldom encounter a SystemV distribution anymore.

In my opinion, the real issue and the root cause of most of the controversy between SystemV and systemd is that there is no choice on the SysAdmin level. The choice of whether to use SystemV or systemd has already been made by the developers, maintainers, and packagers of the various distributions—but with good reason. Scooping out and replacing an init system, by its extreme, invasive nature, brings with it consequences that would be hard to tackle outside the distribution design process.

CHAPTER 1   LEARNING TO LOVE SYSTEMD

Despite the fact that this choice is made for me, my Linux hosts boot up and work, which is what I usually care the most about. As an end user and even as a SysAdmin, my primary concern is whether I can get my work done, work such as writing my books and this chapter, installing updates, and writing scripts to automate everything. So long as I can do my work, I don't really care about the start sequence used by my distro.

I do care when there is a problem during startup or service management. Regardless of which startup system is used on a host, I know enough to follow the sequence of events to find the failure and fix it.

Replacing SystemV

There have been previous attempts at replacing SystemV with something a bit more modern. For about two releases, Fedora used a thing called Upstart to replace the aging SystemV, but it did not replace init and provided no noticeable changes. Because Upstart provided no significant changes to the issues surrounding SystemV, efforts in this direction were quickly dropped in favor of systemd.

Despite the fact that most Linux developers agree that replacing the old SystemV startup is a good idea, many developers and SysAdmins dislike systemd for that. Rather than rehash all the so-called issues that people have—or had—with systemd, I will refer you to two good, if somewhat old, articles that should cover almost everything. Linus Torvalds, the creator of the Linux kernel, seems disinterested. In a 2014 ZDNet article, "Linus Torvalds and others on Linux's systemd," Linus is clear about his feelings.

> *I don't actually have any particularly strong opinions on systemd itself. I've had issues with some of the core developers that I think are much too cavalier about bugs and compatibility, and I think some of the design details are insane (I dislike the binary logs, for example), but those are details, not big issues.*
>
> —Linux Torvalds, ZDNet, 2014

In case you don't know much about Linus, I can tell you that if he does not like something, he is very outspoken, explicit, and quite clear about that dislike. He has become more socially acceptable in his manner of addressing his dislike about things.

In 2013, Poettering wrote a long blog post in which he debunks the myths about systemd while providing insight into some of the reasons for creating it. This is a very good read, and I highly recommend it.

systemd Tasks

Depending upon the options used during the compile process (which are not considered in this series), systemd can have as many as 69 different binary executables that perform the following tasks, among others:

1. The systemd program runs as PID 1 and provides system startup of as many services in parallel as possible, which, as a side effect, speeds overall startup times. It also manages the shutdown sequence.

2. The systemctl program provides a user interface for service management.

3. Support for SystemV and LSB start scripts is offered for backward compatibility.

4. Service management and reporting provide more service status data than SystemV.

5. systemd standardizes configuration and management of system services.

CHAPTER 1   LEARNING TO LOVE SYSTEMD

6. It includes tools for basic system configuration, such as hostname, date, locale, lists of logged-in users, running containers and virtual machines, system accounts, runtime directories and settings, daemons to manage simple network configuration, network time synchronization, log forwarding, and name resolution.

7. It provides for socket management. Many services are launched when a data stream is directed to a socket for that service.

8. systemd timers provide advanced cron-like capabilities to include running a script at times relative to system boot, systemd startup, the last time the timer was started, and more.

9. It provides a tool to analyze dates and times used in timer specifications.

10. Mounting and unmounting of filesystems with hierarchical awareness allows safer cascading of mounted filesystems.

11. It enables the positive creation and management of temporary files, including deletion.

12. An interface to D-Bus provides the ability to run scripts when devices are plugged in or removed. This allows all devices, whether pluggable or not, to be treated as plug-and-play, which considerably simplifies device handling.

13. Its tool to analyze the startup sequence can be used to locate the services that take the most time.

14. It includes journals for storing system log messages and tools for managing the journals.

Over the years, I have read a lot of articles and posts on the Internet about how systemd is replacing everything and trying to take over everything in Linux. And I agree; it is taking over pretty much everything.

But really not "everything-everything." Just everything in that middle ground of services that lies between the kernel itself and things like the GNU core utilities, GUI desktops, and user applications.

Let's start to explore that by examining the structure of our favorite operating system. Figure 1-1 shows the three basic software layers found in Linux. The bottom is the Linux kernel; the middle layer consists of services that may perform startup tasks such as launching various other services like Network Time Protocol (NTP), Dynamic Host Configuration Protocol (DHCP), Domain Name System (DNS), secure shell (SSH), device management, login services, GETTYs, NetworkManager, journal and log management, logical volume management, printing, kernel module management, local and remote filesystems, sound and video, display management, swap space, system statistics collection, and much more.

CHAPTER 1　LEARNING TO LOVE SYSTEMD

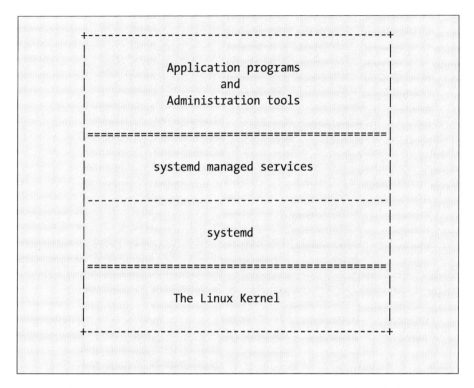

Figure 1-1. *A simple conceptual diagram of systemd and the services it manages with respect to the kernel and application programs such as tools used by the SysAdmin*

It is clear from Figure 1-1 as well as the collective experience as SysAdmins over the last several years that systemd is indeed intended to completely replace the old SystemV init system. But I also know that it significantly extends the capabilities of the init system.

It is also important to recognize that, although Linus Torvalds rewrote the Unix kernel as a hobby—an exercise—he did nothing to change the middle layer of system services and simply recompiled SystemV init to work with his completely new kernel. SystemV is much older than Linux itself and has been much in need of a complete change to something totally new for decades.

So the kernel is new and remains new as it is refreshed frequently through the leadership of Torvalds and the work of thousands of programmers around the planet. There are also tens of thousands of new and powerful application programs at the top layer of Figure 1-1. But until recently there have been no significant enhancements to the init system and management of system services.

Lennart Poettering has done for system services what Linus Torvalds did for the kernel itself. Like Torvalds and the Linux kernel, Poettering has become the leader and arbiter of what happens inside this middle system services layer. And I like what I see.

More Data for the Admin

The new capabilities of systemd include far more status information about services whether running or not. I like having more information about the services I am trying to monitor. For example, let's look at the dhcpd service in Figure 1-2. Were I to use the SystemV command, service dhcpd status, I would simply get a message that the service is running or stopped. Using the systemd command, systemctl status dhcpd, I get much more useful information. The following data is from the main server on my personal network.

CHAPTER 1   LEARNING TO LOVE SYSTEMD

```
[root@yorktown ~]# systemctl status dhcpd
● dhcpd.service - DHCPv4 Server Daemon
     Loaded: loaded (/usr/lib/systemd/system/dhcpd.service; enabled; vendor
             preset: disabled)
     Active: active (running) since Fri 2021-04-09 21:43:41 EDT; 4 days ago
       Docs: man:dhcpd(8)
             man:dhcpd.conf(5)
   Main PID: 1385 (dhcpd)
     Status: "Dispatching packets..."
      Tasks: 1 (limit: 9382)
     Memory: 3.6M
        CPU: 240ms
     CGroup: /system.slice/dhcpd.service
             └─1385 /usr/sbin/dhcpd -f -cf /etc/dhcp/dhcpd.conf -user dhcpd
               -group dhcpd --no-pid

Apr 14 20:51:01 yorktown.both.org dhcpd[1385]: DHCPREQUEST for 192.168.0.7
from e0:d5:5e:a2:de:a4 via eno1
Apr 14 20:51:01 yorktown.both.org dhcpd[1385]: DHCPACK on 192.168.0.7 to
e0:d5:5e:a2:de:a4 via eno1
Apr 14 20:51:14 yorktown.both.org dhcpd[1385]: DHCPREQUEST for 192.168.0.8
from e8:40:f2:3d:0e:a8 via eno1
Apr 14 20:51:14 yorktown.both.org dhcpd[1385]: DHCPACK on 192.168.0.8 to
e8:40:f2:3d:0e:a8 via eno1
<SNIP>
```

Figure 1-2. systemd displays significantly more information about services than the old SystemV

Having all of this information available in a single command is empowering and simplifies the problem determination process for me. I get more information right at the start. I not only see that the service is up and running but some of the most recent log entries as well. The information supplied by this command gives me a more complete picture of how this particular service is faring.

systemd Standardizes Configuration

One of the problems I have had over the years is that, even though "Linux is Linux," not all distributions stored their configuration files in the same places or used the same names or even formats. With the huge numbers of Linux hosts in the world these days, that lack of standardization is a problem. I have also encountered horrible config files and SystemV startup files created by developers who were trying to jump on the Linux bandwagon and had no idea how to create software for Linux and especially not for services that required inclusion in the Linux startup sequence.

The systemd unit files standardize configuration and enforce a startup methodology and organization that provides a level of safety from poorly written SystemV start scripts. They also provide tools the SysAdmin can use to monitor and manage services.

Lennart Poettering wrote a short blog post describing the systemd standard names and locations for common critical configuration files.[2] This standardization makes the SysAdmin's job easier, and it also makes automating administrative tasks easier in environments with multiple Linux distributions. Developers benefit from this standardization as well.

Architecture

Those tasks and more are supported by a number of daemons, control programs, and configuration files. Figure 1-3 shows many of the components that belong to systemd. This is a simplified diagram designed to provide a high-level overview, so it does not include all of the individual programs or files. Nor does it provide any insight into data flow, which is so complex that it would be a useless exercise in the context of this book.

---

[2] Poettering, Lennart, http://0pointer.de/blog/projects/the-new-configuration-files

CHAPTER 1   LEARNING TO LOVE SYSTEMD

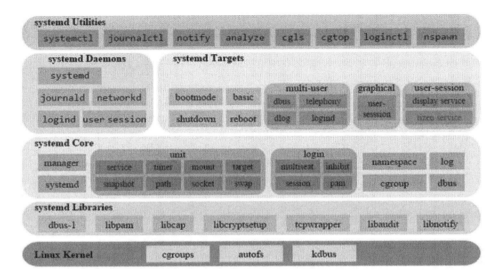

Figure 1-3. Architecture of systemd, by Shmuel Csaba Otto Traian (CC BY-SA 3.0)

A full exposition of systemd would take a book on its own. You do not need to understand the details of how the systemd components in Figure 1-3 fit together; it's enough to know about the programs and components that enable managing various Linux services and deal with log files and journals. But it's clear that systemd is not the monolithic monstrosity it is purported to be by some of its critics.

systemd As PID 1

systemd is PID 1. Some of its functions, which are far more extensive than the old SystemV3 init program, are to manage many aspects of a running Linux host, including mounting filesystems and starting and managing system services required to have a productive Linux host. Any of systemd's tasks that are not related to the startup sequence are outside the scope of this chapter (but some will be explored later in this book).

CHAPTER 1   LEARNING TO LOVE SYSTEMD

First, systemd mounts the filesystems defined by /etc/fstab, including any swap files or partitions. At this point, it can access the configuration files located in /etc, including its own. It uses its configuration link, /etc/systemd/system/default.target, to determine which state or target it should boot the host into. The default.target file is a symbolic link to the true target file. For a desktop workstation, this is typically going to be the graphical. target, which is equivalent to runlevel 5 in SystemV. For a server, the default is more likely to be the multi-user.target, which is like runlevel 3 in SystemV. The emergency.target is similar to single-user mode. Targets and services are systemd units.

Table 1-1 compares the systemd targets with the old SystemV startup runlevels. systemd provides the systemd target aliases for backward compatibility. The target aliases allow scripts—and many SysAdmins—to use SystemV commands like init 3 to change runlevels. Of course, the SystemV commands are forwarded to systemd for interpretation and execution.

Table 1-1. *Comparison of SystemV runlevels with systemd targets and some target aliases*

systemd Targets	Runlevel	Target Aliases	Description
default.target			This target is always aliased with a symbolic link to either multi-user.target or graphical.target. systemd always uses the default.target to start the system. The default.target should never be aliased to halt.target, poweroff.target, or reboot.target.
graphical.target	5	runlevel5.target	Multi-user.target with a GUI.
	4	runlevel4.target	Unused. Runlevel 4 was identical to runlevel 3 in the SystemV world. This target could be created and customized to start local services without changing the default multi-user.target.
multi-user.target	3	runlevel3.target	All services running but command-line interface (CLI) only.
	2	runlevel2.target	Multi-user, without NFS but all other non-GUI services running.
rescue.target	1	runlevel1.target	A basic system including mounting the filesystems with only the most basic services running and a rescue shell on the main console. I find that this target seldom works as it should, so alternate methods are needed.

(*continued*)

CHAPTER 1   LEARNING TO LOVE SYSTEMD

Table 1-1. (*continued*)

systemd Targets	Runlevel	Target Aliases	Description
emergency.target	S		Single-user mode. No services are running; filesystems are not mounted. This is the most basic level of operation with only an emergency shell running on the main console for the user to interact with the system.
halt.target			Halts the system without powering it down.
reboot.target	6	runlevel6.target	Reboot.
poweroff.target	0	runlevel0.target	Halts the system and turns the power off.

Each target has a set of dependencies described in its configuration file. systemd starts the required dependencies, which are the services required to run the Linux host at a specific level of functionality. When all the dependencies listed in the target configuration files are loaded and running, the system is running at that target level. In Table 1-1, the targets with the most system functionality are at the top of the table, with functionality declining toward the bottom of the table.

systemd also looks at the legacy SystemV init directories to see if any startup files exist there. If so, systemd uses them as configuration files to start the services described by the files. The deprecated network service is a good example of one that still uses SystemV startup files in Fedora.

Figure 1-4 is derived from the bootup(7) man page. It shows a map of the general sequence of events during systemd startup and the basic ordering requirements to ensure a successful startup.

CHAPTER 1 LEARNING TO LOVE SYSTEMD

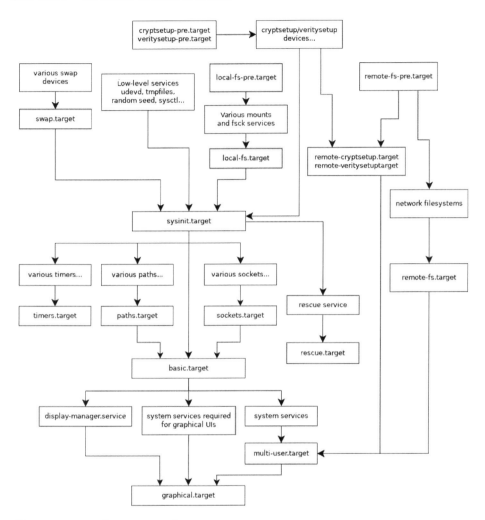

Figure 1-4. The systemd startup map

The sysinit.target and basic.target targets can be considered checkpoints in the startup process. Although one of systemd's design goals is to start system services in parallel, certain services and functional targets must be started before other services and targets can start. These checkpoints cannot be passed until all of the services and targets required by that checkpoint are fulfilled.

The sysinit.target is reached when all of the units it depends on are completed. All of those units, mounting filesystems, setting up swap files, starting udev, setting the random generator seed, initiating low-level services, and setting up cryptographic services (if one or more filesystems are encrypted), must be completed, but, within the sysinit.target, those tasks can be performed in parallel.

The sysinit.target starts up all of the low-level services and units required for the system to be marginally functional and that are required to enable moving onto the basic.target.

After the sysinit.target is fulfilled, systemd then starts all the units required to fulfill the next target. The basic target provides some additional functionality by starting units that are required for all of the next targets. These include setting up things like paths to various executable directories, communication sockets, and timers.

Finally, the user-level targets, multi-user.target or graphical.target, can be initialized. The multi-user.target must be reached before the graphical target dependencies can be met. The underlined targets in Figure 1-4 are the usual startup targets. When one of these targets is reached, startup has completed. If the multi-user.target is the default, then you should see a text-mode login on the console. If graphical.target is the default, then you should see a graphical login; the specific GUI login screen you see depends on your default display manager.

The bootup man page also describes and provides maps of the boot into the initial RAM disk and the systemd shutdown process.

systemd also provides a tool that lists dependencies of a complete startup or for a specified unit. A unit is a controllable systemd resource entity that can range from a specific service, such as httpd or sshd, to timers, mounts, sockets, and more. Try the following command as a non-root user and scroll through the results:

```
$ systemctl list-dependencies graphical.target
```

CHAPTER 1 LEARNING TO LOVE SYSTEMD

Notice that this fully expands the top-level target unit list required to bring the system up to the graphical target run mode. Use the --all option to expand all of the other units as well:

`$ systemctl list-dependencies --all graphical.target`

You can search for strings such as "target," "slice," and "socket" using the search tools of the less command. Try these commands:

`$ systemctl list-dependencies multi-user.target`
`$ systemctl list-dependencies rescue.target`
`$ systemctl list-dependencies local-fs.target`
`$ systemctl list-dependencies dbus.service`

This tool helps me visualize the specifics of the startup dependencies for the host I am working on. Go ahead and spend some time exploring the startup tree for one or more of your Linux hosts. But be careful because the systemctl man page contains this note:

> *Note that this command only lists units currently loaded into memory by the service manager. In particular, this command is not suitable to get a comprehensive list at all reverse dependencies on a specific unit, as it won't list the dependencies declared by units currently not loaded.*
>
> —systemctl man page

Preparation

My best way to learn something new is hands-on. I think most SysAdmins are the same way. We like to do the things we're learning.

Throughout the rest of this book, you'll encounter experiments designed to help you gain that hands-on experience with systemd and its commands. Many of those experiments will be intrusive and inimical to normal operation of a functional system.

I suggest you use a virtual machine with your favorite version of Linux—with systemd, of course—so you can explore it in a safe environment in the event you manage to bork it completely, as I seem to do rather frequently. Your test system needs to have a GUI desktop (such as Xfce, LXDE, GNOME, KDE, or your other favorites) installed.

Take a snapshot of the VM when you get it configured the way you like it, then take snapshots at the end of each chapter. That way, you can always go back as far as necessary.

Summary

Even before getting very deep into systemd, it's obvious that it is both powerful and complex. It is also apparent that systemd is not a single, huge, monolithic, and unknowable binary file. Rather, it is composed of a number of smaller components and sub-commands that are designed to perform specific tasks. Because it's all open source, the source code is available to peruse if you're interested.

systemd has always generated controversy among various groups of Linux developers and SysAdmins. We explored some of the reasons for that rift. Yet I've found things to like about both systemd and SystemV. Although there are Linux distributions that continue to use SystemV init, the complexity of any init service is too great to enable.

We've looked at the functions of systemd and how it differs in scope from SystemV. We've also looked at the much greater amount of information provided to the SysAdmin by systemd than SystemV and the greater level of standardization imposed on services by systemd.

CHAPTER 1   LEARNING TO LOVE SYSTEMD

Exercises

Perform these exercises to complete this chapter:

1. What features do you like about systemd and why?
2. What features do you hate about systemd and why?
3. What is the function of systemd as PID 1?
4. List at least five tasks performed by systemd.
5. How do systemd targets relate to SystemV runlevels?

CHAPTER 2

Linux Boot and Startup

Objectives

In this chapter, you will learn

- The difference between Linux boot and startup
- What happens during the hardware boot sequence
- The functions of and differences between the MBR and GPT
- What happens during the Linux boot sequence
- What happens during the Linux startup sequence
- How to manage and modify the Linux boot and startup sequences
- The function of the display and window managers
- How the login process works for both virtual consoles and a GUI
- What happens when a user logs off

CHAPTER 2   LINUX BOOT AND STARTUP

Overview

This chapter explores the hardware boot sequence, the bootup sequence using the GRUB2 bootloader, and the startup sequence as performed by the systemd initialization system. It covers in detail the sequence of events required to change the state of the computer from off to fully up and running with a user logged in. This knowledge is important to our understanding of systemd's role in the boot and startup of Linux systems.

The complete process that takes a Linux host from an off state to a running state is complex, but it is open and knowable. Before we get into the details, a quick overview of the time the host hardware is turned on until the system is ready for a user to log in will help orient us. Most of the time, we hear about "the boot process" as a single entity, but it is not. There are, in fact, three parts to the complete boot and startup process:

- Hardware boot which initializes the system hardware

- Linux boot in which the GRUB2 bootloader loads the Linux kernel and systemd from a storage drive

- Linux startup in which systemd makes the host ready for productive work

It is important to separate the hardware boot from the Linux boot process from the Linux startup and to explicitly define the demarcation points between them. Understanding these differences and what part each plays in getting a Linux system to a state where it can be productive makes it possible to manage these processes and to better determine the portion in which a problem is occurring during what most people refer to as "boot."

CHAPTER 2　LINUX BOOT AND STARTUP

Hardware Boot

The first step of the Linux boot process really has nothing whatever to do with Linux. This is the hardware portion of the boot process and is the same for any Intel-based operating system.

When power is first applied to the computer, or the VM we have created for this course, it runs the Power On Self-Test (POST) which is part of BIOS or the much newer Unified Extensible Firmware Interface (UEFI). BIOS stands for Basic I/O System, and POST stands for Power On Self-Test. When IBM designed the first PC back in 1981, BIOS was designed to initialize the hardware components. POST is the part of BIOS whose task is to ensure that the computer hardware functioned correctly. If POST fails, the computer may not be usable, and so the boot process does not continue.

Most modern motherboards provide the newer UEFI as a replacement for BIOS. Many motherboards also provide legacy BIOS support, but fewer are now doing so. Both BIOS and UEFI perform the same functions—hardware verification and initialization and loading the bootloader.

BIOS/UEFI POST checks basic operability of the hardware. Then it locates the boot sectors on all attached bootable devices, including rotating HDD or SSD storage devices, DVD or CD ROM, or bootable USB memory sticks. The first boot sector it finds that contains a valid master boot record (MBR)[1] is loaded into RAM, and control is then transferred to the RAM copy of the boot sector.

---

[1] Wikipedia, "Master Boot Record," https://en.wikipedia.org/wiki/Master_boot_record

The BIOS/UEFI user interface can be used to configure the system hardware for things like overclocking, specifying CPU cores as active or inactive, specific devices from which the system might boot, and the sequence in which those devices are to be searched for a bootable boot sector. I do not create or boot from bootable CD or DVD devices anymore. I only use bootable USB thumb drives to boot from external, removable devices.

Because I sometimes do boot from an external USB drive—or in the case of a VM, a bootable ISO image like that of the Live USB device—I always configure my systems to boot first from the external USB device and then from the appropriate internal disk drive. This is not considered secure in most commercial environments, but I do a lot of boots to external USB drives. In most environments, you will want to be more secure and set the host to boot from the internal boot device only. In environments that need to be even more secure, you can use a BIOS password to prevent unauthorized users from accessing BIOS to change the default boot sequence.

Hardware boot ends when the boot sector assumes control of the system.

The Boot Sector

The boot sector is always located in the first sector of the storage device whether HDD or SSD, and it contains the partition table as part of the master boot record (MBR). This MBR partitioning methodology dates back to 1983 and imposes limits on modern storage hardware to less than its full capabilities.

Modern partitioning schemes use the GUID Partition Table[2] (GPT) to overcome those limitations.

In this section, we look very briefly at both MBR and GPT.

---

[2] Wikipedia, "GUID Partition Table," https://en.wikipedia.org/wiki/GUID_Partition_Table. This entry contains an excellent description of the MBR, its problems, and the function and structure of the GPT.

The MBR

The MBR[3] is very small—only 512 bytes. Therefore, the space is very limited and must contain both a tiny bit of code, GRUB stage 1, as well as the partition table for the drive. The partition table defines the partitions that subdivide the space on the storage drive.

The historical MBR is capable of supporting four primary partitions although one partition could be created as a so-called extended partition which supported additional logical partitions so that the space on the drive could be further subdivided. The total disk size supported by the MBR methodology is approximately 2.2 TB (2.2×10^{12}) which is smaller than many storage devices currently available.

The GPT

The GPT is a new, modern standard for disk partition tables. Designed both for much greater disk sizes as well as systemic redundancy, it is larger than the MBR, so it supports much larger storage devices—up to 9.44 zettabytes, 9.44×10^{21}.

GPT uses an MBR in the first sector of the disk although it is used as a protective structure to provide an identifier so that system tools don't see the drive as an empty storage device.

Functional Impact MBR vs. GPT

Most of the time, the difference between MBR and GPT is not relevant to the operation of Linux hosts or the task of problem-solving. The function of both is to partition storage devices into usable chunks and to provide a tiny bit of code to provide a transition between the BIOS/UEFI hardware boot and the main portion of the GRUB bootloader.

---

[3] Wikipedia, "Disk Partitioning – Partition Table," https://en.wikipedia.org/wiki/Disk_partitioning#Partition_table

Using different disk partitioning strategies during the Linux installation can make a difference between whether the Anaconda installer installs an MBR or GPT. Either works with the Linux filesystems typically used today, EXT4, BTRFS, ZFS, and others. The only functional difference is that GPT supports extremely large capacity storage devices. The kinds of devices that—for now—would certainly not be found outside the data center even in large businesses, let alone homes and small to medium businesses.

Linux Boot

The boot sector that is loaded by BIOS is stage 1 of the GRUB[4] bootloader. The Linux boot process itself is composed of multiple stages of GRUB. We consider each stage in this section.

GRUB

The primary function of the GRUB bootloader is to get the Linux kernel loaded into memory and running.

GRUB2 stands for "GRand Unified Bootloader, version 2," and it is now the primary bootloader for most current Linux distributions. GRUB2 is the program which makes the computer just smart enough to find the operating system kernel and load it into memory. Because it is easier to write and say GRUB than GRUB2, I may use the term GRUB in this document, but I will be referring to GRUB2 unless specified otherwise.

GRUB2 provides the same boot functionality as GRUB Legacy, but GRUB2 also provides a mainframe-like command-based pre-OS environment and allows more flexibility during the pre-boot phase. GRUB2 is configured with /boot/grub2/grub.cfg.

---

[4]GNU, *GRUB*, https://www.gnu.org/software/grub/manual/grub

CHAPTER 2   LINUX BOOT AND STARTUP

GRUB has been designed to be compatible with the multiboot specification which allows GRUB to boot many versions of Linux and other free operating systems; it can also chain load the boot record of proprietary operating systems. GRUB can also allow the user to choose to boot from among several different kernels for any given Linux distribution. This affords the ability to boot to a previous kernel version if an updated one fails somehow or is incompatible with an important piece of software. I have used this capability several times over the years.

GRUB can be configured using the /boot/grub/grub.conf file. The configuration of GRUB or GRUB2 and the use of GRUB2 commands are outside the scope of this book. As mentioned in the POST section, at the end of POST, BIOS/UEFI searches the attached disks for a boot record, located in the GPT. BIOS/UEFI loads the first one it finds into memory and then starts execution of the boot record.

The GUID Partition Table

Before going further, let's look at the GUID Partition Table that replaces the legacy MBR partition table. The GUID Partition Table (GPT) shown in Figure 2-1 is a relatively new, modern standard for disk partition tables. GPT is part of the Unified Extensible Firmware Interface (UEFI) specification.

Designed both for much greater disk sizes and systemic redundancy, it is larger than the legacy MBR, so it supports much larger storage devices up to 9.44 zettabytes, or 9.44×10^{21}. The partition table provides pointers to up to 256 partition entries. Each entry defines a partition in the data area of the storage device.

CHAPTER 2   LINUX BOOT AND STARTUP

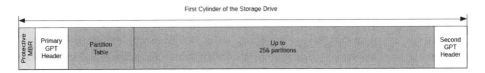

Figure 2-1. *The GUID Partition Table takes the entire first cylinder of the storage device and provides for a large number of partitions*

GPT does use an MBR in the first sector of the disk although it is partially designed as a protective structure to provide an identifier so that system tools that only recognize MBR partitions don't see the drive as an empty storage device. The MBR—whether GPT or legacy version—is the starting point for Linux boot and startup.

You can determine whether a storage device was created with a legacy MBR or GPT by using the **gdisk** command.

EXPERIMENT 2-1: IS MY STORAGE DEVICE GPT?

Let's look at a storage device to determine whether it's formatted MBR or GPT. This experiment must be performed as root.

First, identify your storage devices.

```
# lsblk
NAME                    MAJ:MIN RM   SIZE RO TYPE MOUNTPOINTS
sda                       8:0    0 931.5G  0 disk
└─vg03-Virtual          253:7    0 931.5G  0 lvm  /Virtual
sdb                       8:16   0   2.7T  0 disk
├─vg04-stuff            253:8    0   250G  0 lvm  /stuff
└─vg04-VMArchives       253:9    0   800G  0 lvm  /VMArchives
sdc                       8:32   0   3.6T  0 disk
└─sdc1                    8:33   0   3.6T  0 part
  └─vg_Backups-Backups  253:4    0   3.6T  0 lvm
```

```
sdd                     8:48    0    1.8T   0 disk
└─sdd1                  8:49    0    1.8T   0 part
sr0                     11:0    1   1024M   0 rom
sr1                     11:1    1    668M   0 rom
zram0                  252:0    0      8G   0 disk [SWAP]
nvme0n1                259:0    0  476.9G   0 disk
└─vg02-home            253:2    0    250G   0 lvm  /home
nvme1n1                259:1    0  476.9G   0 disk
├─nvme1n1p1            259:2    0      5G   0 part /boot/efi
├─nvme1n1p2            259:3    0      5G   0 part /boot
└─nvme1n1p3            259:4    0  466.9G   0 part
  ├─vg01-root          253:0    0     10G   0 lvm  /
  ├─vg01-usr           253:1    0     60G   0 lvm  /usr
  ├─vg01-var           253:3    0     50G   0 lvm  /var
  ├─vg01-tmp           253:5    0     15G   0 lvm  /tmp
  └─vg01-ansible       253:6    0     15G   0 lvm  <SNIP>
```

I first selected /dev/nvme0n1. Your device names will probably be different. But this one is good for illustrative purposes. Now use gdisk to determine the device format. Your results will be different from mine.

gdisk /dev/nvme0n1
```
GPT fdisk (gdisk) version 1.0.10

Partition table scan:
  MBR: not present
  BSD: not present
  APM: not present
  GPT: not present

Creating new GPT entries in memory.

Command (? for help):
```

CHAPTER 2   LINUX BOOT AND STARTUP

Notice that the scan shows no known partition tables. That's because this storage device uses logical volume management (LVM) on a raw disk. That means it has no traditional partitions.

```
# gdisk /dev/nvme1n1
GPT fdisk (gdisk) version 1.0.10

Partition table scan:
  MBR: protective
  BSD: not present
  APM: not present
  GPT: present

Found valid GPT with protective MBR; using GPT.

Command (? for help):
```

This storage device I scanned on my primary workstation has a GPT partitioning table scheme. You can see the protective MBR and the GPT line indicates that a GPT partition is present.

One thing to be aware of when scanning drives with gdisk is the instance in which all of the partition table formats show "not present." If that occurs, it is most likely because the storage device is an LVM physical volume (PV).

The GUID MBR contains a small executable image, which is installed from the boot.img file. This boot image is loaded into RAM and locates the core.img file which is the next stage of the boot process. Storage devices that use the legacy MBR and partition table instead of the GUID MBR and partitioning structure can still use GRUB2, but the locations of some files are different. When using the GPT, the core.img file is located in the BIOS boot partition.

The core.img program is smart enough to locate and load the files for the final stage of GRUB. All of the files for GRUB stage 2 are located in the /boot/grub2 directory and several subdirectories. GRUB2 does not have an image file. Instead, it consists mostly of runtime kernel modules that are loaded as needed from the /boot/efi/EFI directory.

The function of GRUB2 stage 2 is to locate and load a Linux kernel into RAM and turn control of the computer over to the kernel. The kernel and its associated files are located in the /boot directory. The kernel files are identifiable as they are all named starting with vmlinuz. You can list the contents of the /boot directory to see the currently installed kernels on your system.

GRUB supports booting from one of a selection of Linux kernels. The Red Hat package manager, DNF, supports keeping multiple versions of the kernel so that if a problem occurs with the newest one, an older version of the kernel can be booted. By default, GRUB provides a pre-boot menu of the installed kernels, including a rescue option and, if configured, a recovery option.

The Kernel

All Linux kernels are in a self-extracting, compressed format to save space. The kernels are located in the /boot directory, along with an initial RAM disk image, and device maps of the hard drives.

After the selected kernel is loaded into memory and begins executing, it must first extract itself from the compressed version of the file before it can perform any useful work. After the kernel has extracted itself, it loads systemd and turns control over to it.

This is the end of the boot process. At this point, the Linux kernel and systemd are running but unable to perform any productive tasks for the end user because nothing else is running.

CHAPTER 2   LINUX BOOT AND STARTUP

Linux Startup

The startup process follows the boot process and brings the Linux computer up to an operational state in which it is usable for productive work. The startup process begins when the kernel takes control of the system.

> **EXPERIMENT 2-2: EXPLORING TEXT MODE STARTUP**
>
> Because of the speed with which Linux boots and the large number of informational messages it emits into the data stream, it is not possible for us mere "humons[5]"[sic] to follow most of it. However, the Linux kernel developers have provided us with an excellent alternative in the dmesg command.
>
> The dmesg command lists all of the startup messages that were displayed on the screen and lets us explore what happens during startup. This includes all kernel messages such as locating memory and devices, as well as the startup of system services performed by systemd.
>
> Perform this experiment as root user.
>
> ```
> [root@testvm1 ~]# dmesg | less
> [    0.000000] Linux version 6.1.7-200.fc37.x86_64 [    0.000000]
>    Linux version 6.11.4-201.fc40.x86_64 (mockbuild@49ea9c9b44
>    de4986ad76c1a7822f2cd3) (gcc (GCC) 14.2.1 20240912 (Red Hat
>    14.2.1-3), GNU ld version 2.41-37.fc40) #1 SMP PREEMPT_DYNAMIC
>    Sun Oct 20 15:04:22 UTC 2024
> [    0.000000] Command line: BOOT_IMAGE=(hd0,gpt2)/vmlinuz-
>    6.11.4-201.fc40.x86_64 root=/dev/mapper/vg01-root ro rd.lvm.
>    lv=vg01/root rd.lvm.lv=vg01/usr selinux=0
> [    0.000000] BIOS-provided physical RAM map:
> ```

---

[5] Refer to *Star Trek: Deep Space Nine (DS9)*.

CHAPTER 2   LINUX BOOT AND STARTUP

[0.000000] BIOS-e820: [mem 0x0000000000000000-0x000000000009fbff] usable
[0.000000] BIOS-e820: [mem 0x000000000009fc00-0x000000000009ffff] reserved
[0.000000] BIOS-e820: [mem 0x00000000000f0000-0x00000000000fffff] reserved
[0.000000] BIOS-e820: [mem 0x0000000000100000-0x00000000dffeffff] usable
[0.000000] BIOS-e820: [mem 0x00000000dfff0000-0x00000000dfffffff] ACPI data
[0.000000] BIOS-e820: [mem 0x00000000fec00000-0x00000000fec00fff] reserved
[0.000000] BIOS-e820: [mem 0x00000000fee00000-0x00000000fee00fff] reserved
[0.000000] BIOS-e820: [mem 0x00000000fffc0000-0x00000000ffffffff] reserved
[0.000000] BIOS-e820: [mem 0x0000000100000000-0x000000021fffffff] usable
[0.000000] NX (Execute Disable) protection: active
[0.000000] APIC: Static calls initialized
[0.000000] SMBIOS 2.5 present.
[0.000000] DMI: innotek GmbH VirtualBox/VirtualBox, BIOS VirtualBox 12/01/2006
[0.000000] DMI: Memory slots populated: 0/0
[0.000000] Hypervisor detected: KVM
[0.000000] kvm-clock: Using msrs 4b564d01 and 4b564d00
[0.000005] kvm-clock: using sched offset of 14727133304 cycles
[0.000012] clocksource: kvm-clock: mask: 0xffffffffffffffff max_cycles: 0x1cd42e4dffb, max_idle_ns: 881590591483 ns
[0.000018] tsc: Detected 2868.906 MHz processor
[0.002686] e820: update [mem 0x00000000-0x00000fff] usable ==> reserved
[0.002696] e820: remove [mem 0x000a0000-0x000fffff] usable
[0.002705] last_pfn = 0x220000 max_arch_pfn = 0x400000000

35

CHAPTER 2   LINUX BOOT AND STARTUP

```
[    0.002811] MTRR map: 5 entries (3 fixed + 2 variable; max 35),
      built from 16 variable MTRRs
[    0.002817] x86/PAT: Configuration [0-7]: WB  WC  UC- UC
      WB  WP  UC- WT
[    0.002941] e820: update [mem 0xe0000000-0xffffffff] usable ==>
      reserved
[    0.002951] last_pfn = 0xe0000 max_arch_pfn = 0x400000000
[    0.019740] found SMP MP-table at [mem 0x0009fbf0-0x0009fbff]
[    0.020703] RAMDISK: [mem 0x33f0e000-0x35f7efff]
<SNIP>
```

The numbers like [0.002696] are the time in nanoseconds (millionths) since the kernel started running.

Page through the data and look for events such as memory initialization, CPU discovery, filesystem mounts, network interface card (NIC) configurations, and any other.

systemd

systemd is the mother of all processes. Its process ID (PID) is always 1. It is responsible for bringing the Linux host up to a state in which productive work can be done. Some of its functions, which are far more extensive than the old SystemV init program, are to manage many aspects of a running Linux host, including mounting filesystems and starting and managing system services required to have a productive Linux host. Any of systemd's tasks that are not related to the startup sequence are outside the scope of this chapter, but we will explore them in later chapters.

   systemd mounts the filesystems as defined by the /etc/fstab file (filesystem table), including any swap files or partitions. At this point, it can access the configuration files located in /etc, including its own. It uses its configuration link, /etc/systemd/system/default.target, to determine

CHAPTER 2 LINUX BOOT AND STARTUP

which state or target into which it should boot the host. The default.target file is a symbolic link—a pointer—to the true target file. For a desktop workstation, this is typically going to be the graphical.target, which is equivalent to runlevel 5 in SystemV. For a server, the default is more likely to be the multi-user.target which is like runlevel 3 in SystemV. The emergency.target is similar to single-user mode. Targets and services are systemd units.

Table 2-1 is a comparison of the systemd targets with the old SystemV startup runlevels. The systemd target aliases are provided by systemd for backward compatibility. The target aliases allow scripts—and many SysAdmins like myself—to use SystemV commands like init 3 to change targets. Of course, the SystemV commands are forwarded to systemd for interpretation and execution.

Table 2-1. *Comparison of SystemV runlevels with systemd targets and some target aliases*

systemd Targets	SystemV Runlevel	Target Aliases	Description
default.target			This target is always aliased with a symbolic link to either multi-user.target or graphical.target. systemd always uses the default.target to start the system. The default.target should never be aliased to halt.target, poweroff.target, or reboot.target.
graphical.target	5	runlevel5.target	Multi-user.target with a GUI.

(*continued*)

37

CHAPTER 2   LINUX BOOT AND STARTUP

Table 2-1. (*continued*)

systemd Targets	SystemV Runlevel	Target Aliases	Description
	4	runlevel4.target	Unused. Runlevel 4 was identical to runlevel 3 in the SystemV world. This target could be created and customized to start local services without changing the default multi-user.target.
multi-user.target	3	runlevel3.target	Multi-user with all services running but command-line interface (CLI) only.
	2	runlevel2.target	Multi-user, without NFS but all other non-GUI services running.
rescue.target	1	runlevel1.target	A basic system including mounting the filesystems with only the most basic services running and a rescue shell on the main console.
emergency.target	S		No services are running; filesystems are not mounted. This is the most basic level of operation with only an emergency shell running on the main console for the user to interact with the system. Single-user mode in SystemV.
halt.target			Halts the system without powering it down.
reboot.target	6	runlevel6.target	Reboot.
poweroff.target	0	runlevel0.target	Halts the system and turns the power off.

Each target has a set of dependencies described in its configuration file. systemd starts the required dependencies. These dependencies are the services required to run the Linux host at a specific level of functionality. When all of the dependencies listed in the target configuration files are loaded and running, the system is running at that target level.

systemd also looks at the legacy SystemV init directories to see if any startup files exist there. If so, systemd uses those as configuration files to start the services described by the files. The deprecated network service is a good example of one of those that still use SystemV startup files in Fedora.

Figure 2-2 is copied directly from the bootup man page.[6] It shows a map of the general sequence of events during systemd startup and the basic ordering requirements to ensure a successful startup.

The sysinit.target and basic.target targets can be considered as checkpoints in the startup process. Although systemd has as one of its design goals to start system services in parallel, there are still certain services and functional targets that must be started before other services and targets can be started. These checkpoints cannot be passed until all of the services and targets required by that checkpoint are fulfilled.

The sysinit.target is reached when all of the units on which it depends are completed. All of those units, mounting filesystems, setting up swap files, starting udev, setting the random generator seed, initiating low-level services, and setting up cryptographic services if one or more filesystems are encrypted, must be completed, but within the sysinit.target those tasks can be performed in parallel.

The sysinit.target starts up all of the low-level services and units required for the system to be marginally functional and that are required to enable moving on to the basic.target.

---

[6] Use the command **man bootup**.

After the sysinit.target is fulfilled, systemd next starts the basic.target, starting all of the units required to fulfill it. The basic target provides some additional functionality by starting units that are required for all of the next targets. These include setting up things like paths to various executable directories, communication sockets, and timers.

Finally, the user-level targets, multi-user.target and graphical.target, are initialized. The multi-user.target must be reached before the graphical target dependencies can be met. The underlined targets in Figure 2-2 are the usual startup targets. When one of these targets is reached, then startup has completed. If the multi-user.target is the default, then you should see a text mode login on the console. If graphical.target is the default, then you should see a graphical login; the specific GUI login screen you see will depend upon the default display manager.

The bootup man page also describes and provides maps of the boot into the initial RAM disk and the systemd shutdown process.

CHAPTER 2 LINUX BOOT AND STARTUP

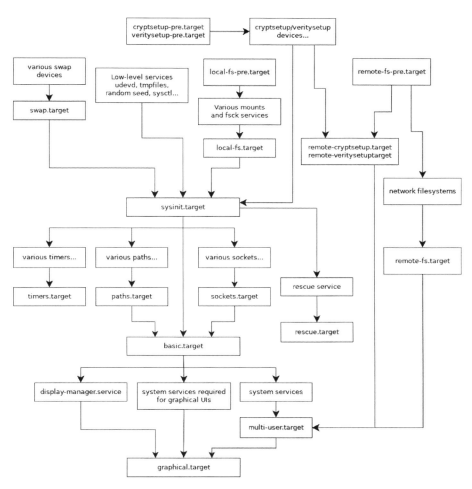

Figure 2-2. *The systemd startup map from the bootup man page*

CHAPTER 2   LINUX BOOT AND STARTUP

EXPERIMENT 2-3: CHANGING THE DEFAULT TARGET

So far, we have only booted to the graphical.target, so let's change the default target to multi-user.target to boot into a console interface rather than a GUI interface.

As the root user on testvm1, change to the directory in which systemd configuration is maintained and do a long listing.

```
[root@testvm1 ~]# cd /etc/systemd/system/ ; ll
total 56
drwxr-xr-x. 2 root root 4096 Nov  5 04:17 basic.target.wants
drwxr-xr-x. 2 root root 4096 Nov  5 04:17 bluetooth.target.wants
lrwxrwxrwx. 1 root root   37 Nov  5 04:17 ctrl-alt-del.target ->
/usr/lib/systemd/system/reboot.target
<SNIP>
lrwxrwxrwx. 1 root root   40 Jan 17 07:39 default.target ->
/usr/lib/systemd/system/graphical.target
drwxr-xr-x. 2 root root 4096 Nov  5 04:18 'dev-virtio\x2dports-
org.qemu.guest_agent.0.device.wants'
lrwxrwxrwx  1 root root   39 Feb  7 16:18 display-manager.
service -> /usr/lib/systemd/system/lightdm.service
drwxr-xr-x. 2 root root 4096 Nov  5 04:17 getty.target.wants
drwxr-xr-x. 2 root root 4096 Jan 17 07:54 graphical.target.wants
drwxr-xr-x. 2 root root 4096 Nov  5 04:18 local-fs.target.wants
drwxr-xr-x. 2 root root 4096 Jan 25 13:52 multi-user.target.wants
drwxr-xr-x. 2 root root 4096 Nov  5 04:17 network-online.
target.wants
drwxr-xr-x. 2 root root 4096 Nov  5 04:18 remote-fs.target.wants
drwxr-xr-x. 2 root root 4096 Nov  5 04:18 sockets.target.wants
drwxr-xr-x. 2 root root 4096 Jan 17 02:53 sysinit.target.wants
drwxr-xr-x. 2 root root 4096 Jan 20 11:28 sysstat.service.wants
drwxr-xr-x. 2 root root 4096 Nov  5 04:18 timers.target.wants
drwxr-xr-x. 2 root root 4096 Nov  5 04:18 vmtoolsd.service.
requires
```

CHAPTER 2 LINUX BOOT AND STARTUP

The default.target entry is a symbolic link to the directory, /lib/systemd/system/graphical.target. List that directory to see what else is there.

[root@testvm1 system]# **ls -l /lib/systemd/system/ | less**

You should see files, directories, and more links in this listing, but look for multi-user.target and graphical.target. Now display the contents of default.target which is a link to the file, /lib/systemd/system/graphical.target. The cat command shows the content of the linked file. You can see that this link provides access to a file that is actually located in a different directory from the PWD—just as if it were in the PWD.

```
[root@testvm1 system]# cat default.target
#  SPDX-License-Identifier: LGPL-2.1+
#
#  This file is part of systemd.
#
#  systemd is free software; you can redistribute it and/or
   modify it
#  under the terms of the GNU Lesser General Public License
   as published by
#  the Free Software Foundation; either version 2.1 of the
   License, or
#  (at your option) any later version.

[Unit]
Description=Graphical Interface
Documentation=man:systemd.special(7)
Requires=multi-user.target
Wants=display-manager.service
Conflicts=rescue.service rescue.target
After=multi-user.target rescue.service rescue.target
display-manager.service
AllowIsolate=yes
[root@testvm1 system]#
```

This link to the graphical.target file now describes all of the prerequisites and needs that the graphical user interface requires. To enable the host to boot to multi-user mode, we need to delete the existing link and then create a new one that points to the correct target. Make pwd /etc/systemd/system if it is not already.

```
# rm -f default.target
# ln -s /lib/systemd/system/multi-user.target default.target
```

List the default.target link to verify that it links to the correct file.

```
# ls -l default.target
lrwxrwxrwx 1 root root 37 Nov 28 16:08 default.target -> /lib/systemd/system/multi-user.target
[root@testvm1 system]#
```

If your link does not look exactly like that, delete it and try again. List the content of the default.target link.

```
[root@testvm1 system]# cat default.target
#  SPDX-License-Identifier: LGPL-2.1+
#
#  This file is part of systemd.
#
#  systemd is free software; you can redistribute it and/or
   modify it
#  under the terms of the GNU Lesser General Public License
   as published by
#  the Free Software Foundation; either version 2.1 of the
   License, or
#  (at your option) any later version.

[Unit]
Description=Multi-User System
Documentation=man:systemd.special(7)
```

```
Requires=basic.target
Conflicts=rescue.service rescue.target
After=basic.target rescue.service rescue.target
AllowIsolate=yes
[root@testvm1 system]#
```

The default.target has different requirements in the [Unit] section. It does not require the graphical display manager.

Reboot. Your VM should boot to the console login for virtual console 1 which is identified on the display as tty1. Now that you know what is necessary to change the default target, change it back to the graphical.target using a command designed for the purpose. Let's first check the current default target.

```
# systemctl get-default
multi-user.target
```

Now change the default target with the command used explicitly for that purpose.

```
# systemctl set-default graphical.target
Removed /etc/systemd/system/default.target.
Created symlink /etc/systemd/system/default.target → /usr/lib/systemd/system/graphical.target.
[root@testvm1 ~]#
```

Having changed the default target using both methods, you now understand the details of what is happening when using the systemctl command. Understanding these details can help you when trying to locate the true source of a problem.

Type the following command to go directly to the display manager login page without having to reboot:

```
# systemctl isolate default.target
```

CHAPTER 2 LINUX BOOT AND STARTUP

I am unsure why the term "isolate" was chosen for this sub-command by the developers of systemd. However, its effect is to switch targets from one target to another, in this case from the emergency target to the graphical target.

The command above is equivalent to the old **init 5** command in the days of SystemV start scripts and the init program.

GRUB and the systemd init system are key components in the boot and startup phases of most modern Linux distributions. These two components work together smoothly to first load the kernel and then to start up all of the system services required to produce a functional GNU/Linux system.

Although I do find both GRUB and systemd more complex than their predecessors, they are also just as easy to learn and manage. The man pages have a great deal of information about systemd, and freedesktop.org has a website that describes the complete startup process,[7] and a complete set of systemd man pages[8] is also online.

Graphical Login

There are still two components that figure into the very end of the boot and startup process for the graphical.target, the display manager (dm) and the window manager (wm). These two programs, regardless of which ones you use on your Linux GUI desktop system, always work closely together to make your GUI login experience smooth and seamless before you even get to your desktop.

---

[7] Freedesktop.org, systemd bootup process, https://www.freedesktop.org/software/systemd/man/bootup.html

[8] Freedesktop.org, systemd index of man pages, https://www.freedesktop.org/software/systemd/man/index.html

CHAPTER 2 LINUX BOOT AND STARTUP

Display Manager

A display manager[9] is a program with the sole function of providing the GUI login screen for Linux. After login to a GUI desktop, the display manager turns control over to the window manager. When you log out of the desktop, the display manager is given control again to display the login screen and wait for another login.

There are several display managers; some are provided with their respective desktops. For example, the gdm display manager is provided with the GNOME desktop. Other display managers are not directly associated with a specific desktop. Any of the display managers can be used for your login screen regardless of which desktop you are using. And not all desktops have their own display managers. Such is the flexibility of Linux and well-written, modular code.

The typical desktops and display manager combinations are shown in Table 2-2. The display manager for the first desktop that is installed, that is, GNOME, KDE, etc., becomes the default one. For Fedora, this is usually gdm which is the GNOME display manager. If GNOME is not installed, then the display manager for the installed desktop is the default. If the desktop selected during installation does not have a default display manager, then gdm is installed and used. If you use KDE as your desktop, the new SDDM[10] is the default display manager.

---

[9] Wikipedia, "X Display Manager," https://en.wikipedia.org/wiki/X_display_manager_(program_type)

[10] Wikipedia, "Simple Desktop Display Manager," https://en.wikipedia.org/wiki/Simple_Desktop_Display_Manager

Table 2-2. *A short list of display managers*

Desktop	Display Manager	Comments
GNOME	gdm	GNOME Display Manager
	lightdm	Lightweight Display Manager
LXDE	lxdm	LXDE Display Manager
KDE	sddm	Simple Desktop Display Manager (Fedora 21 and above)
	xdm	Default X Window System Display Manager

Regardless of which display manager is configured as the default at installation time, later installation of additional desktops does not automatically change the display manager used. If you want to change the display manager, you must do it yourself from the command line. Any display manager can be used, regardless of which window manager and desktop is used.

Window Manager

The function of a window manager[11] is to manage the creation, movement, and destruction of windows on a GUI desktop, including the GUI login screen. The window manager works with the Xwindow[12] system or the newer Wayland[13] to perform these tasks. These graphical subsystems provide all of the primitives and functions needed to generate the graphics for the Linux graphical user interface.

---

[11] Wikipedia, "X Window Manager," https://en.wikipedia.org/wiki/X_window_manager

[12] Wikipedia, "X Window System," https://en.wikipedia.org/wiki/X_Window_System

[13] Wikipedia, "Wayland," https://en.wikipedia.org/wiki/Wayland_(display_server_protocol)

The window manager also controls the appearance of the windows it generates. This includes the functional and decorative aspects of the windows, such as the look of buttons, sliders, window frames, pop-up menus, and more.

As with almost every other component of Linux, there are many different window managers from which to choose. The list in Table 2-3 represents only a sample of the available window managers. Some of these window managers are stand-alone, that is, they are not associated with a desktop and can be used to provide a simple graphical user interface without the more complex, feature-rich, and more resource-intensive overhead of a full desktop environment. Stand-alone window managers should not be used with any of the desktop environments.

Table 2-3. *A short list of window managers*

Desktop	Window Manager	Comments
	Fluxbox	
	FVWM	
	IceWM	
KDE	Kwin	Starting with KDE Plasma 4 in 2008
GNOME	Mutter	Default starting with GNOME 3
LXDE	Openbox	
	twm	A very old and simple tiling window manager. Some distros use it as a fallback in case no other window manager or desktop is available
Xfce	xfwm4	

Most window managers are not directly associated with any specific desktop. In fact, some window managers can be used without any type of desktop software, such as KDE or GNOME, to provide a very minimalist GUI experience for users. Many desktop environments support the use of more than one window manager.

How Do I Deal with All These Choices?

In most modern distributions, the choices are made for you at installation time and are based on your selection of desktops and the preferences of the packagers of your distribution. The desktop, window manager, and the display manager can be easily changed.

Now that systemd has become the standard startup system in many distributions, you can set the preferred display manager in /etc/systemd/system which is where the basic system startup configuration is located. There is a symbolic link (symlink) named display-manager.service that points to one of the display manager service units in /usr/lib/systemd/system. Each installed display manager has a service unit located there. To change the active display manager, remove the existing display-manager.service link and replace it with the one you want to use.

EXPERIMENT 2-4: DISPLAY AND WINDOW MANAGERS

Perform this experiment as root. We will install additional display managers and stand-alone window managers, then switch between them.

Check and see which window managers are already installed. The RPMs in which the window managers are packaged have inconsistent naming, so it is difficult to locate them using a simple DNF search unless you already know their RPM package names which, after a bit of research, I do.

CHAPTER 2   LINUX BOOT AND STARTUP

`dnf list fluxbox fvwm icewm xorg-x11-twm xfwm4`
Last metadata expiration check: 0:19:40 ago on Sun 05 Feb 2023 01:37:32 PM EST.
Installed Packages
xfwm4.x86_64   4.16.1-6.fc37   @anaconda
Available Packages
fluxbox.x86_64   1.3.7-20.fc37   fedora
fvwm.x86_64   2.6.9-8.fc37   fedora
icewm.x86_64   3.3.1-1.fc37   updates

Now let's look at some of the display managers.

`dnf list gdm lightdm lxdm sddm xfdm xorg-x11-xdm`
Last metadata expiration check: 0:20:23 ago on Sun 05 Feb 2023 01:37:32 PM EST.
Installed Packages
lightdm.x86_64   1.32.0-2.fc37   @anaconda
Available Packages
gdm.i686   1:43.0-3.fc37   fedora
gdm.x86_64   1:43.0-3.fc37   fedora
lightdm.i686   1.32.0-2.fc37   fedora
lxdm.x86_64   0.5.3-22.D20220831git2d4ba970.fc37   fedora
sddm.i686   0.19.0^git20221025.fc24321-1.fc37   fedora
sddm.x86_64   0.19.0^git20221025.fc24321-1.fc37   fedora

Each display manager is started as a systemd service, so another way to determine which ones are installed is to check the /usr/lib/systemd/system/ directory. The lightdm display manager shows up twice as installed and available because there was an update for it at the time this task was performed.

`cd /usr/lib/systemd/system/ ; ll *dm.service`
-rw-r--r--. 1 root root 1081 Jul 21 2022 lightdm.service
[root@testvm1 system]#

51

Like my VM, yours should have only a single dm, the lightdm. Let's install lxdm as the additional display manager, with FVWM, fluxbox, and icewm for window managers.

```
# dnf install -y lxdm fvwm fluxbox icewm
```

Now we must restart the display manager service to display the newly installed window managers in the display manager selection tool. The simplest way is to log out of the desktop and restart the dm from a virtual console session.

```
# systemctl restart display-manager.service
```

Or we could do this by switching to the multi-user target and then back to the graphical target. Do this, too, just to see what switching between these targets looks like.

```
# systemctl isolate multi-user.target
# systemctl isolate graphical.target
```

But this second method is a lot more typing. Log out, if necessary, to switch back to the lightdm login on vc1 and look in the upper-right corner of the lightdm login screen. The leftmost icon, which on my VM looks like a sheet of paper with a wrench,[14] allows us to choose the desktop or window manager we want to use before we log in. Click this icon and choose FVWM from the menu in Figure 2-3, then log in.

---

[14] The icon on your version of lightdm might be different. This icon is used to show the currently selected DM, so it will change when you select a different one.

CHAPTER 2　LINUX BOOT AND STARTUP

Figure 2-3. *The lightdm display manager menu now shows the newly installed window managers*

Explore this window manager by using a left-click on the desktop, open an Xterm instance, and locate the menu option that gives access to application programs. Figure 2-4 shows the FVWM desktop (this is not a desktop environment like KDE or GNOME) with an open Xterm instance and a menu tree that is opened with a left-click on the display. A different menu is opened with a right-click.

FVWM is a very basic but usable window manager. Like most window managers, it provides menus to access various functions and a graphical display that supports simple windowing functionality. FVWM also provides multiple windows in which to run programs for some task management capabilities.

Notice that the XDGMenu in Figure 2-4 also contains Xfce applications. The Start Here menu item leads to the FVWM menus that include all of the standard Linux applications that are installed on the host.

CHAPTER 2   LINUX BOOT AND STARTUP

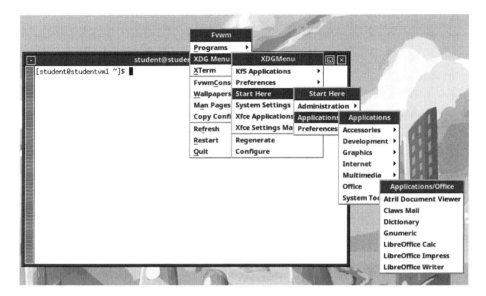

Figure 2-4. *The FVWM window manager with an Xterm instance and some of the available menus*

After spending a bit of time exploring the FVWM interface, log out. Can't find the way to do that? Neither could I as it is very nonintuitive. Left-click the desktop and open the FVWMConsole. Then type in the command **Quit**—yes, with the uppercase Q—and press **Enter**.

We could also open an Xterm session and use the following command which kills all instances of the FVWM window manager belonging to the student user:

`killall fvwm`

Try each of the other window managers, exploring the basic functions of launching applications and a terminal session. When you have finished that, exit whichever window manager you are in and log in again using the Xfce desktop environment.

CHAPTER 2   LINUX BOOT AND STARTUP

Change the display manager to one of the new ones we have installed. Each display manager has the same function, to provide a GUI for login and some configuration such as the desktop environment or window manager to start as the user interface. Change into the /etc/systemd/system/ directory and list the link for the display manager service.

cd /etc/systemd/system/ ; ll display-manager.service
```
total 60
lrwxrwxrwx. 1 root root 39 Nov  5 04:18 display-manager.
service -> /usr/lib/systemd/system/lightdm.service
```

Locate all of the display manager services in the /usr/lib/systemd/system/ directory.

ll /usr/lib/systemd/system/*dm.service
```
-rw-r--r--. 1 root root 1081 Jul 21  2022 /usr/lib/systemd/
system/lightdm.service
-rw-r--r--  1 root root  384 Sep 11 02:19 /usr/lib/systemd/
system/lxdm.service
```

And make the change.

rm -f display-manager.service
ln -s /usr/lib/systemd/system/lxdm.service display-manager.service
ll display-manager.service
```
lrwxrwxrwx 1 root root 36 Feb  5 16:08 display-manager.
service -> /usr/lib/systemd/system/lxdm.service
```

As far as I can tell from my experiments at this point, rebooting the host is the only way to reliably activate the new dm. Go ahead and reboot your VM now to do that. Figure 2-5 shows what the lxdm display manager looks like.

55

CHAPTER 2　LINUX BOOT AND STARTUP

Figure 2-5. *The lxdm display manager looks a bit different from lightdm but performs the same function to allow you to select a window manager and to log in*

Log in using lxdm. Then log out and switch back to the lightdm.

Different distributions and desktops have various means of changing the window manager, but, in general, changing the desktop environment also changes the window manager to the default one for that desktop.

For current releases of Fedora Linux, the desktop environment can be changed on the display manager login screen. If stand-alone display managers are also installed, they also appear in the list with the desktop environments.

There are many different choices for display and window managers available. When you install most modern distributions with any kind of desktop, the choices of which ones to install and activate are usually made by the installation program. For most users, there should never be any need to change these choices. For others who have different needs, or for those who are simply more adventurous, there are many options and combinations from which to choose. With a little research, you can make some interesting changes.

Console Login

Not all Linux systems use or even have a graphical interface installed. Login to these hosts is through the Linux virtual console.

A console is a special terminal because it is the primary terminal connected to a host. It is the terminal at which the system operator would sit to enter commands and perform tasks that were not allowed at other terminals connected the host. The console is also the only terminal on which the host would display system-level error messages when problems occurred.

Figure 2-6 shows Unix developers Ken Thompson and Dennis Ritchie at a DEC computer running Unix. Thompson is sitting at a teletype terminal used as a console to interface with the computer.

CHAPTER 2   LINUX BOOT AND STARTUP

Figure 2-6. *Unix developers Ken Thompson and Dennis Ritchie. Thompson is sitting at a teletype terminal used as a console to interface with a DEC computer running Unix. Peter Hamer— Uploaded by Magnus Manske*

There can be many terminals connected to mainframe and Unix hosts, but only one can act as a console. On most mainframes and Unix hosts, the console was connected through a dedicated connection that was designated specifically for the console. Like Unix, Linux has runlevels, and some of the runlevels such as runlevel 1, single-user mode, and recovery mode are used only for maintenance. In these runlevels, only the console is functional to allow the SysAdmin to interact with the system and perform maintenance.

Note KVM stands for Keyboard, Video, and Mouse, the three devices that most people use to interact with their computers.

On a PC, the physical console is usually the keyboard, monitor (video), and sometimes the mouse (KVM) that are directly attached to the computer. These are the physical devices used to interact with BIOS during the BIOS boot sequence and can be used during the early stages of the Linux boot process to interact with GRUB and choose a different kernel to boot or modify the boot command to boot into a different runlevel.

Because of the close physical connection to the computer of the KVM devices, the SysAdmin must be physically present at this console during the boot process in order to interact with the computer. Remote access is not available to the SysAdmin during the boot process and only becomes available when the SSHD service is up and running.

Virtual Consoles

Modern personal computers and servers that run Linux do not usually have dumb terminals that can be used as a console. Linux typically provides the capability for multiple virtual consoles to allow for multiple logins from a single, standard PC keyboard and monitor. Most Linux distributions usually provide for six or seven virtual consoles for text mode logins. If a graphical interface is used, the first virtual console, vc1, becomes the first graphical (GUI) session after the X Window System (X) starts, and vc7 becomes the second GUI session.

Each virtual console is assigned to a function key corresponding to the console number. So vc1 would be assigned to function key F1 and so on. It is easy to switch to and from these sessions. On a physical computer, you can hold down the **Ctrl+Alt** keys and press **F2** to switch to vc2 as shown in Figure 2-7. Then hold down the **Ctrl+Alt** keys and press **F1** to switch to vc1

CHAPTER 2 LINUX BOOT AND STARTUP

and what is usually the graphical desktop interface. We will cover how to do this on a VM in Experiment 2-5. If there is no GUI running, vc1 will be simply another text console.

```
Fedora 27 (Twenty Seven)
Kernel 4.13.12-300.fc27.x86_64 on an x86_64 (tty2)

testvm1 login: _
```

Figure 2-7. *Login prompt for virtual console 2*

Virtual consoles provide a means to access multiple consoles using a single physical system console, the keyboard, video display, and mouse (KVM). This gives administrators more flexibility to perform system maintenance and problem-solving. There are some other means for additional flexibility, but virtual consoles are always available if you have physical access to the system or directly attached KVM device or some logical KVM extension such as Integrated Lights Out (ILO). Other means such as the screen command might not be available in some environments, and a GUI desktop will probably not be available on most servers.

Using Virtual Consoles

> **EXPERIMENT 2-5: USING VIRTUAL CONSOLES**
>
> For this experiment, you will use one of the virtual consoles to log in to the command line as root. The command line is where you will do most of your work as a system administrator. You will have an opportunity to use a terminal session in the GUI desktop later, but this is what your system will look like if you do not have a GUI.

Press Ctrl+Alt+F2 to access virtual console 2.

Log in to virtual console session 2 as root. Type **root** on the Login line and press the **Enter** key. Type in your root password and press **Enter** again. You should now be logged in and at the command prompt.

Enter a couple simple commands, then enter **exit** to log out of the virtual console.

Although these virtual consoles can be handy in some situations such as recovering from a system crash of some sort, the experiments in this book can all be performed using a GUI terminal emulator on your desktop.

How Logins Work

After a Linux host is turned on, it boots and goes through the startup process. When the startup process is completed, we are presented with a graphical or command-line login screen. Without a login prompt, it is impossible to log in to a Linux host.

systemd manages logins using the systemd-logind.service. This service keeps track of user logins, processes, and idle states. How the login prompt is displayed and how a new one is displayed after a user logs out is the final stage of understanding the Linux startup.

Let's take a quick look at the systemd-logind.service.

CHAPTER 2   LINUX BOOT AND STARTUP

EXPERIMENT 2-6: EXPLORING SYSTEMD-LOGIND.SERVICE

In a root terminal session, view the status of the systemd-logind.service.

```
# systemctl status systemd-logind.service
● systemd-logind.service - User Login Management
     Loaded: loaded (/usr/lib/systemd/system/systemd-logind.
     service; static)
    Drop-In: /usr/lib/systemd/system/systemd-logind.
    service.d
             └─10-grub2-logind-service.conf
             /usr/lib/systemd/system/service.d
             └─10-timeout-abort.conf
     Active: active (running) since Thu 2024-10-24 10:55:38
     EDT; 24h ago
       Docs: man:sd-login(3)
             man:systemd-logind.service(8)
             man:logind.conf(5)
             man:org.freedesktop.login1(5)
   Main PID: 1060 (systemd-logind)
     Status: "Processing requests..."
      Tasks: 1 (limit: 9471)
   FD Store: 0 (limit: 512)
     Memory: 1.8M (peak: 2.3M)
        CPU: 7.484s
     CGroup: /system.slice/systemd-logind.service
             └─1060 /usr/lib/systemd/systemd-logind

Oct 24 10:55:38 testvm1.both.org systemd[1]: Starting
systemd-logind.service - User Login Management...
Oct 24 10:55:38 testvm1.both.org systemd-logind[1060]: New
seat seat0.
```

CHAPTER 2 LINUX BOOT AND STARTUP

```
Oct 24 10:55:38 testvm1.both.org systemd-logind[1060]:
Watching system buttons on /dev/input/event0 (Power Button)
Oct 24 10:55:38 testvm1.both.org systemd-logind[1060]:
Watching system buttons on /dev/input/event1 (Sleep Button)
Oct 24 10:55:38 testvm1.both.org systemd-logind[1060]:
Watching system buttons on /dev/input/event2 (AT Translated
Set 2 keyboard)
Oct 24 10:55:38 testvm1.both.org systemd[1]: Started
systemd-logind.service - User Login Management.
Oct 24 10:55:44 testvm1.both.org systemd-logind[1060]: New
session c1 of user lightdm.
Oct 24 11:20:14 testvm1.both.org systemd-logind[1060]: New
session 2 of user root.
```

CLI Login Screen

The CLI login screen is initiated by a program called a getty, which stands for GEt TTY. The historical function of a getty was to wait for a connection from a remote dumb terminal to come in on a serial communications line. The getty program would spawn the login screen and wait for a login to occur. When the remote user logged in, the getty would terminate, and the default shell for the user account would launch and allow the user to interact with the host on the command line. When the user logged out, the init program would spawn a new getty to listen for the next connection.

We now use an agetty, which is an advanced form of getty, in combination with the systemd service manager to handle the Linux virtual consoles as well as the increasingly rare incoming modem lines. The steps listed below shows the sequence of events in a modern Linux computer:

1. systemd starts the systemd-getty-generator daemon.

2. The systemd-getty-generator spawns an agetty on each of the virtual consoles using the serial-getty@. service.

63

CHAPTER 2   LINUX BOOT AND STARTUP

3. The agettys wait for virtual console connection, that is, the user switching to one of the VCs.

4. The agetty presents the text mode login screen on the display.

5. The user logs in.

6. The default shell specified in /etc/passwd is started.

7. The shell configuration scripts run.

8. The user works in the shell session.

9. The user logs off.

10. If present, the user's logout script runs. For Bash, this is .bash_logout.

11. The systemd-getty-generator spawns an agetty on the logged-out virtual console.

12. Go to step 3.

Starting with step 3, this is a circular process that repeats as long as the host is up and running. New login screens are displayed on a virtual console immediately after the user logs out of the old session.

GUI Login Screen

The GUI login screen as displayed by the display manager is handled in much the same way as the systemd-getty-generator handles the text mode login:

1. The specified display manager (dm) is launched by systemd at the end of the startup sequence.

2. The display manager displays graphical login screen, usually on virtual console 1.

3. The dm waits for a login.

4. The user logs in.

5. The specified window manager is started.

6. The specified desktop GUI, if any, is started.

7. The user performs work in the window manager/desktop.

8. The user logs out.

9. systemd respawns the display manager.

10. Go to step 2.

The steps are almost the same, and the display manager functions as a graphical version of the agetty.

Summary

We have explored the Linux boot and startup processes in some detail. This chapter explored reconfiguration of the GRUB bootloader to display the kernel boot and startup messages as well as to create recovery mode entries, ones that actually work, for the GRUB menu.

We installed and explored some different window managers as an alternative to more complex desktop environments. The desktop environments do depend upon at least one of the window managers for their low-level graphical functions while providing useful, needed, and sometimes fun features. We also discovered how to change the default display manager to provide a different GUI login screen as well as how the GUI and command-line logins work.

This chapter has also introduced some of the systemd tools to perform basic tasks like viewing and changing the default target and restarting a service.

CHAPTER 2   LINUX BOOT AND STARTUP

Exercises

Perform these exercises to complete this chapter:

1. Describe the Linux boot process.

2. Describe the Linux startup process.

3. What does GRUB do?

4. Where is stage 1 of GRUB located on the hard drive?

5. What is the function of systemd during startup?

6. Where are the systemd startup target files and links located?

7. What is the function of an agetty?

8. Describe the function of a display manager.

9. What Linux component attaches to a virtual console and displays the text mode login screen?

10. List and describe the Linux components involved and the sequence of events that take place when a user logs in to a virtual console until they log out.

11. What happens when the display manager service is restarted from a root terminal session on the desktop using the command **systemctl restart display-manager.service**?

CHAPTER 3

Understanding Linux Startup with systemd

Objectives

In this chapter, you will learn

- The files and tools that manage the Linux startup sequence

- How to change the default startup target (runlevel in SystemV terms)

- How to manually switch to a different target without going through a reboot

- To use the systemctl command, which is the primary means of interacting with and sending commands to systemd

- To use journalctl, which provides access to the systemd journals that contain huge amounts of system history data such as kernel and service messages (both informational and error messages)

CHAPTER 3   UNDERSTANDING LINUX STARTUP WITH SYSTEMD

Overview

systemd's startup provides important clues to help you solve problems when they occur. In this chapter, we'll start exploring the files and tools that manage the Linux startup sequence. We'll explore the systemd startup sequence, how to change the default startup target (runlevel in SystemV terms), and how to manually switch to a different target without going through a reboot.

We'll also look at two important systemd tools. The first is the systemctl command, which is the primary means of interacting with and sending commands to systemd. The second is journalctl, which provides access to the systemd journals that contain huge amounts of system history data such as kernel and service messages (both informational and error messages).

Be sure to use a non-production system or VM for testing and experimentation. Your test system needs to have a GUI desktop (such as Xfce, LXDE, GNOME, KDE, or another) installed.

Exploring Linux Startup with systemd

Before you can observe the startup sequence, you need to do a couple of things to make the boot and startup sequences open and visible. Normally, most distributions use a startup animation or splash screen to hide the detailed messages that would otherwise be displayed during a Linux host's startup and shutdown. This is called the Plymouth boot screen on Red Hat–based distros. Those hidden messages can provide a great deal of information about startup and shutdown to a SysAdmin looking for information to troubleshoot a bug or to just learn about the startup sequence. You can change this using the GRUB (Grand Unified Bootloader) configuration.

CHAPTER 3 UNDERSTANDING LINUX STARTUP WITH SYSTEMD

EXPERIMENT 3-1: MODIFY GRUB TO SHOW STARTUP MESSAGES

The main GRUB configuration file is /boot/grub2/grub.cfg, but, because this file can be overwritten when the kernel version is updated, you do not want to change it. Instead, modify the /etc/default/grub file, which is used to modify the default settings of grub.cfg.

Start by looking at the current, unmodified version of the /etc/default/grub file. Note that the three lines starting with the GRUB_CMDLINE_LINUX line is wrapped in the listing shown here.

```
[root@testvm1 default]# cd /etc/default ; cat grub
GRUB_TIMEOUT=5
GRUB_DISTRIBUTOR="$(sed 's, release .*$,,g' /etc/system-
release)"
GRUB_DEFAULT=saved
GRUB_DISABLE_SUBMENU=true
GRUB_TERMINAL_OUTPUT="console"
GRUB_CMDLINE_LINUX="resume=/dev/mapper/fedora_testvm1-swap
\ rd.lvm.lv=fedora_testvm1/root rd.lvm.lv=fedora_testvm1/
swap \ rd.lvm.lv=fedora_testvm1/usr rhgb quiet"
GRUB_DISABLE_RECOVERY="true"
[root@testvm1 default]#
```

Chapter 6 of the GRUB documentation contains a list of all the possible entries in the /etc/default/grub file, but I focus on the following two items:

• Change GRUB_TIMEOUT, the number of seconds for the GRUB menu countdown, from five to ten to give a bit more time to respond to the GRUB bootup menu before the countdown hits zero.

CHAPTER 3 UNDERSTANDING LINUX STARTUP WITH SYSTEMD

- Delete the last two parameters on GRUB_CMDLINE_LINUX, which lists the command-line parameters that are passed to the kernel at boot time.

One of these parameters, rhgb, stands for Red Hat Graphical Boot, and it displays the little Fedora icon animation during the kernel initialization instead of showing boot-time messages. The other, the quiet parameter, prevents displaying the startup messages that document the progress of the startup and any errors that occur. I delete both rhgb and quiet because SysAdmins need to see these messages. If something goes wrong during boot, the messages displayed on the screen can point to the cause of the problem.

After you make these changes, your GRUB file will look like this:

```
[root@testvm1 default]# cat grub
GRUB_TIMEOUT=10
GRUB_DISTRIBUTOR="$(sed 's, release .*$,,g' /etc/system-release)"
GRUB_DEFAULT=saved
GRUB_DISABLE_SUBMENU=true
GRUB_TERMINAL_OUTPUT="console"
GRUB_CMDLINE_LINUX="rd.lvm.lv=vg01/root rd.lvm.lv=vg01/usr selinux=0"
GRUB_DISABLE_RECOVERY="false"
[root@testvm1 default]#
```

The grub2-mkconfig program generates the grub.cfg configuration file using the contents of the /etc/default/grub file to modify some of the default GRUB settings. The grub2-mkconfig program sends its output to STDOUT. It has a -o option that allows you to specify a file to send the data stream to, but it is just as easy to use redirection. Run the following command to update the /boot/grub2/grub.cfg configuration file:

```
# grub2-mkconfig > /boot/grub2/grub.cfg
```

CHAPTER 3   UNDERSTANDING LINUX STARTUP WITH SYSTEMD

Reboot your test system to view the startup messages that would otherwise be hidden behind the Plymouth boot animation. But what if you need to view the startup messages and have not disabled the Plymouth boot animation? Or you have, but the messages stream by too fast to read? (Which they do.)

There are a couple of options, and both involve log files and systemd journals—which are your friends. You can use the less command to view the contents of the /var/log/messages file. This file contains boot and startup messages as well as messages generated by the operating system during normal operation. You can also use the **journalctl** command without any options to view the systemd journal, which contains essentially the same information:

journalctl
<SNIP>
Oct 20 18:13:45 david.both.org kernel: Linux version 6.11.3-200.fc40.x86_64 (mockbuild@4786ea1e4860458caf0f0f3344c01d01) (gcc (GCC) 14.2.1 2024>
Oct 20 18:13:45 david.both.org kernel: Command line: BOOT_IMAGE=(hd9,gpt2)/vmlinuz-6.11.3-200.fc40.x86_64 root=/dev/mapper/vg01-root ro rd.lvm.>
Oct 20 18:13:45 david.both.org kernel: BIOS-provided physical RAM map:
Oct 20 18:13:45 david.both.org kernel: BIOS-e820: [mem 0x0000000000000000-0x000000000009ffff] usable
Oct 20 18:13:45 david.both.org kernel: BIOS-e820: [mem 0x00000000000a0000-0x00000000000fffff] reserved
Oct 20 18:13:45 david.both.org kernel: BIOS-e820: [mem 0x0000000000100000-0x000000003bc91fff] usable
<SNIP>
Oct 20 18:13:45 david.both.org kernel: BIOS-e820: [mem 0x00000000fed00000-0x00000000fed00fff] reserved
Oct 20 18:13:45 david.both.org kernel: BIOS-e820: [mem 0x00000000fee00000-

CHAPTER 3   UNDERSTANDING LINUX STARTUP WITH SYSTEMD

```
Oct 20 18:13:45 david.both.org kernel: e820: update [mem
0x32bc8018-0x32bd8e57] usable ==> usable
Oct 20 18:13:45 david.both.org kernel: e820: update [mem
0x32baa018-0x32bc7257] usable ==> usable
Oct 20 18:13:45 david.both.org kernel: extended physical
RAM map:
Oct 20 18:13:45 david.both.org kernel: reserve setup_data:
[mem 0x0000000000000000-0x000000000009ffff] usable
<SNIP>
Oct 20 18:13:45 david.both.org kernel: tcp_listen_
portaddr_hash hash table entries: 32768 (order: 7, 524288
bytes, linear)
Oct 20 18:13:45 david.both.org kernel: Table-perturb hash
table entries: 65536 (order: 6, 262144 bytes, linear)
Oct 20 18:13:45 david.both.org kernel: TCP established hash
table entries: 524288 (order: 10, 4194304 bytes, linear)
Oct 20 18:13:45 david.both.org kernel: TCP bind hash table
entries: 65536 (order: 9, 2097152 bytes, linear)
Oct 20 18:13:45 david.both.org kernel: TCP: Hash tables
configured (established 524288 bind 65536)
<SNIP>
```

I truncated this data stream because it can be hundreds of thousands or even millions of lines long. (The journal listing on my primary workstation is 1,399,459 lines long.) Explore this journal data on your test system because it contains a lot of information that can be very useful when doing problem determination. Knowing what this data looks like for a normal boot and startup can help you locate problems when they occur.

We'll explore more of the systemd journals, the journalctl command, and how to sort through the data stream to find what you want in more detail as we proceed through this book.

After GRUB loads the kernel into memory, it must first extract itself from the compressed version of the file before it can perform any useful work. After the kernel has extracted itself and started running, it loads systemd and turns control over to it.

This is the end of the boot process. At this point, the Linux kernel and systemd are running but unable to perform any productive tasks for the end user because nothing else is running, there's no shell to provide a command line, no background processes to manage the network or other communication links, and nothing that enables the computer to perform any productive function.

systemd can now load the functional units required to bring the system up to a selected target run state.

Targets

A systemd target represents a Linux system's current or desired run state. Much like SystemV start scripts, targets define the services that must be present for the system to run and be active in that state. Table 3-1 shows the possible run-state targets of a Linux system using systemd. As seen in Chapter 2, and in the systemd bootup man page (man bootup), there are other intermediate targets that are required to enable various necessary services. These can include swap.target, timers.target, local-fs.target, and more. Some targets (like basic.target) are used as checkpoints to ensure that all the required services are up and running before moving on to the next higher-level target.

Unless otherwise changed at boot time in the GRUB menu, systemd always starts the default.target. The default.target file is a symbolic link to the true target file. For a desktop workstation, this is typically going to be the graphical.target, which is equivalent to runlevel 5 in SystemV. For a server, the default is more likely to be the multi-user.target, which is like runlevel 3 in SystemV. The emergency.target file is similar to single-user mode. Targets and services are systemd units.

CHAPTER 3   UNDERSTANDING LINUX STARTUP WITH SYSTEMD

Table 3-1 compares the systemd targets with the old SystemV startup runlevels. The systemd target aliases are provided by systemd for backward compatibility. The target aliases allow scripts—and SysAdmins—to use SystemV commands like init 3 to change runlevels. SystemV commands are forwarded to systemd for interpretation and execution.

Table 3-1. *Comparison of SystemV runlevels with systemd targets and target aliases. Reproduced here for ease of reference*

systemd Targets	SystemV Runlevel	Target Aliases	Description
default.target			This target is always aliased with a symbolic link to either multi-user.target or graphical.target. systemd always uses the default.target to start the system. The default.target should never be aliased to halt.target, poweroff.target, or reboot.target.
graphical.target	5	runlevel5.target	Multi-user.target with a GUI.
	4	runlevel4.target	Unused. Runlevel 4 was identical to runlevel 3 in the SystemV world. This target could be created and customized to start local services without changing the default multi-user.target.
multi-user.target	3	runlevel3.target	Multi-user with all services running but command-line interface (CLI) only.
	2	runlevel2.target	Multi-user, without NFS but all other non-GUI services running.

(*continued*)

Table 3-1. (*continued*)

systemd Targets	SystemV Runlevel	Target Aliases	Description
rescue.target	1	runlevel1.target	A basic system including mounting the filesystems with only the most basic services running and a rescue shell on the main console.
emergency.target	S		No services are running; filesystems are not mounted. This is the most basic level of operation with only an emergency shell running on the main console for the user to interact with the system. Single-user mode in SystemV.
halt.target			Halts the system without powering it down.
reboot.target	6	runlevel6.target	Reboot.
poweroff.target	0	runlevel0.target	Halts the system and turns the power off.

Each target has a set of dependencies described in its configuration file. systemd starts the required dependencies, which are the services required to run the Linux host at a specific level of functionality. When all of the dependencies listed in the target configuration files are loaded and running, the system is running at that target level.

CHAPTER 3   UNDERSTANDING LINUX STARTUP WITH SYSTEMD

Exploring the Current Target

Many Linux distributions default to installing a GUI desktop interface so that the installed systems can be used as workstations. I always install from a Fedora Live boot USB drive with an Xfce or LXDE desktop. Even when I'm installing a server or other infrastructure type of host (such as the ones I use for routers and firewalls), I use one of these installations that installs a GUI desktop.

I could install a server without a desktop (and that would be typical for data centers), but that does not meet my needs. It is not that I need the GUI desktop itself, but the LXDE installation includes many of the other tools I use that are not in a default server installation. This means less work for me after the initial installation.

But just because I have a GUI desktop does not mean it makes sense to use it. I have a 16-port KVM that I can use to access the KVM interfaces of most of my Linux systems, but the vast majority of my interaction with them is via a remote SSH connection from my primary workstation. This is more secure, and it uses fewer system resources to run multi-user.target compared to graphical.target.

> **EXPERIMENT 3-2: EXPLORING THE CURRENT TARGET**

To begin, check the default target to verify that it is the graphical.target:

```
# systemctl get-default
graphical.target
```

Now verify the currently running target. It should be the same as the default target. You can still use the old method, which displays the old SystemV runlevels. Note that the previous runlevel is on the left; it is N (which means None), indicating that the runlevel has not changed since the host was booted. The number 5 indicates the current target, as defined in the old SystemV terminology:

CHAPTER 3 UNDERSTANDING LINUX STARTUP WITH SYSTEMD

runlevel
N 5
#

Note that the runlevel man page indicates that runlevels are obsolete and provides a conversion table. You can also use the systemd method. There is no one-line answer here, but it does provide the answer in systemd terms:

systemctl list-units --type target

```
UNIT                    LOAD   ACTIVE SUB    DESCRIPTION
basic.target            loaded active active Basic System
cryptsetup.target       loaded active active Local
                                             Encrypted Volumes
getty.target            loaded active active Login Prompts
graphical.target        loaded active active Graphical
                                             Interface
local-fs-pre.target     loaded active active Local File
                                             Systems (Pre)
local-fs.target         loaded active active Local
                                             File Systems
multi-user.target       loaded active active Multi-User System
network-online.target   loaded active active Network is Online
network.target          loaded active active Network
nfs-client.target       loaded active active NFS client
                                             services
nss-user-lookup.target  loaded active active User and Group
                                             Name Lookups
paths.target            loaded active active Paths
remote-fs-pre.target    loaded active active Remote File
                                             Systems (Pre)
remote-fs.target        loaded active active Remote
                                             File Systems
```

```
rpc_pipefs.target       loaded active active rpc_pipefs.target
slices.target           loaded active active Slices
sockets.target          loaded active active Sockets
sshd-keygen.target      loaded active active sshd-
                                              keygen.target
swap.target             loaded active active Swap
sysinit.target          loaded active active System
                                              Initialization
timers.target           loaded active active Timers

LOAD   = Reflects whether the unit definition was
properly loaded.
ACTIVE = The high-level unit activation state, i.e.
generalization of SUB.
SUB    = The low-level unit activation state, values depend
on unit type.

21 loaded units listed. Pass --all to see loaded but
inactive units, too.
To show all installed unit files use 'systemctl list-
unit-files'.
```

This shows all of the currently loaded and active targets. You can also see the graphical.target and the multi-user.target. The multi-user.target is required before the graphical.target can be loaded. In this example, the graphical.target is active.

Switching to a Different Target

There are times when I've needed to change the running target while the host is running. This doesn't change the default target, and the system will start the default target the next time it's rebooted.

> **EXPERIMENT 3-3: CHANGING TARGETS**

Making the switch to the multi-user.target is easy using the isolate sub-command. That seems like a strange word for this sub-command, but it's what we have.

`systemctl isolate multi-user.target`

The display should now change from the GUI desktop or login screen to a virtual console. Log in and list the currently active systemd units to verify that graphical.target is no longer running:

`systemctl list-units --type target`

Be sure to use the **runlevel** command to verify that it shows both previous and current "runlevels":

`runlevel`
5 3

You could still use the **init** command to change "runlevels."

Changing the Default Target

Now, change the default target to the multi-user.target so that it will always boot into the multi-user.target for a console command-line interface rather than a GUI desktop interface.

CHAPTER 3 UNDERSTANDING LINUX STARTUP WITH SYSTEMD

EXPERIMENT 3-4: CHANGING THE DEFAULT TARGET

As the root user on your test host, change to the directory where the systemd configuration is maintained and do a quick listing:

```
# cd /etc/systemd/system/ ; ll
total 60
lrwxrwxrwx. 1 root root     9 Jun 10 13:58  abrtd.service -> /dev/null
lrwxrwxrwx. 1 root root     9 Jun 10 13:58  abrt-journal-core.service -> /dev/null
lrwxrwxrwx. 1 root root     9 Jun 10 13:58  abrt-oops.service -> /dev/null
lrwxrwxrwx. 1 root root     9 Jun 10 13:58  abrt-xorg.service -> /dev/null
<SNIP>
lrwxrwxrwx. 1 root root    40 Jun 10 11:26  default.target -> /usr/lib/systemd/system/graphical.target
drwxr-xr-x. 2 root root  4096 Apr 14  2024 'dev-virtio\x2dports-org.qemu.guest_agent.0.device.wants'
lrwxrwxrwx. 1 root root    39 Jun 10 14:00  display-manager.service -> /usr/lib/systemd/system/lightdm.service
drwxr-xr-x. 2 root root  4096 Apr 14  2024  getty.target.wants
drwxr-xr-x. 2 root root  4096 Aug 24 09:20  graphical.target.wants
drwxr-xr-x. 2 root root  4096 Aug 27 08:13  multi-user.target.wants
drwxr-xr-x. 2 root root  4096 Apr 14  2024  network-online.target.wants
drwxr-xr-x. 2 root root  4096 Apr 14  2024  remote-fs.target.wants
```

CHAPTER 3   UNDERSTANDING LINUX STARTUP WITH SYSTEMD

```
drwxr-xr-x. 2 root root 4096 Apr 14  2024   sockets.
target.wants
drwxr-xr-x. 2 root root 4096 Jun 10 13:46   sysinit.
target.wants
drwxr-xr-x. 2 root root 4096 Jun 10 13:57   sysstat.
service.wants
drwxr-xr-x. 2 root root 4096 Apr 14  2024   systemd-homed.
service.wants
drwxr-xr-x. 2 root root 4096 Apr 14  2024   systemd-journald.
service.wants
drwxr-xr-x. 2 root root 4096 Apr 14  2024   timers.
target.wants
drwxr-xr-x  2 root root 4096 Aug 24 09:21   user@.
service.wants
drwxr-xr-x. 2 root root 4096 Apr 14  2024   vmtoolsd.service.
requires
root@testvm1:/etc/systemd/system#
```

I shortened this listing to highlight a few important things that will help explain how systemd manages the boot process. You should be able to see the entire list of directories and links on your virtual machine. The default.target entry is a symbolic link (symlink, soft link) to the directory /lib/systemd/system/graphical.target. List that directory to see what else is there:

ll /lib/systemd/system/ | less

You should see files, directories, and more links in this listing, but look specifically for multi-user.target and graphical.target. Now display the contents of default.target, which is a link to /lib/systemd/system/graphical.target:

cat default.target
```
#   SPDX-License-Identifier: LGPL-2.1-or-later
#
```

```
#  This file is part of systemd.
#
#  systemd is free software; you can redistribute it and/or modify it
#  under the terms of the GNU Lesser General Public License as published by
#  the Free Software Foundation; either version 2.1 of the License, or
#  (at your option) any later version.

[Unit]
Description=Graphical Interface
Documentation=man:systemd.special(7)
Requires=multi-user.target
Wants=display-manager.service
Conflicts=rescue.service rescue.target
After=multi-user.target rescue.service rescue.target display-manager.service
AllowIsolate=yes
```

This link to the graphical.target file describes all of the prerequisites and requirements that the graphical user interface requires. We'll explore at least some of these options in future articles. To enable the host to boot to multi-user mode, you need to delete the existing link and create a new one that points to the correct target. Make the PWD /etc/systemd/system, if it is not already:

rm -f default.target
ln -s /lib/systemd/system/multi-user.target default.target

List the default.target link to verify that it links to the correct file:

ll default.target

CHAPTER 3 UNDERSTANDING LINUX STARTUP WITH SYSTEMD

```
lrwxrwxrwx 1 root root 37 Nov 28 16:08 default.target ->
/lib/systemd/system/multi-user.target
```

List the content of the default.target link:

cat default.target
```
#  SPDX-License-Identifier: LGPL-2.1+
#
#  This file is part of systemd.
#
#  systemd is free software; you can redistribute it and/or modify it
#  under the terms of the GNU Lesser General Public License as published by
#  the Free Software Foundation; either version 2.1 of the License, or
#  (at your option) any later version.

[Unit]
Description=Multi-User System
Documentation=man:systemd.special(7)
Requires=basic.target
Conflicts=rescue.service rescue.target
After=basic.target rescue.service rescue.target
AllowIsolate=yes
```

If your link does not look exactly like this, delete it and try again.

The default.target—which is really a link to the multi-user.target at this point—now has different requirements in the [Unit] section. It does not require the graphical display manager.

Reboot your virtual machine which should boot to the console login for virtual console 1, which is identified on the display as tty1. Now that you know how to change the default target, change it back to the graphical.target using the command designed for the purpose.

First, check the current default target, then set the graphical.target as the default.

systemctl get-default
multi-user.target
systemctl set-default graphical.target
Removed /etc/systemd/system/default.target.
Created symlink /etc/systemd/system/default.target → /usr/lib/systemd/system/graphical.target.

Enter the following command to go directly to the graphical.target and the display manager login page without having to reboot:

systemctl isolate default.target

I do not know why the term "isolate" was chosen for this sub-command by systemd's developers. My research indicates that it may refer to running the specified target but "isolating" and terminating all other targets that are not required to support the target. However, the effect is to switch targets from one run target to another—in this case, from the multi-user target to the graphical target. The command above is equivalent to the old init 5 command in SystemV start scripts and the init program.

Log in to the GUI desktop, and verify that it is working as it should.

Summary

In this chapter, we explored the Linux systemd startup sequence and started to work with two important systemd tools, systemctl and journalctl. We also learned how to switch from one target to another and to change the default target.

Exercises

Perform these exercises to complete this chapter:

1. Which file did you use to configure GRUB2 and why?
2. What is the function of GRUB2?
3. What is the default target?
4. Change the default target to rescue.target and reboot the computer.
5. Can you change to the multi-user.target without changing the default?
6. Change the default target to graphical.target and reboot.
7. Why might you use the computer in rescue.target?
8. Why might you run the computer in multi-user.target?

CHAPTER 4

How to Manage Startup Using systemd

Objectives

In this chapter, you will learn

- How systemd determines the order services start, even though it is a massively parallel system
- To use systemd tools to create a new systemd unit that runs a simple program at startup time
- To use the boot messages to view text added by the new program and service unit
- To use journalctl to view the messages created by the start and end of the new service unit and the program output
- To configure service units to start at specific stages of the Linux systemd startup

Chapter 4   How to Manage Startup Using systemd

Overview

While setting up a new Linux system recently, I wanted to know how to ensure that dependencies for services and other units were up and running before those dependent services and units start. Specifically, I needed more knowledge of how systemd manages the startup sequence, especially in determining the order services are started in what is essentially a parallel system.

You may know that SystemV orders the startup sequence by naming the startup scripts with an SXX prefix, where XX is a number from 00 to 99. SystemV then uses the Linux natural sort order by name and runs each start script in alphanumerical sequence for the desired runlevel.

But systemd uses unit files, which can be created or modified by a SysAdmin, to define subroutines for not only initialization but also for regular operation. We'll create a service unit file that runs a simple test program at startup. You can also change certain configuration settings in the unit file and use the systemd journal to view the location of your changes in the startup sequence.

Preparation

Make sure you have removed rhgb and quiet from the GRUB_CMDLINE_LINUX= line in the /etc/default/grub file, as we did in Experiment 3-1. This enables you to observe the Linux startup message stream, which you'll need for some of the experiments in this chapter.

Also, ensure that SELinux won't prevent the shell script we'll create from running. Verify the current SELinux status so you can restore that status at the end of this chapter.

```
# sestatus
SELinux status:                 enabled
SELinuxfs mount:                /sys/fs/selinux
```

CHAPTER 4 HOW TO MANAGE STARTUP USING SYSTEMD

```
SELinux root directory:         /etc/selinux
Loaded policy name:             targeted
Current mode:                   enforcing
Mode from config file:          enforcing
Policy MLS status:              enabled
Policy deny_unknown status:     allowed
Memory protection checking:     actual (secure)
Max kernel policy version:      33
```

If SELinux is in enforcing mode, run the following command to set SELinux to permissive:

```
# setenforce Permissive
```

The Program

In this experiment, you will create a simple program that enables you to observe a message during startup on the console and later in the systemd journal.

EXPERIMENT 4-1: CREATE THE PROGRAM

Create the shell program /usr/local/bin/hello.sh and add the following content. We want to ensure that the output resulting from this little program is visible during startup and that you can easily find it when looking through the systemd journal. You will use a version of the "Hello world" program with some bars around it, so it stands out. Make sure the file is executable and has user and group ownership by root with 700 permissions for security.

```
#!/usr/bin/bash
# Simple program to use for testing startup configurations
# with systemd.
# # Copyright David Both, 2025
```

89

```
# GNU All-Permissive License:
# Copying and distribution of this file, with or without
# modification, are permitted in any medium without royalty
# provided the copyright notice and this notice are
preserved.
# This file is offered as-is, without any warranty.

echo "################################"
echo "######### Hello World! ########"
echo "################################"
```

Run this program from the command line to verify that it works correctly.

```
# hello.sh
################################
######### Hello World! ########
################################
```

This program could be created in any scripting or compiled language. The hello.sh program could also be located in other places based on the Linux filesystem hierarchical structure (FHS). I place it in the /usr/local/bin directory so that it can be easily run from the command line without having to prepend a path when I type the command.

I find that many of the shell programs I create need to be run from the command line and by other tools such as systemd.

The Service Unit

Before we create our service unit, let's explore what a service unit is and how it relates to getting a Linux host up and running.

A unit is "a service, a socket, a device, a mount point, an automount point, a swap file or partition, a start-up target, a watched file system path, a timer controlled and supervised by systemd, a resource management slice or a group of externally created processes"—the systemd.unit man page.

A unit file is a plain-text ini-style file that contains data that defines a unit.

And a service unit file defines the type of service unit being created, how it's used, the programs it runs, and the systemd target that it's triggered or started by.

There are eight service types, and you can find an explanation of each (along with the other parts of a service unit file) in the systemd.service(5) man page. Kernel and service developers are the usual users of system types.

These are typically only used by SysAdmins when creating a new service unit file for local use such as the oneshot service, timers, and mounts. The types I use most frequently are simple, exec, oneshot, and dbus. We'll explore each of those in this book. We've already seen the oneshot type in Chapter 3.

Table 4-1 lists all eight service types with a brief explanation of each.

Table 4-1. *The eight types of systemd services*

Service Type	Description
simple	This is the default type. systemd assumes the unit is to be started immediately after the program has begun executing. This is usually the main process of the program.
exec	Similar to simple, but systemd considers the unit started immediately after the main service binary has been executed. The service manager will delay starting of follow-up units until that point. Note that this means systemctl start command lines for exec services will report failure when the service's binary cannot be invoked successfully.
forking	systemd considers the unit started immediately after the binary that forked off by the manager exits. The use of this type is discouraged; use notify, notify-reload, or dbus instead.
oneshot	Similar to simple; however, the service manager will consider the unit up after the main process exits. It will then start follow-up units.
dbus	Similar to simple; however, units of this type must have the BusName= specified, and the service manager will consider the unit up when the specified bus name has been acquired.
notify	Similar to exec; however, it is expected that the service sends a "READY=1" notification message via sd_notify(3) or an equivalent call when it has finished starting up. systemd will proceed with starting follow-up units after this notification message has been sent.

(*continued*)

Table 4-1. (*continued*)

Service Type	Description
notify-reload	Similar to notify, with one difference: the SIGHUP UNIX process signal is sent to the service's main process when the service is asked to reload, and the manager will wait for a notification about the reload being finished.
idle	Similar to simple; however, actual execution of the service program is delayed until all active jobs are dispatched. This may be used to avoid interleaving of output of shell services with the status output on the console. Note that this type is useful only to improve console output; it is not useful as a general unit ordering tool.

You can find more information in the resources at the end of this chapter.

Creating the Service Unit

Service unit files use the form and structure of standard ini files. Commands start with a pound sign (#), and section names are enclosed in [square brackets]. Our unit file is about the most simple possible. It has three sections:

- **[unit]**: This is a short description of the unit used as an identifier for us SysAdmins. It will appear in systemd status reports for the service.

- **[Service]**: Defines the type of unit as a service and provides the service type, oneshot in this instance, and the fully qualified path to the program to run.

- **[Install]**: Specifies the target unit that will trigger the service unit. The oneshot type is intended for services where the program launched by the service unit file is the main process and must complete before systemd starts any dependent process. We don't have any dependent processes that need to wait for this one to complete.

EXPERIMENT 4-2: CREATE THE SERVICE UNIT

Create the service unit file /usr/local/lib/systemd/system/hello.service with the following content. This is a location explicitly specified by the Linux Filesystem Hierarchical Standard[1] to be used for locally created system files. systemd checks this directory for those local files.

This file does not need to be executable, but for security, it does need user and group ownership by root and 754 permissions.

```
# Simple service unit file to use for testing
# startup configurations with systemd.
# Copyright David Both, 2025

# GNU All-Permissive License:
# Copying and distribution of this file, with or without
# modification, are permitted in any medium without royalty
# provided the copyright notice and this notice are
preserved.
# This file is offered as-is, without any warranty.
#
```

---

[1] Both, David, *The Linux Philosophy for SysAdmins, Tenet 04 — Use the Linux FHS*, https://www.both.org/?p=6982

CHAPTER 4   HOW TO MANAGE STARTUP USING SYSTEMD

```
[Unit]
Description=My hello shell script

[Service]
Type=oneshot
ExecStart=/usr/local/bin/hello.sh

[Install]
WantedBy=multi-user.target
```

You can verify the logic and syntax of the service unit.

systemd-analyze verify /etc/systemd/system/hello.service

Adhering to the Linux philosophy tenet, "silence is golden," a lack of output messages means that there are no errors in the scanned file.

You can also verify that the service unit file performs as expected by viewing the service status. Any syntactical errors will also show up here.

systemctl status hello.service
```
○ hello.service - My hello shell script
     Loaded: loaded (/etc/systemd/system/hello.service;
             disabled; preset: disabled)
    Drop-In: /usr/lib/systemd/system/service.d
             └─10-timeout-abort.conf
     Active: inactive (dead)
[root@testvm1 ~]#
```

As curious as I am, I wanted to see what an error might look like. So, I deleted the "o" from the Type=oneshot line, so it looked like Type=neshot, and ran the command again:

systemctl status hello.service
```
○ hello.service - My hello shell script
```

CHAPTER 4　HOW TO MANAGE STARTUP USING SYSTEMD

```
     Loaded: loaded (/usr/local/lib/systemd/system/hello.
             service; disabled; preset: disabled)
    Drop-In: /usr/lib/systemd/system/service.d
             └─10-timeout-abort.conf
     Active: inactive (dead)
Oct 28 06:51:44 testvm1.both.org systemd[1]: /usr/local/lib/
systemd/system/hello.service:11: Failed to parse service
type, ignoring: neshot
root@testvm1:~#
```

These results told me precisely where the error was and made it very easy to resolve the problem.

Be aware that even after you restore the hello.service file to its original form, the error reports will persist. These are part of the journal and represent the historical error reports. Be sure to examine the timestamps to determine the age of the errors. So long as no new errors are reported, everything is good.

Run the command **systemctl daemon-reload** after changing a unit file or creating a new one. This notifies systemd that the changes have been made, and it can prevent certain types of issues with managing altered services or units. Run this command now.

Experiment a bit by introducing some other errors into the hello.service file to see what kinds of results you get.

Start the Service

Now you are ready to start the new service and check the status to see the result. You can start or restart a oneshot service as many times as you want since it runs once and then exits.

EXPERIMENT 4-3: STARTING THE SERVICE

We will not enable the service for now, just start it so that it will run once each time we start it. You can run this "oneshot" service type multiple times without problems.

Start the service (as shown below), and then check the status. Depending upon how much you experimented with errors, your results may differ from mine, and the timestamps will be different.

```
# systemctl start hello.service
# systemctl status hello.service
o hello.service - My hello shell script
     Loaded: loaded (/usr/local/lib/systemd/system/hello.
             service; disabled; preset: disabled)
    Drop-In: /usr/lib/systemd/system/service.d
             └─10-timeout-abort.conf
     Active: inactive (dead)

Oct 29 06:33:09 testvm1.both.org systemd[1]: Starting hello.
service - My hello shell script...
Oct 29 06:33:09 testvm1.both.org hello.sh[130983]:
################################
Oct 29 06:33:09 testvm1.both.org hello.sh[130983]: #########
Hello World! ########
Oct 29 06:33:09 testvm1.both.org hello.sh[130983]:
################################
Oct 29 06:33:09 testvm1.both.org systemd[1]: hello.service:
Deactivated successfully.
Oct 29 06:33:09 testvm1.both.org systemd[1]: Finished hello.
service - My hello shell script.
```

Notice in the status command's output that the systemd messages indicate that the hello.sh script started and the service completed. You can also see the output from the script. This display is generated from the journal entries of the most recent invocations of the service. Try starting the service several times, and then run the status command again to see what I mean.

You can also look at the journal contents directly. There are multiple ways to do this. One way is to specify the record type identifier, in this case, the name of the shell script. I rebooted while writing this section, so this shows the journal entries for previous reboots as well as the current session.

```
# journalctl -t hello.sh
Oct 27 17:58:11 testvm1.both.org hello.sh[128976]:
################################
Oct 27 17:58:11 testvm1.both.org hello.sh[128976]: #########
Hello World! ########
Oct 27 17:58:11 testvm1.both.org hello.sh[128976]:
################################
Oct 27 17:58:12 testvm1.both.org hello.sh[128980]:
################################
Oct 27 17:58:12 testvm1.both.org hello.sh[128980]: #########
Hello World! ########
Oct 27 17:58:12 testvm1.both.org hello.sh[128980]:
################################
-- Boot e257de57d9e2430ca25873e18a1d628b --
Oct 28 06:53:33 testvm1.both.org hello.sh[1632]:
################################
Oct 28 06:53:33 testvm1.both.org hello.sh[1632]: #########
Hello World! ########
Oct 28 06:53:33 testvm1.both.org hello.sh[1632]:
################################
Oct 28 06:54:31 testvm1.both.org hello.sh[1638]:
################################
```

CHAPTER 4   HOW TO MANAGE STARTUP USING SYSTEMD

```
Oct 28 06:54:31 testvm1.both.org hello.sh[1638]: #########
Hello World! ########
Oct 28 06:54:31 testvm1.both.org hello.sh[1638]:
################################
Oct 28 06:54:31 testvm1.both.org hello.sh[1642]:
################################
Oct 28 06:54:31 testvm1.both.org hello.sh[1642]: #########
Hello World! ########
Oct 28 06:54:31 testvm1.both.org hello.sh[1642]:
################################
Oct 28 06:54:33 testvm1.both.org hello.sh[1646]:
################################
Oct 28 06:54:33 testvm1.both.org hello.sh[1646]: #########
Hello World! ########
Oct 28 06:54:33 testvm1.both.org hello.sh[1646]:
################################
-- Boot d04572266a83472a929037300b9ae756 --
Oct 28 07:03:21 testvm1.both.org hello.sh[1509]:
################################
Oct 28 07:03:21 testvm1.both.org hello.sh[1509]: #########
Hello World! ########
Oct 28 07:03:21 testvm1.both.org hello.sh[1509]:
################################
Oct 28 07:03:22 testvm1.both.org hello.sh[1513]:
################################
Oct 28 07:03:22 testvm1.both.org hello.sh[1513]: #########
Hello World! ########
Oct 28 07:03:22 testvm1.both.org hello.sh[1513]:
################################
Oct 29 06:31:45 testvm1.both.org hello.sh[130958]:
################################
```

Oct 29 06:31:45 testvm1.both.org hello.sh[130958]: #########
Hello World! ########
Oct 29 06:31:45 testvm1.both.org hello.sh[130958]:
################################
Oct 29 06:33:09 testvm1.both.org hello.sh[130983]:
################################
Oct 29 06:33:09 testvm1.both.org hello.sh[130983]: #########
Hello World! ########
Oct 29 06:33:09 testvm1.both.org hello.sh[130983]:
################################

To locate the systemd records for the hello.service unit, you can search on systemd. You can use SHIFT+G to page to the end of the journal entries and then scroll back to locate the ones you are interested in. Use the -b option to show only the entries for the most recent boot.

journalctl -b -t systemd
<snip>
Oct 29 06:31:45 testvm1.both.org systemd[1]: Starting hello.service - My hello shell script...
Oct 29 06:31:45 testvm1.both.org systemd[1]: hello.service: Deactivated successfully.
Oct 29 06:31:45 testvm1.both.org systemd[1]: Finished hello.service - My hello shell script.
Oct 29 06:32:44 testvm1.both.org systemd[1]: Starting packagekit.service - PackageKit Daemon...
Oct 29 06:32:44 testvm1.both.org systemd[1]: Started packagekit.service - PackageKit Daemon.
Oct 29 06:33:09 testvm1.both.org systemd[1]: Starting hello.service - My hello shell script...
Oct 29 06:33:09 testvm1.both.org systemd[1]: hello.service: Deactivated successfully.

Oct 29 06:33:09 testvm1.both.org systemd[1]: Finished hello.
service - My hello shell script.

I kept the other journal entries to give you an idea of what you might find. This command spews all of the journal lines pertaining to systemd—109,183 lines when I wrote this. Fortunately, the entries for our new service are at the end of the data stream. Use uppercase "G" to take the pager to the end of the data stream. You could use the pager's search facility, which is usually **less**, or you can use the built-in grep feature. The -g (or --grep=) option uses Perl-compatible regular expressions:

```
# journalctl -b -t systemd -g "hello"
Oct 28 07:03:14 testvm1.both.org systemd[1]: Configuration
file /usr/local/lib/systemd/system/hello.service is marked
executable. Please remove ex>
Oct 28 07:03:14 testvm1.both.org systemd[1]: Configuration
file /usr/local/lib/systemd/system/hello.service is marked
executable. Please remove ex>
Oct 28 07:03:21 testvm1.both.org systemd[1]: Configuration
file /usr/local/lib/systemd/system/hello.service is marked
executable. Please remove ex>
Oct 28 07:03:21 testvm1.both.org systemd[1]: Starting hello.
service - My hello shell script...
Oct 28 07:03:21 testvm1.both.org systemd[1]: hello.service:
Deactivated successfully.
Oct 28 07:03:21 testvm1.both.org systemd[1]: Finished hello.
service - My hello shell script.
Oct 28 07:03:22 testvm1.both.org systemd[1]: Configuration
file /usr/local/lib/systemd/system/hello.service is marked
executable. Please remove ex>
Oct 28 07:03:22 testvm1.both.org systemd[1]: Starting hello.
service - My hello shell script...
```

```
Oct 28 07:03:22 testvm1.both.org systemd[1]: hello.service:
Deactivated successfully.
Oct 28 07:03:22 testvm1.both.org systemd[1]: Finished hello.
service - My hello shell script.
Oct 28 07:03:24 testvm1.both.org systemd[1]: Configuration
file /usr/local/lib/systemd/system/hello.service is marked
executable. Please remove ex>
Oct 28 07:03:24 testvm1.both.org systemd[1]: Configuration
file /usr/local/lib/systemd/system/hello.service is marked
executable. Please remove ex>
Oct 29 06:31:45 testvm1.both.org systemd[1]: Starting hello.
service - My hello shell script...
Oct 29 06:31:45 testvm1.both.org systemd[1]: hello.service:
Deactivated successfully.
Oct 29 06:31:45 testvm1.both.org systemd[1]: Finished hello.
service - My hello shell script.
Oct 29 06:33:09 testvm1.both.org systemd[1]: Starting hello.
service - My hello shell script...
Oct 29 06:33:09 testvm1.both.org systemd[1]: hello.service:
Deactivated successfully.
Oct 29 06:33:09 testvm1.both.org systemd[1]: Finished hello.
service - My hello shell script.
```

You could use the standard GNU grep command, but that would not show the log metadata in the first line.

Notice the error messages in the lines from October 28 indicating I had the hello.service file set as executable. I fixed that so that the lines from October 29 don't contain those error messages. This is a good illustration why we should check the logs and journals because they have a lot of good information that can help us to ensure that things are configured correctly.

CHAPTER 4   HOW TO MANAGE STARTUP USING SYSTEMD

You can narrow things down a bit by specifying a date and time range. For example, I will start with a time just before the minute the entries above are from. Note that the --since= option must be enclosed in quotes and that this option can also be expressed as -S "<time specification>".

The date and time will be different on your host, so be sure to use the timestamps that match the times in your journals.

journalctl --since="2024-10-29 06:30:00"

The since specification skips all of the entries before that time, but there may be a lot of entries after that time that you don't need. You can also use the until option to trim off the entries that come a bit after the time you are interested in. I want the entire time when the event occurred and as little more as possible.

journalctl --since="2024-10-29 06:30:00" --until="2024-10-29 06:33:10"

If there were a lot of activity in this time period, you could further narrow the resulting data stream using a combination with the -u option to specify the unit.

journalctl --since="2024-10-29 06:30:00" --until="2024-10-29 06:33:10" -u hello

```
Oct 29 06:31:45 testvm1.both.org systemd[1]: Starting hello.
service - My hello shell script...
Oct 29 06:31:45 testvm1.both.org hello.sh[130958]:
###############################
Oct 29 06:31:45 testvm1.both.org hello.sh[130958]: #########
Hello World! ########
Oct 29 06:31:45 testvm1.both.org hello.sh[130958]:
###############################
```

```
Oct 29 06:31:45 testvm1.both.org systemd[1]: hello.service:
Deactivated successfully.
Oct 29 06:31:45 testvm1.both.org systemd[1]: Finished hello.
service - My hello shell script.
Oct 29 06:33:09 testvm1.both.org systemd[1]: Starting hello.
service - My hello shell script...
Oct 29 06:33:09 testvm1.both.org hello.sh[130983]:
#################################
Oct 29 06:33:09 testvm1.both.org hello.sh[130983]: #########
Hello World! ########
Oct 29 06:33:09 testvm1.both.org hello.sh[130983]:
#################################
Oct 29 06:33:09 testvm1.both.org systemd[1]: hello.service:
Deactivated successfully.
Oct 29 06:33:09 testvm1.both.org systemd[1]: Finished hello.
service - My hello shell script.
#
```

Your results should be similar to mine. You can see from this series of experiments that the service executed properly.

Reboot—Finally

So far, you have not rebooted the host where you installed your service. So we'll do that now because, after all, this is about running a program at startup.

EXPERIMENT 4-4: EXPLORING THE REBOOT

First, you need to enable the service to launch during the startup sequence:

`systemctl enable --now hello.service`
Created symlink /etc/systemd/system/multi-user.target.wants/
hello.service → /usr/local/lib/systemd/system/hello.service.
#

Notice that the link was created in the /etc/systemd/system/multi-user.target.wants directory. This is because the service unit file specifies that the service is "wanted" by the multi-user.target.

Reboot, and be sure to watch the data stream during the startup sequence to see the "Hello world" message. Wait … you did not see it? Well, neither did I. Although it went by very fast, I did see systemd's message that it was starting the hello.service.

Look at the journal since the latest system boot. You can use the less pager's search tool to find "Hello" or "hello," to get a feel for what the entries pertaining to your service look like.

`journalctl -b`

You can see that systemd started the hello.service unit, which ran the hello.sh shell script with the output recorded in the journal. If you were able to catch it during boot, you would also have seen the systemd message indicating that it was starting the script and another message indicating that the service succeeded. By looking at the first systemd message in the data stream above, you can see that systemd started your service very soon after reaching the basic system target.

I would like to see the message displayed at startup as well. There is a way to make that happen. Add the following line to the [Service] section of the hello.service file:

StandardOutput=journal+console

The hello.service file now looks like this:

```
# Simple service unit file to use for testing
# startup configurations with systemd.
# By David Both
# Licensed under GPL V2
#
[Unit]
Description=My hello shell script

[Service]
Type=oneshot
ExecStart=/usr/local/bin/hello.sh
StandardOutput=journal+console

[Install]
WantedBy=multi-user.target
```

After adding this line, reboot the system, and watch the data stream as it scrolls up the display during the boot process. You should see the message in its little box. After the startup sequence completes, view the journal for the most recent boot and locate the entries for your new service.

Changing the Sequence

Now that your service is working, you can look at where it starts in the startup sequence and experiment with changing it. It's important to remember that systemd's intent is to start as many services and other unit types in parallel within each of the major targets: basic.target, multi-user.target, and graphical.target. You have just seen the journal entries for the most recent boot, which should look similar to my journal in the output above.

CHAPTER 4 HOW TO MANAGE STARTUP USING SYSTEMD

systemd started your test service soon after it reached the target basic system. This is what you specified in the service unit file in the WantedBy line, so it is correct.

> **EXPERIMENT 4-5: CHANGE THE SEQUENCE IN WHICH HELLO. SERVICE STARTS**

Before you change anything, list the contents of the /etc/systemd/system/multi-user.target.wants directory, and you will see a symbolic (soft) link to the service unit file. The [Install] section of the service unit file specifies which target will start the service, and running the systemctl enable hello.service command creates the link in the appropriate "target wants" directory.

```
hello.service -> /usr/local/lib/systemd/system/hello.service
```

Certain services need to start during the basic.target, and others do not need to start unless the system is starting the graphical.target. Let's assume we don't need our service to start until the graphical.target.

Disable the hello.service to remove the old link from the multi-user.target.wants directory, then change the WantedBy line to this:

```
WantedBy=graphical.target
```

Re-enable the service to add the new link in the graphical.targets.wants directory. I have noticed that if I forget to disable the service before changing the target that wants it, I can run the systemctl disable command, and the links will be removed from both "target wants" directories. Then, I just need to re-enable the service and reboot.

One concern with starting services in the graphical.target is that if the host boots to multi-user.target, this service will not start automatically. That may be what you want if the service requires a GUI desktop interface, but it also may not be what you want.

107

CHAPTER 4   HOW TO MANAGE STARTUP USING SYSTEMD

Look at the journal entries for the graphical.target and the multi-user.target using the **-o short-monotonic** option that displays the number of seconds after kernel startup with microsecond precision.

`journalctl -b -o short-monotonic`

Some results for multi-user.target. The times on your test system will be different from mine.

```
[   17.264730] testvm1.both.org systemd[1]: Starting My hello shell script...
[   17.265561] testvm1.both.org systemd[1]: Starting IPv4 firewall with iptables...
<SNIP>
[   19.478468] testvm1.both.org systemd[1]: Starting LSB: Init script for live image....
[   19.507359] testvm1.both.org iptables.init[844]: iptables: Applying firewall rules: [  OK  ]
[   19.507835] testvm1.both.org hello.sh[843]: ################################
[   19.507835] testvm1.both.org hello.sh[843]: ######### Hello World! ########
[   19.507835] testvm1.both.org hello.sh[843]: ################################
<SNIP>
[   21.482481] testvm1.both.org systemd[1]: hello.service: Succeeded.
[   21.482550] testvm1.both.org smartd[856]: Opened configuration file /etc/smartmontools/smartd.conf
[   21.482605] testvm1.both.org systemd[1]: Finished My hello shell script.
```

CHAPTER 4   HOW TO MANAGE STARTUP USING SYSTEMD

And some results for graphical.target:

```
[   19.436815] testvm1.both.org systemd[1]: Starting My
hello shell script...
[   19.437070] testvm1.both.org systemd[1]: Starting IPv4
firewall with iptables...
<SNIP>
[   19.612614] testvm1.both.org hello.sh[841]:
################################
[   19.612614] testvm1.both.org hello.sh[841]: #########
Hello World! ########
[   19.612614] testvm1.both.org hello.sh[841]:
################################
[   19.629455] testvm1.both.org audit[1]: SERVICE_START
pid=1 uid=0 auid=4294967295 ses=4294967295 msg='unit=hello
comm="systemd" exe="/usr/lib/systemd/systemd" hostname=?
addr=? terminal=? res=success'
[   19.629569] testvm1.both.org audit[1]: SERVICE_STOP
pid=1 uid=0 auid=4294967295 ses=4294967295 msg='unit=hello
comm="systemd" exe="/usr/lib/systemd/systemd" hostname=?
addr=? terminal=? res=success'
[   19.629682] testvm1.both.org systemd[1]: hello.service:
Succeeded.
[   19.629782] testvm1.both.org systemd[1]: Finished My
hello shell script.
```

Despite having the graphical.target "want" in the unit file, the hello.service unit runs about 19.5 or 19.6 seconds into startup. But hello.service starts at about 17.24 seconds in the multi-user.target and 19.43 seconds in the graphical target.

109

CHAPTER 4 HOW TO MANAGE STARTUP USING SYSTEMD

What does this mean? Look at the /etc/systemd/system/default.target link. The contents of that file show that systemd first starts the default target—the graphical.target—which then pulls in the multi-user.target.

```
# cat default.target
#  SPDX-License-Identifier: LGPL-2.1+
#
#  This file is part of systemd.
#
#  systemd is free software; you can redistribute it and/or modify it
#  under the terms of the GNU Lesser General Public License as published by
#  the Free Software Foundation; either version 2.1 of the License, or
#  (at your option) any later version.

[Unit]
Description=Graphical Interface
Documentation=man:systemd.special(7)
Requires=multi-user.target
Wants=display-manager.service
Conflicts=rescue.service rescue.target
After=multi-user.target rescue.service rescue.target display-manager.service
AllowIsolate=yes
[root@testvm1 system]#
```

Whether it starts the service with the graphical.target or the multi-user.target, the hello.service unit runs at about 19.5 or 19.6 seconds into startup. Based on this and the journal results (especially the ones using the monotonic output), you know that both of these targets are starting in parallel. Look at one more thing from the journal output.

[28.397330] testvm1.both.org systemd[1]: Reached target
Multi-User System.
[28.397431] testvm1.both.org systemd[1]: Reached target
Graphical Interface.

Both targets finish at almost the same time. This is consistent because the graphical.target pulls in the multi-user.target and cannot finish until the multi-user.target is reached, that is, finished. But hello.service finishes much earlier than this.

What all this means is that these two targets start up pretty much in parallel. If you explore the journal entries, you will see various targets and services from each of those primary targets starting mostly in parallel. It is clear that the multi-user.target does not need to complete before the graphical.target starts. Therefore, simply using these primary targets to sequence the startup does not work very well, although it can be useful for ensuring that units are started only when they are needed for the graphical.target.

Before continuing, revert the hello.service unit file to WantedBy=multi-user.target.

Ensure a Service Starts After the Network Is Running

One common startup sequence issue is ensuring that a unit starts after the network is up and running. This article at systemd.io, "Network Configuration Synchronization Points,"[2] says there is no real consensus on when a network is considered "up." However, the article provides three options, and the one that meets the needs of a fully operational network

---

[2] systemd.io, "Network Configuration Synchronization Points," https://systemd.io/NETWORK_ONLINE/

CHAPTER 4　HOW TO MANAGE STARTUP USING SYSTEMD

is network-online.target. Also, be aware that network.target is used during shutdown rather than startup, so it will not do you any good when you are trying to sequence the startup.

Our hello.service doesn't really require the network service, but we can use it as a test for one that does. Because setting WantedBy=graphical. target does not ensure that the service will be started after the network is up and running, you need another way to ensure that it is. Fortunately, there is an easy way to do this.

EXPERIMENT 4-6: ENSURE THAT A SERVICE STARTS AFTER THE NETWORK IS ACTIVE

Before making any other changes, be sure to examine the journal and verify that the hello.service unit starts well before the network. You can look for the network-online.target in the journal to check.

Add the following two lines to the [Unit] section of the hello.service unit file:

```
After=network-online.target
Wants=network-online.target
```

Both of these entries are required to make this work. Reboot your test host and look for the entries for your service in the journals. I've included some of the NetworkManager entries to verify that hello.service starts after it.

```
<SNIP>
[   26.083349] testvm1.both.org NetworkManager[842]: <info>  [1589227764.0301] manager: NetworkManager state is now CONNECTED_GLOBAL
[   26.085818] testvm1.both.org NetworkManager[842]: <info>  [1589227764.0331] manager: startup complete
[   26.089911] testvm1.both.org systemd[1]: Finished Network Manager Wait Online.
```

[26.090254] testvm1.both.org systemd[1]: Reached target Network is Online.
[26.090399] testvm1.both.org audit[1]: SERVICE_START pid=1 uid=0 auid=4294967295 ses=4294967295 msg='unit=NetworkManager-wait-online comm="systemd" exe="/usr/lib/systemd/systemd" hostname=? addr=? termina>"'
[26.091991] testvm1.both.org systemd[1]: Starting My hello shell script...
[26.095864] testvm1.both.org sssd[be[implicit_files]][1007]: Starting up
[26.290539] testvm1.both.org systemd[1]: Condition check resulted in Login and scanning of iSCSI devices being skipped.
[26.291075] testvm1.both.org systemd[1]: Reached target Remote File Systems (Pre).
[26.291154] testvm1.both.org systemd[1]: Reached target Remote File Systems.
[26.292671] testvm1.both.org systemd[1]: Starting Notify NFS peers of a restart...
[26.294897] testvm1.both.org systemd[1]: iscsi.service: Unit cannot be reloaded because it is inactive.
[26.304682] testvm1.both.org hello.sh[1010]: ###############################
[26.304682] testvm1.both.org hello.sh[1010]: ######### Hello World! ########
[26.304682] testvm1.both.org hello.sh[1010]: ###############################
[26.306569] testvm1.both.org audit[1]: SERVICE_START pid=1 uid=0 auid=4294967295 ses=4294967295 msg='unit=hello comm="systemd" exe="/usr/lib/systemd/systemd" hostname=? addr=? terminal=? res=success'

```
[   26.306669] testvm1.both.org audit[1]: SERVICE_STOP
pid=1 uid=0 auid=4294967295 ses=4294967295 msg='unit=hello
comm="systemd" exe="/usr/lib/systemd/systemd" hostname=?
addr=? terminal=? res=success'
[   26.306772] testvm1.both.org systemd[1]: hello.service:
Succeeded.
[   26.306862] testvm1.both.org systemd[1]: Finished My
hello shell script.
[   26.584966] testvm1.both.org sm-notify[1011]: Version
2.4.3 starting
<SNIP>
```

This confirms that the hello.service unit started after the network-online. target. This is exactly what you want. You may also have seen the "Hello World" message as it passed by during startup. Notice also that the timestamp is later in the startup than it was before.

If you changed it, set SELinux back to the mode it was when you checked at the beginning of this chapter.

setenforce enforcing

Summary

We've explored Linux startup with systemd and unit files and journals in greater detail and discovered what happens when errors are introduced into the service file. As a SysAdmin, I find that this type of experimentation helps me understand the behaviors of a program or service when it breaks, and breaking things intentionally is a good way to learn in a safe environment.

CHAPTER 4   HOW TO MANAGE STARTUP USING SYSTEMD

As these experiments have proved, just adding a service unit to either the multi-user.target or the graphical.target does not define its place in the start sequence. It merely determines whether a unit starts as part of the graphical.target or the non-graphical multi-user.target. The reality is that the startup targets—multi-user.target and graphical.target—and all of their Wants and Requires, start up pretty much in parallel. The best way to ensure that a unit starts in a specific order is to determine the unit it is dependent on and configure the new unit to "Want" and "After" the unit upon which it is dependent.

Exercises

Perform these exercises to complete this chapter:

1. Name and describe at least three types of service units.

2. Why did we use the oneshot service unit type for the new service?

3. What target should be specified in the service unit file so that the service will start both in graphical.target and multi-user.target?

4. What tool can be used to verify that a service has started properly in the specified target?

115

CHAPTER 5

Manage systemd Units with systemctl

Objectives

In this chapter, you will learn

- The practical structure of the systemd suite of programs
- More advanced usage of the systemctl program
- How to obtain more information about systemd service units
- How to create a mount unit that mounts a storage device during Linux startup

Overview

In previous chapters, we explored the Linux systemd startup sequence and were introduced to systemd units. In this chapter, we'll explore systemd units in more detail and how to use the **systemctl** command to explore and manage units. We'll also learn to stop and disable units and how to create a new systemd mount unit to mount a new filesystem and enable it to initiate during startup.

Preparation

All of the experiments in this chapter should be done as the root user (unless otherwise specified). Some of the commands that simply list various systemd units can be performed by non-root users, but the commands that make changes cannot. Make sure to do all of these experiments only on non-production hosts or virtual machines (VMs).

EXPERIMENT 5-1: PREPARATION

One of these experiments requires the sysstat package. As root, install it before you move on. For Fedora and other Red Hat–based distributions, you can install sysstat with this command:

`dnf -y install sysstat`

The sysstat RPM installs several statistical tools that can be used for problem determination. One is System Activity Report (SAR), which records many system performance data points at regular intervals (every ten minutes by default). Rather than run as a daemon in the background, the sysstat package installs two systemd timers. One timer runs every ten minutes to collect data, and the other runs once a day to aggregate the daily data. In this chapter, I will look briefly at these timers but wait to explain how to create a timer in a future article.

---

systemd Suite

The fact is systemd is more than just one program. It is a large suite of programs all designed to work together to manage nearly every aspect of a running Linux system. A full exposition of systemd would take a book on its own. Most of us do not need to understand all of the details about how

CHAPTER 5 MANAGE SYSTEMD UNITS WITH SYSTEMCTL

all of systemd's components fit together, so I will focus on the programs and components that enable you to manage various Linux services and deal with log files and journals.

Practical Structure

The structure of systemd—outside of its executable files—is contained in its many configuration files. Although these files have different names and identifier extensions, they are all called "unit" files. Units are the basis of everything systemd. Unit files are ASCII plain-text files that are accessible to and can be created or modified by a SysAdmin. There are a number of unit file types, and each has its own man page. Table 5-1 lists some of these unit file types by their filename extensions and a short description of each.

Table 5-1. Some systemd unit file types

systemd Unit	Description
.automount	The **.automount** units are used to implement on-demand (i.e., plug and play) and mounting of filesystem units in parallel during startup.
.device	The **.device** unit files define hardware and virtual devices that are exposed to the SysAdmin in the **/dev/directory**. Not all devices have unit files; typically, block devices such as hard drives, network devices, and some others have unit files.
.mount	The **.mount** unit defines a mount point on the Linux filesystem directory structure.

(continued)

119

CHAPTER 5 MANAGE SYSTEMD UNITS WITH SYSTEMCTL

Table 5-1. (*continued*)

systemd Unit	Description
.scope	The **.scope** unit defines and manages a set of system processes. This unit is not configured using unit files; rather, it is created programmatically. Per the **systemd.scope** man page, "The main purpose of scope units is grouping worker processes of a system service for organization and for managing resources."
.service	The **.service** unit files define processes that are managed by systemd. These include services such as crond cups (Common Unix Printing System), iptables, multiple logical volume management (LVM) services, NetworkManager, and more.
.slice	The **.slice** unit defines a "slice," which is a conceptual division of system resources that are related to a group of processes. You can think of all system resources as a pie and this subset of resources as a "slice" out of that pie.
.socket	The **.socket** units define inter-process communication sockets, such as network sockets.
.swap	The **.swap** units define swap devices or files.
.target	The **.target** units define groups of unit files that define startup synchronization points, runlevels, and services. Target units define the services and other units that must be active in order to start successfully.
.timer	The **.timer** unit defines timers that can initiate program execution at specified times.

systemctl

systemd provides the **systemctl** command that is used to start and stop services, configure them to launch (or not) at system startup, and monitor the current status of running services.

> **EXPERIMENT 5-2: MANAGING SYSTEMD SERVICES**
>
> In a terminal session as the root user, ensure that root's home directory (~) is the Present Working Directory[1] (PWD). To begin looking at units in various ways, list all of the loaded and active systemd units. **systemctl** automatically pipes its stdout[2] data stream through the **less** pager, so you don't have to do that yourself. I've trimmed the output data stream considerably but left enough so you can see the wide range of systemd units. Your own system will display a long list of units.
>
> ```
> # systemctl
>   UNIT                         LOAD    ACTIVE SUB
>     DESCRIPTION       >
>  <SNIP>
>   lightdm.service              loaded active running
>     Light Display Man>
>   lm_sensors.service           loaded active exited
>     Hardware Monitori>
>  <SNIP>
>   NetworkManager.service       loaded active running
>     Network Manager
>  <SNIP>
> ```

---

[1] Wikipedia, "Present Working Directory," https://en.wikipedia.org/wiki/Pwd
[2] Wikipedia, "Standard Output," https://en.wikipedia.org/wiki/Standard_streams#Standard_output_(stdout)

```
  sshd.service                    loaded active running
    OpenSSH server da>
<SNIP>
  dev-zram0.swap                  loaded active active
    Compressed Swap o>
  basic.target                    loaded active active
    Basic System
  cryptsetup.target               loaded active active
    Local Encrypted V>
  getty.target                    loaded active active
    Login Prompts
  graphical.target                loaded active active
    Graphical Interfa>
  integritysetup.target           loaded active active
    Local Integrity P>
  local-fs-pre.target             loaded active active
    Preparation for L>
  local-fs.target                 loaded active active
    Local File Systems
  multi-user.target               loaded active active
    Multi-User System
  network-online.target           loaded active active
    Network is Online
<SNIP>
  sysstat-collect.timer           loaded active waiting
    Run system activi>
  sysstat-summary.timer           loaded active waiting
    Generate summary >
  systemd-tmpfiles-clean.timer loaded active waiting
    Daily Cleanup of >
  unbound-anchor.timer            loaded active waiting
    daily update of t>
```

```
LOAD   = Reflects whether the unit definition was
properly loaded.
ACTIVE = The high-level unit activation state, i.e.
generalization of SUB.
SUB    = The low-level unit activation state, values depend
on unit type.
200 loaded units listed. Pass --all to see loaded but
inactive units, too.
```

As you scroll through the data in your terminal session, look for some specific things. The first section lists devices such as hard drives, sound cards, network interface cards, and TTY devices. Another section shows the filesystem mount points. Other sections include various services and a list of all loaded and active targets.

The **sysstat** timers at the bottom of the output are used to collect and generate daily system activity summaries for SAR. SAR is a very useful problem-solving tool. You can learn more about it in Chapter 13 of my book *Using and Administering Linux: Volume 1, Zero to SysAdmin: Getting Started.*[3] Near the very bottom, three lines describe the meanings of the statuses (loaded, active, and sub). Press **q** to exit the pager.

Use the following command (as suggested in the last line of the output above) to see all the units that are installed, whether or not they are loaded. I won't reproduce the output here, because you can scroll through it on your own. The systemctl program has an excellent tab-completion facility that makes it easy to enter complex commands without needing to memorize all the options:

```
# systemctl list-unit-files
```

---

[3] Both, David, *Using and Administering Linux: Volume 1, Zero to SysAdmin: Getting Started, 2nd Edition*, Apress, 2023, 395-400.

You can see that some units are disabled. Table 1 in the man page for systemctl lists and provides short descriptions of the entries you might see in this listing. Use the **-t** (type) option to view just the timer units:

```
# systemctl list-unit-files -t timer
UNIT FILE                          STATE
chrony-dnssrv@.timer               disabled
dnf-makecache.timer                enabled
fstrim.timer                       disabled
logrotate.timer                    disabled
logwatch.timer                     disabled
mdadm-last-resort@.timer           static
mlocate-updatedb.timer             enabled
sysstat-collect.timer              enabled
sysstat-summary.timer              enabled
systemd-tmpfiles-clean.timer       static
unbound-anchor.timer               enabled
```

You could do the same thing with this alternative, which provides considerably more detail:

```
# systemctl list-timers
Thu 2020-04-16 09:06:20 EDT  3min 59s left   n/a                       n/a              systemd-tmpfiles-clean.timer systemd-tmpfiles-clean.service
Thu 2020-04-16 10:02:01 EDT  59min left      Thu 2020-04-16 09:01:32 EDT  49s ago       dnf-makecache.timer          dnf-makecache.service
Thu 2020-04-16 13:00:00 EDT  3h 57min left   n/a                       n/a              sysstat-collect.timer        sysstat-collect.service
```

CHAPTER 5   MANAGE SYSTEMD UNITS WITH SYSTEMCTL

```
Fri 2020-04-17 00:00:00 EDT   14h left        Thu 2020-04-16
12:51:37 EDT   3h 49min left mlocate-updatedb.timer
mlocate-updatedb.service
Fri 2020-04-17 00:00:00 EDT   14h left        Thu 2020-04-16
12:51:37 EDT   3h 49min left unbound-anchor.timer
unbound-anchor.service
Fri 2020-04-17 00:07:00 EDT   15h
left      n/a                         n/a               sysstat-
summary.timer           sysstat-summary.service

6 timers listed.
Pass --all to see loaded but inactive timers, too.
```

Although there is no option to do **systemctl** list-mounts, you can list the mount point unit files:

```
# systemctl list-unit-files -t mount
UNIT FILE                        STATE
-.mount                          generated
boot.mount                       generated
dev-hugepages.mount              static
dev-mqueue.mount                 static
home.mount                       generated
proc-fs-nfsd.mount               static
proc-sys-fs-binfmt_misc.mount    disabled
run-vmblock\x2dfuse.mount        disabled
sys-fs-fuse-connections.mount    static
sys-kernel-config.mount          static
sys-kernel-debug.mount           static
tmp.mount                        generated
usr.mount                        generated
var-lib-nfs-rpc_pipefs.mount     static
var.mount                        generated
15 unit files listed.
```

The STATE column in this data stream is interesting and requires a bit of explanation. The "generated" states indicate that the mount unit was generated on the fly during startup using the information in **/etc/fstab**. The program that generates these mount units is **/lib/systemd/system-generators/systemd-fstab-generator,** along with other tools that generate a number of other unit types. The "static" mount units are for filesystems like **/proc** and **/sys**, and the files for these are located in the **/usr/lib/systemd/system** directory.

Now, look at the service units. This command will show all services installed on the host, whether or not they are active:

`systemctl --all -t service`

The bottom of this listing of service units displays 166 as the total number of loaded units on my host. Your number will probably differ.

Unit files do not have a filename extension (such as **.unit**) to help identify them, so you can generalize that most configuration files that belong to systemd are unit files of one type or another. The few remaining files are mostly **.conf** files located in **/etc/systemd**. Unit files are stored in the **/usr/lib/systemd** directory and its subdirectories, while the **/etc/systemd/** directory and its subdirectories contain symbolic links to the unit files necessary to the local configuration of this host.

To explore this, make **/etc/systemd** the PWD and list its contents. Then make **/etc/systemd/system** the PWD and list its contents, and list the contents of at least a couple of the current PWD's subdirectories. Take a look at the **default.target** file, which determines which runlevel target the system will boot to. In the second article in this series, I explained how to change the default target from the GUI (**graphical.target**) to the command-line only (**multi-user.target**) target. The **default.target** file on my test VM is simply a symlink to **/usr/lib/systemd/system/graphical.target**.

Take a few minutes to examine the contents of the **/etc/systemd/system/default.target** file:

```
# cat default.target
#  SPDX-License-Identifier: LGPL-2.1+
#
#  This file is part of systemd.
#
#  systemd is free software; you can redistribute it and/or
   modify it
#  under the terms of the GNU Lesser General Public License
   as published by
#  the Free Software Foundation; either version 2.1 of the
   License, or
#  (at your option) any later version.

[Unit]
Description=Graphical Interface
Documentation=man:systemd.special(7)
Requires=multi-user.target
Wants=display-manager.service
Conflicts=rescue.service rescue.target
After=multi-user.target rescue.service rescue.target
display-manager.service
AllowIsolate=yes
```

Note that this requires the **multi-user.target**; the **graphical.target** cannot start if the **multi-user.target** is not already up and running. It also says it "wants" the **display-manager.service** unit. A "want" does not need to be fulfilled in order for the unit to start successfully. If the "want" cannot be fulfilled, it will be ignored by systemd, and the rest of the target will start regardless.

The subdirectories in **/etc/systemd/system** are lists of wants for various targets. Take a few minutes to explore the files and their contents in the **/etc/systemd/system/graphical.target.wants** directory.

The **systemd.unit** man page contains a lot of good information about unit files, their structure, the sections they can be divided into, and the options that can be used. It also lists many of the unit types, all of which have their own man pages. If you want to interpret a unit file, this would be a good place to start.

Service Units

A Fedora installation usually installs and enables services that particular hosts do not need for normal operation. Conversely, sometimes it doesn't include services that need to be installed, enabled, and started. Services that are not needed for the Linux host to function as desired, but which are installed and possibly running, represent a security risk and should—at minimum—be stopped and disabled and—at best—should be uninstalled.

EXPERIMENT 5-3: MANAGING SERVICE UNITS

The **systemctl** command is used to manage systemd units, including services, targets, mounts, and more. Take a closer look at the list of services to identify services that will never be used.

```
# systemctl --all -t service
UNIT                              LOAD      ACTIVE   SUB
  DESCRIPTION
<snip>
chronyd.service                   loaded    active   running
  NTP client/server
```

CHAPTER 5   MANAGE SYSTEMD UNITS WITH SYSTEMCTL

```
crond.service                loaded     active    running
  Command Scheduler
cups.service                 loaded     active    running
  CUPS Scheduler
dbus-daemon.service          loaded     active    running
  D-Bus System Message Bus
<SNIP>
● ip6tables.service          not-found  inactive  dead
  ip6tables.service
● ipset.service              not-found  inactive  dead
  ipset.service
● iptables.service           not-found  inactive  dead
  iptables.service
<SNIP>
firewalld.
service                      loaded     active    running  firewalld
  - dynamic firewall daemon
<SNIP>
● ntpd.service               not-found  inactive  dead
  ntpd.service
● ntpdate.service            not-found  inactive  dead
  ntpdate.service
pcscd.service                loaded     active    running
  PC/SC Smart Card Daemon
```

I have pruned most of the output from the command to save space. The services that show "loaded active running" are obvious. The "not-found" services are ones that systemd is aware of but are not installed on the Linux host. If you want to run those services, you must install the packages that contain them.

CHAPTER 5   MANAGE SYSTEMD UNITS WITH SYSTEMCTL

This data stream is piped to the **less** pager, so you can page up and down and search for text strings in the stream. Start a search just as you would in less, using the / (slash), and then typing the search string.

Find the **pcscd.service** unit. This is the PC/SC smart card daemon. Its function is to communicate with smart card readers. Many Linux hosts—including VMs—have no need for this reader nor the service that is loaded and taking up memory and CPU resources. You can stop this service and disable it, so it will not restart on future reboots. First, check its status:

systemctl status pcscd.service
```
● pcscd.service - PC/SC Smart Card Daemon
     Loaded: loaded (/usr/lib/systemd/system/pcscd.service;
             indirect; preset: disabled)
    Drop-In: /usr/lib/systemd/system/service.d
             └─10-timeout-abort.conf, 50-keep-warm.conf
     Active: active (running) since Thu 2024-11-21 12:14:01
EST; 1s ago
 Invocation: 651b0198bdcb49f8ba99b1290f04c817
TriggeredBy: ● pcscd.socket
       Docs: man:pcscd(8)
   Main PID: 265754 (pcscd)
      Tasks: 3 (limit: 9470)
     Memory: 912K (peak: 1.5M)
        CPU: 22ms
     CGroup: /system.slice/pcscd.service
             └─265754 /usr/sbin/pcscd --foreground
               --auto-exit
Nov 21 12:14:01 testvm1.both.org systemd[1]: Started pcscd.
service - PC/SC Smart Card Daemon.
```

Nov 21 12:14:01 testvm1.both.org (pcscd)[265754]: pcscd.
service: Referenced but unset environment variable evaluates
to an empty string: PC>
lines 1-17/17 (END)

This data illustrates the additional information systemd provides vs. SystemV, which only reports whether or not the service is running. Note that specifying the **.service** unit type in the command is optional. Now stop and disable the service, then recheck its status:

systemctl disable --now pcscd
Removed '/etc/systemd/system/sockets.target.wants/pcscd.socket'.
Disabling 'pcscd.service', but its triggering units are still active:
pcscd.socket
systemctl status pcscd
○ pcscd.service - PC/SC Smart Card Daemon
     Loaded: loaded (/usr/lib/systemd/system/pcscd.service;
             indirect; preset: disabled)
    Drop-In: /usr/lib/systemd/system/service.d
             └─10-timeout-abort.conf, 50-keep-warm.conf
     Active: inactive (dead) since Thu 2024-11-21 12:15:02
             EST; 19min ago
   Duration: 1min 1.116s
 Invocation: 651b01o pcscd.service - PC/SC Smart Card Daemon
     Loaded: loaded (/usr/lib/systemd/system/pcscd.service;
             indirect; preset: disabled)
    Drop-In: /usr/lib/systemd/system/service.d
             └─10-timeout-abort.conf, 50-keep-warm.conf
     Active: inactive (dead) since Thu 2024-11-21 12:15:02
             EST; 19min ago

```
     Duration: 1min 1.116s
   Invocation: 651b0198bdcb49f8ba99b1290f04c817
  TriggeredBy: ● pcscd.socket
         Docs: man:pcscd(8)
     Main PID: 265754 (code=exited, status=0/SUCCESS)
     Mem peak: 1.5M
          CPU: 23ms
```

The short log entry display for most services prevents having to search through various log files to locate this type of information. Note the error message indicating that the pcscd.socket can activate the service. Sockets are used for many services so that the service doesn't necessarily need to run all the time. A message or request sent to the socket starts the corresponding service.

We don't want the smart card daemon to start at all, so disable the socket and verify its new status.

```
# systemctl disable --now pcscd.socket
Removed '/etc/systemd/system/sockets.target.wants/pcscd.socket'.
root@testvm1:~# systemctl status pcscd.socket
○ pcscd.socket - PC/SC Smart Card Daemon Activation Socket
     Loaded: loaded (/usr/lib/systemd/system/pcscd.socket;
             disabled; preset: enabled)
     Active: inactive (dead)
   Triggers: ● pcscd.service
     Listen: /run/pcscd/pcscd.comm (Stream)

Nov 20 06:58:37 testvm1.both.org systemd[1]: Listening on pcscd.socket - PC/SC Smart Card Daemon Activation Socket.
Nov 21 12:38:32 testvm1.both.org systemd[1]: pcscd.socket: Deactivated successfully.
```

```
Nov 21 12:38:32 testvm1.both.org systemd[1]: Closed pcscd.
socket - PC/SC Smart Card Daemon Activation Socket.
Nov 21 12:38:40 testvm1.both.org systemd[1]: Listening on
pcscd.socket - PC/SC Smart Card Daemon Activation Socket.
Nov 21 12:38:44 testvm1.both.org systemd[1]: pcscd.socket:
Deactivated successfully.
Nov 21 12:38:44 testvm1.both.org systemd[1]: Closed pcscd.
socket - PC/SC Smart Card Daemon Activation Socket.
root@testvm1:~#
```

Mounts the Old Way

A mount unit defines all of the parameters required to mount a filesystem on a designated mount point. systemd can manage mount units with more flexibility than those using the **/etc/fstab** filesystem configuration file. Despite this, systemd still uses the **/etc/fstab** file for filesystem configuration and mounting purposes. systemd uses the **systemd-fstab-generator** tool to create transient mount units from the data in the **fstab** file.

EXPERIMENT 5-4: MOUNTING A NEW FILESYSTEM

In this experiment, we'll create a new partition, filesystem, and an fstab entry to mount it.

Note The volume group and logical volume names may be different on your test system. Be sure to use the names that are pertinent to your system.

CHAPTER 5   MANAGE SYSTEMD UNITS WITH SYSTEMCTL

You will need to create a new partition or logical volume, then make an EXT4 filesystem on it. Add a label to the filesystem, **TestFS**, and create a directory for a mount point **/TestFS**. To try this on your own, first, verify that you have free space on the volume group. Here is what that looks like on my VM where I have some space available on the volume group to create a new logical volume:

```
# lsblk
NAME              MAJ:MIN RM   SIZE RO TYPE MOUNTPOINTS
sda                 8:0    0   120G  0 disk
├─sda1              8:1    0    2M   0 part
├─sda2              8:2    0    5G   0 part /boot
└─sda3              8:3    0   115G  0 part
  ├─vg01-root    253:0    0    5G   0 lvm  /
  ├─vg01-usr     253:1    0    30G  0 lvm  /usr
  ├─vg01-var     253:2    0    30G  0 lvm  /var
  ├─vg01-home    253:3    0    5G   0 lvm  /home
  └─vg01-tmp     253:4    0    10G  0 lvm  /tmp
sr0                11:0    1  1024M  0 rom
zram0             252:0    0   7.7G  0 disk [SWAP]
root@testvm1:~# vgs
  VG   #PV #LV #SN Attr   VSize   VFree
  vg01   1   5   0 wz--n- 114.99g 34.99g
```

Then create a new volume on VG01 named TestFS. It does not need to be large; 1GB is fine. Then create a filesystem, add the filesystem label, and create the mount point.

```
# lvcreate -L 1G -n TestFS vg01
  Logical volume "TestFS" created.
# mkfs -t ext4 /dev/mapper/vg01-TestFS
mke2fs 1.45.3 (14-Jul-2019)
Creating filesystem with 262144 4k blocks and 65536 inodes
```

CHAPTER 5   MANAGE SYSTEMD UNITS WITH SYSTEMCTL

```
Filesystem UUID: 8718fba9-419f-4915-ab2d-8edf811b5d23
Superblock backups stored on blocks:
     32768, 98304, 163840, 229376

Allocating group tables: done
Writing inode tables: done
Creating journal (8192 blocks): done
Writing superblocks and filesystem accounting
information: done
```

e2label /dev/mapper/vg01-TestFS TestFS
mkdir /TestFS

Now, mount the new filesystem:

mount /TestFS/
```
mount: /TestFS/: can't find in /etc/fstab.
```

That's what I did and it won't work because I didn't have an entry in **/etc/fstab**. You can mount the new filesystem even without the entry in **/etc/fstab** using both the device name (as it appears in **/dev**) and the mount point. Mounting in this manner is simpler than it used to be—it used to require the filesystem type as an argument. The mount command is now smart enough to detect the filesystem type and mount it accordingly.

Try it again.

mount /dev/mapper/vg01-TestFS /TestFS/
lsblk
```
NAME              MAJ:MIN RM   SIZE RO TYPE MOUNTPOINT
sda                 8:0    0   120G  0 disk
├─sda1              8:1    0    4G   0 part /boot
└─sda2              8:2    0   116G  0 part
  ├─VG01-root     253:0    0    5G   0 lvm  /
  ├─VG01-swap     253:1    0    8G   0 lvm  [SWAP]
  ├─VG01-usr      253:2    0   30G   0 lvm  /usr
```

135

CHAPTER 5   MANAGE SYSTEMD UNITS WITH SYSTEMCTL

```
  ├─VG01-home    253:3    0   20G  0 lvm  /home
  ├─VG01-var     253:4    0   20G  0 lvm  /var
  ├─VG01-tmp     253:5    0   10G  0 lvm  /tmp
  └─VG01-TestFS  253:6    0    1G  0 lvm  /TestFS
sr0              11:0     1 1024M  0 rom
zram0            252:0    0  7.7G  0 disk [SWAP]
```

Now the new filesystem is mounted in the proper location. List the mount unit files.

`systemctl list-unit-files -t mount`

This command does not show a file for the **/TestFS** filesystem because no file exists for it. The command **systemctl status TestFS.mount** does not display any information about the new filesystem either. You can try it using wildcards with the **systemctl status** command:

`systemctl status *mount`
* usr.mount - /usr
    Loaded: loaded (/etc/fstab; generated)
    Active: active (mounted)
     Where: /usr
      What: /dev/mapper/VG01-usr
      Docs: man:fstab(5)
            man:systemd-fstab-generator(8)

<SNIP>
* TestFS.mount - /TestFS
    Loaded: loaded (/proc/self/mountinfo)
    Active: active (mounted) since Fri 2020-04-17 16:02:26
            EDT; 1min 18s ago
     Where: /TestFS
      What: /dev/mapper/VG01-TestFS

- run-user-0.mount - /run/user/0
  Loaded: loaded (/proc/self/mountinfo)
  Active: active (mounted) since Thu 2020-04-16 08:52:29
          EDT; 1 day 5h ago
   Where: /run/user/0
    What: tmpfs

- var.mount - /var
  Loaded: loaded (/etc/fstab; generated)
  Active: active (mounted) since Thu 2020-04-16 12:51:34
          EDT; 1 day 1h ago
   Where: /var
    What: /dev/mapper/VG01-var
    Docs: man:fstab(5)
          man:systemd-fstab-generator(8)
   Tasks: 0 (limit: 19166)
  Memory: 212.0K
     CPU: 5ms
  CGroup: /system.slice/var.mount

This command provides some very interesting information about your system's mounts, and your new filesystem shows up here. The **/var** and **/usr** filesystems are identified as being generated from **/etc/fstab**, while your new filesystem simply shows that it is loaded and provides the location of the info file in the **/proc/self/mountinfo** file.

Next, automate this mount. First, do it the old-fashioned way by adding an entry in **/etc/fstab**. Later, I'll show you how to do it the new way, which will teach you more about creating units and integrating them into the startup sequence.

Unmount **/TestFS** and add the following line to the **/etc/fstab** file:

/dev/mapper/vg01-TestFS   /TestFS   ext4   defaults   1 2

CHAPTER 5 MANAGE SYSTEMD UNITS WITH SYSTEMCTL

After changing fstab, use "systemctl daemon-reload" to reload the daemon configurations, including the filesystems in /etc/fstab.

```
# systemctl daemon-reload
```

Now, mount the filesystem with the simpler version of the **mount** command and list the mount units again.

```
# mount /TestFS
```

```
# systemctl status *mount
<SNIP>
● TestFS.mount - /TestFS
     Loaded: loaded (/etc/fstab; generated)
     Active: active (mounted) since Thu 2024-11-21 16:37:23
             EST; 2min 41s ago
 Invocation: 45988dea733a4bf39d9aafae1597037d
      Where: /TestFS
       What: /dev/mapper/vg01-TestFS
       Docs: man:fstab(5)
             man:systemd-fstab-generator(8)
<SNIP>
```

The information for this mount did not change because the filesystem was manually mounted. Reboot and run the command again, and this time specify **TestFS.mount** rather than using the wildcard. The results for this mount are now consistent with it being mounted at startup:

```
# systemctl status TestFS.mount
● TestFS.mount - /TestFS
   Loaded: loaded (/etc/fstab; generated)
   Active: active (mounted) since Fri 2020-04-17 16:30:21
           EDT; 1min 38s ago
    Where: /TestFS
     What: /dev/mapper/VG01-TestFS
```

CHAPTER 5   MANAGE SYSTEMD UNITS WITH SYSTEMCTL

```
     Docs: man:fstab(5)
           man:systemd-fstab-generator(8)
    Tasks: 0 (limit: 19166)
   Memory: 72.0K
      CPU: 6ms
   CGroup: /system.slice/TestFS.mount

Apr 17 16:30:21 testvm1 systemd[1]: Mounting /TestFS...
Apr 17 16:30:21 testvm1 systemd[1]: Mounted /TestFS.
```

Creating a Mount Unit

Mount units may be configured either with the traditional **/etc/fstab** file or with systemd units. Fedora uses the **fstab** file as it is created during the installation. However, systemd uses the **systemd-fstab-generator** program to translate the **fstab** file into systemd units for each entry in the **fstab** file. Now that you know you can use systemd **.mount** unit files for filesystem mounting, let's create a mount unit for the new filesystem.

> **EXPERIMENT 5-5: MOUNTING WITH SYSTEMD**
>
> First, unmount **/TestFS**. Edit the **/etc/fstab** file and delete or comment out the **TestFS** line. Now, create a new file with the name **TestFS.mount** in the **/usr/local/lib/systemd/system** directory.[4] Edit it to contain the configuration data below. The unit filename and the name of the mount point *must* be identical, or the mount will fail.

---

[4] The /usr/local/lib/systemd/system is the correct location to place locally created systemd unit files.

```
# This mount unit is for the TestFS filesystem
# Copyright David Both, 2025
# GNU All-Permissive License:
# Copying and distribution of this file, with or without
# modification, are permitted in any medium without royalty
# provided the copyright notice and this notice are
  preserved.
# This file is offered as-is, without any warranty.
# This file should be located in the
# /usr/local/lib/systemd/system directory

[Unit]
Description=TestFS Mount

[Mount]
What=/dev/mapper/VG01-TestFS
Where=/TestFS
Type=ext4
Options=defaults

[Install]
WantedBy=multi-user.target
```

The **Description** line in the **[Unit]** section is for us humans, and it provides the name that's shown when you list mount units with **systemctl -t mount**. The data in the **[Mount]** section of this file contains essentially the same data that would be found in the **fstab** file.

You can verify the logic and syntax of the service unit.

systemd-analyze verify /etc/systemd/system/TestFS.service

Adhering to the Linux philosophy tenet, "silence is golden," a lack of output messages means that there are no errors in the scanned file.

CHAPTER 5 MANAGE SYSTEMD UNITS WITH SYSTEMCTL

Now enable the mount unit.

 # systemctl enable TestFS.mount
Created symlink /etc/systemd/system/multi-user.target.wants/
TestFS.mount → /etc/systemd/system/TestFS.mount.

This creates the symlink in the **/etc/systemd/system** directory, which will cause this mount unit to be mounted on all subsequent boots. The filesystem has not yet been mounted, so you must "start" it:

 # systemctl start TestFS.mount

You could also enable and start the mount unit at the same time.

 # systemctl enable --now TestFS.mount

Verify that the filesystem has been mounted:

 # systemctl status TestFS.mount
```
● TestFS.mount - TestFS Mount
   Loaded: loaded (/etc/systemd/system/TestFS.mount;
           enabled; vendor preset: disabled)
   Active: active (mounted) since Sat 2020-04-18 09:59:53
           EDT; 14s ago
    Where: /TestFS
     What: /dev/mapper/VG01-TestFS
    Tasks: 0 (limit: 19166)
   Memory: 76.0K
      CPU: 3ms
   CGroup: /system.slice/TestFS.mount

Apr 18 09:59:53 testvm1 systemd[1]: Mounting TestFS Mount...
Apr 18 09:59:53 testvm1 systemd[1]: Mounted TestFS Mount.
```

This experiment has been specifically about creating a unit file for a mount, but can be applied to other types of unit files as well. The details will be different, but the concepts are the same. Yes, I know it is still easier to add a line to the **/etc/fstab** file than it is to create a mount unit. But this is a good example of how to create a unit file because systemd does not have generators for every type of unit.

Summary

In this chapter, we looked at the practical structure of systemd. We explored systemd units in more detail and learned how to use the systemctl command to explore and manage units. We also explored how to stop and disable units and created a systemd mount unit to mount a new filesystem and enable it to initiate during startup.

Exercises

Perform these exercises to complete this chapter:

1. Define the term "Unit" as it applies to systemd.

2. Describe the process that systemd uses to mount filesystems that don't have a mount unit.

3. What's the point of using a mount unit for mounting new filesystems when the mount generator works just as well?

CHAPTER 5   MANAGE SYSTEMD UNITS WITH SYSTEMCTL

4. Why do we place locally created systemd unit files in the /usr/local/lib/systemd/system directory?

5. Create a small, new partition or logical volume on your test host. Configure it to mount using a systemd mount unit.

6. Verify that it's necessary to have a line in /etc/fstab for filesystems whether they're mounted the historical way or using systemd mount units.

CHAPTER 6

Control Your Computer Time and Date with systemd

Objectives

In this chapter, you will learn

- To list the typical reasons that time is important to computers
- To list and describe the two different times that modern Linux hosts maintain
- To define Network Time Protocol (NTP)
- To describe the NTP server hierarchy
- How to keep your Linux computer time in sync with the NTP servers
- To use chrony and systemd-timesyncd to manage the time services
- To use your Linux host as a time server for an internal network

CHAPTER 6   CONTROL YOUR COMPUTER TIME AND DATE WITH SYSTEMD

Overview

Does anybody really know what time it is? Does anybody really care?

—Chicago, 1969

Perhaps that rock group didn't care what time it was, but our computers and devices really need to know the exact time.

Most people are concerned with time. We get up in time to perform our morning rituals and commute to work, take a break for lunch, meet a project deadline, celebrate birthdays and holidays, catch a plane, and so much more.

Some of us are even obsessed with time. My watch is solar-powered and obtains the exact time from the National Institute of Standards and Technology (NIST) in Fort Collins, Colorado, via the WWVB time signal radio station located there. The time signals are synced to the atomic clock, also located in Fort Collins. My Fitbit syncs up to my phone, which is synced to a Network Time Protocol (NTP) server, which is ultimately synced to the atomic clock.

And, of course, I have an NTP time server in my home network, and all my other hosts get their time from that.

Although we SysAdmins use command-line programs and Bash scripts to automate the tasks we perform as SysAdmins, what happens when tasks need to be performed at times that are not convenient for us as humans? For example, if we do backups at 01:01AM every morning, or run a maintenance script at 03:00AM every Sunday, I most definitely do not want to get out of bed to perform those tasks.

Linux provides multiple tools and ways in which we can use those tools to run tasks at specified times in the future, repeating as needed or just for a one-time occurrence. However, keeping accurate time is critical to ensuring that scheduled jobs run at the correct times.

CHAPTER 6   CONTROL YOUR COMPUTER TIME AND DATE WITH SYSTEMD

This chapter starts by looking at computer times, NTP, and the use of chrony to synchronize the time our computer keeps with a standardized time reference such as an atomic clock. We'll then move on to using systemd-timesyncd.

Why Time Is Important to Computers

There are many reasons our devices and computers need the exact time. For example, in banking, stock markets, and other financial businesses, transactions must be maintained in the proper order, and exact time sequences are critical for that.

Our phones, tablets, cars, GPS systems, and computers all require precise time and date settings. I want the clock on my computer desktop to be correct, so I can count on my local calendar application to pop up reminders at the correct time. More importantly, the correct time also ensures old-style cron jobs and systemd timers trigger at the correct time.

The correct time is also important for logging, so it's easier to locate specific log entries based on the time. For one example, I once worked in DevOps (it was not called that at the time) for the State of North Carolina email system. We used to process more than 20 million emails per day. Following the trail of email through a series of servers or determining the exact sequence of events by using log files on geographically dispersed hosts can be much easier when the computers in question keep exact times.

Multiple Times

Linux hosts have two times to consider: system time and RTC time. RTC stands for real-time clock, which is a fancy and not particularly accurate name for the system hardware clock.

The hardware clock runs continuously, even when the computer is turned off, powered by the battery on the system motherboard. The RTC's primary function is to keep the time when a connection to a time server is not available. In the dark ages of personal computers, there was no Internet to connect to a time server, so the only time a computer had available was the internal clock. Operating systems had to rely on the RTC at boot time, and the user had to manually set the system time using the hardware BIOS configuration interface to ensure it was correct.

The hardware clock doesn't understand the concept of time zones; only the time is stored in the RTC, not the time zone nor an offset from UTC (Universal Coordinated Time, which is also known as GMT, or Greenwich Mean Time). The RTC time can be set with a tool I'll cover later in this chapter.

The system time is the time known by the operating system. It is the time you see on the GUI clock on your desktop, in the output from the date command, in timestamps for logs, and in file access, modify, and change times.

The rtc man page contains a more complete discussion of the RTC and system clocks and RTC's functionality.

NTP

NTP is the Network Time Protocol[1] that is used by computers worldwide to synchronize their times with Internet standard reference clocks via a hierarchy of NTP servers.

There are multiple tools available for management of NTP timekeeping. We look at two, chrony and systemd-timesync.

---

[1]Wikipedia, `https://en.wikipedia.org/wiki/Network_Time_Protocol`

The NTP Server Hierarchy

The NTP server hierarchy is built in layers called strata. Each stratum is a layer of NTP servers. The primary servers are at stratum 1, and they are connected directly to various national time services at stratum 0 via satellite, radio, or even modems over phone lines in some cases. Those time services at stratum 0 may be an atomic clock, a radio receiver that is tuned to the signals broadcast by an atomic clock, or a GPS receiver using the highly accurate clock signals broadcast by GPS satellites.

To prevent time requests from time servers lower in the hierarchy, that is, with a higher stratum number, from overwhelming the primary reference servers, there are several thousand public NTP stratum 2 servers that are open and available for all to use. Many users and organizations, myself included, with large numbers of their own hosts that need an NTP server, set up their own time servers so that only one local host actually accesses the stratum 2 time servers. The remaining hosts in our networks are all configured to use the local time server, which, in my case, is a stratum 3 server.

NTP Implementation Options

The original NTP implementation is ntpd, the NTP daemon, and it has been joined by two newer ones, chronyd and systemd-timesyncd. All three keep the local host's time synchronized with an NTP time server. The systemd-timesyncd service is not as robust as chronyd, but it is sufficient for most purposes. It can perform large time jumps if the RTC is far out of sync, and it can adjust the system time gradually to stay in sync with the NTP server if the local system time drifts a bit. The systemd-timesync service cannot be used as a time server.

Chrony is an NTP implementation containing two programs: the chronyd daemon and a command-line interface called chronyc. Chrony has some features that make it the best choice for many environments, chiefly:

- Chrony can synchronize to the time server much faster than the old ntpd service. This is good for laptops or desktops that do not run constantly.

- It can compensate for fluctuating clock frequencies, such as when a host hibernates or enters sleep mode or when the clock speed varies due to frequency stepping that slows clock speeds when loads are low.

- It handles intermittent network connections and bandwidth saturation.

- It adjusts for network delays and latency.

- After the initial time sync, chrony never stops the clock. This ensures stable and consistent time intervals for many system services and applications.

- Chrony can work even without a network connection. In this case, the local host or server can be updated manually using the **date** command.

- Chrony can act as an NTP server.

Just to be clear, NTP is a protocol that is implemented on a Linux host using either chrony or the systemd-timesyncd.service.

The NTP, chrony, and systemd-timesyncd RPM packages are available in standard Linux distribution repositories. The systemd-udev RPM is a rule-based device node and kernel event manager that is installed by default with Fedora but not enabled.

You can install all three and switch between them, but that's a lot of work and not worth the trouble. Modern releases of Fedora and RHEL have moved from NTP to chrony as their default timekeeping implementation. They also install systemd-timesyncd. I find that chrony works well, provides a better interface than the NTP service, presents much more information, and increases control, which are all advantages for the SysAdmin.

NTP Client Configuration

The NTP client configuration is simple and requires little or no change. The NTP server can be defined by the SysAdmin during the Linux installation, or it can be provided by the DHCP server at boot time. The default /etc/chrony.conf file shown in its entirety in Figure 6-1 requires no alterations to work properly as a client. For Fedora, chrony uses the Fedora NTP pool. RHEL also has its own NTP server pool. Like many Red Hat–based distributions, the configuration file is well commented.

```
# Use public servers from the pool.ntp.org project.
# Please consider joining the pool (http://www.pool.ntp.org/join.html).
pool 2.fedora.pool.ntp.org iburst

# Record the rate at which the system clock gains/losses time.
driftfile /var/lib/chrony/drift

# Allow the system clock to be stepped in the first three updates
# if its offset is larger than 1 second.
makestep 1.0 3

# Enable kernel synchronization of the real-time clock (RTC).

# Enable hardware timestamping on all interfaces that support it.
#hwtimestamp *

# Increase the minimum number of selectable sources required to adjust
# the system clock.
#minsources 2

# Allow NTP client access from local network.
#allow 192.168.0.0/16

# Serve time even if not synchronized to a time source.
#local stratum 10

# Specify file containing keys for NTP authentication.
keyfile /etc/chrony.keys

# Get TAI-UTC offset and leap seconds from the system tz database.
leapsectz right/UTC

# Specify directory for log files.
logdir /var/log/chrony

# Select which information is logged.
#log measurements statistics tracking
```

Figure 6-1. The default chrony.conf configuration file

If an NTP server is defined during installation, it will be the first entry in chrony.conf. It will be preceded by a comment that the device was defined during installation, as in Figure 6-2. This is also the case if the DHCP service provides the IP address of a time server.

```
# These servers were defined in the installation:
server yorktown.both.org iburst
<SNIP>
```

Figure 6-2. *These two lines are added at the beginning of the chrony. conf configuration file if a time server is specified during installation*

NTP Server Pools

Line 3 of the default chrony.conf file lists a server that's part of a pool of Fedora NTP time servers. There are many server pools[2] with thousands of servers worldwide.

The objective for the server pools is to spread the load of millions of NTP clients so that no one server becomes overloaded with requests. Pools also provide multiple servers so that, if one is unavailable, others will be.

Most Linux distributions have their own pool of servers. Fedora and Red Hat are no exceptions. GitHub has a long list of top public server pools,[3] and all the major distributions and a number of lesser ones have pools listed. We'll use the list of Fedora pools in an experiment.

---

[2] NTP Pool Project, https://www.ntppool.org/en/
[3] GitHub NTP Server pools, https://gist.github.com/bakursait/1ccca11ccf4 6d5a6337600e6497ca3be

Chapter 6 Control Your Computer Time and Date with Systemd

Chrony

The chrony daemon, chronyd, runs in the background and monitors the time and status of the time server specified in the chrony.conf file. If the local time needs to be adjusted, chronyd does so smoothly without the programmatic trauma that would occur if the clock were to be instantly reset to a new time.

Chrony also provides the chronyc tool that allows us to monitor the current status of chrony and to make changes if necessary. The chronyc utility can be used as a command that accepts sub-commands, or it can be used as an interactive text mode program. We will use it both ways.

Yes, this book is about systemd, and chrony is not part of it. Why explore the chrony time and date services?

For now, at least, chrony is the default timekeeping service for Fedora and other distributions, so learning to use that provides both insight into the current service as well as a baseline from which to consider systemd-timesyncd. A big part of understanding systemd is knowing how to use it to interact with other services. The primary use of systemd is to run services that aren't systemd. The systemd timers are an important aspect of systemd, and their correct functioning is dependent upon accurate timekeeping. The systemd journal also relies on an accurate system clock.

The command we use to interact with chrony is **chronyc**, and it can be used directly on the command line or in scripts. It can also be used interactively in a Captive User Interface[4] (CUI).

---

[4] A Captive User Interface (CUI) is one in which the program takes control of the terminal, and all user input is through that interface, in this case, chronyc. There is no access to shell commands when using a CUI, unless the CUI provides for it.

CHAPTER 6　CONTROL YOUR COMPUTER TIME AND DATE WITH SYSTEMD

Using chronyc from the Command Line

Chronyc is used on the command line with a number of sub-commands that also can be used in scripts. I find this to be the method I use most frequently, so let's explore it first.

> **EXPERIMENT 6-1: GETTING STARTED WITH CHRONY**

Let's start by verifying that the chrony service is running on a newly installed Fedora 41 host. It should be on most current distributions.

```
# systemctl status chronyd
● chronyd.service - NTP client/server
     Loaded: loaded (/usr/lib/systemd/system/chronyd.
             service; enabled; preset: enabled)
    Drop-In: /usr/lib/systemd/system/service.d
             └─10-timeout-abort.conf
     Active: active (running) since Tue 2024-11-12 13:00:09
             EST; 19min ago
 Invocation: 2b74de9054d64b27ab824bc9d997f8dd
       Docs: man:chronyd(8)
             man:chrony.conf(5)
    Process: 1077 ExecStart=/usr/sbin/chronyd $OPTIONS
(code=exited, status=0/SUCCESS)
   Main PID: 1180 (chronyd)
      Tasks: 1 (limit: 19131)
     Memory: 4.6M (peak: 5.3M)
        CPU: 165ms
     CGroup: /system.slice/chronyd.service
             └─1180 /usr/sbin/chronyd -F 2

Nov 12 13:00:09 f41vm.both.oreg systemd[1]: Started chronyd.
service - NTP client/server.
```

CHAPTER 6   CONTROL YOUR COMPUTER TIME AND DATE WITH SYSTEMD

```
Nov 12 13:00:09 f41vm.both.oreg chronyd[1180]: chronyd
version 4.6.1 starting (+CMDMON +NTP +REFCLOCK +RTC +PRIVDROP
+SCFILTER +SIGND +ASYNCDNS +NTS +SECH>
Nov 12 13:00:09 f41vm.both.oreg chronyd[1180]: Using leap
second list /usr/share/zoneinfo/leap-seconds.list
Nov 12 13:00:09 f41vm.both.oreg chronyd[1180]: Frequency
18715.289 +/- 0.989 ppm read from /var/lib/chrony/drift
Nov 12 13:00:09 f41vm.both.oreg chronyd[1180]: Loaded
seccomp filter (level 2)
Nov 12 13:00:12 f41vm.both.oreg chronyd[1180]: Source
192.168.0.52 offline
Nov 12 13:00:13 f41vm.both.oreg chronyd[1180]: Source
192.168.0.52 online
Nov 12 13:00:13 f41vm.both.oreg chronyd[1180]: Could not add
source 192.168.0.52 : Already in use
Nov 12 13:00:17 f41vm.both.oreg chronyd[1180]: Selected
source 192.168.0.52
Nov 12 13:00:17 f41vm.both.oreg chronyd[1180]: System clock
TAI offset set to 37 seconds
```

However, this shows the systemd view of the chronyd.service and little about the timekeeping status of chrony.

The chrony service provides a command that can be used both interactively and directly on the command line. This command, **chronyc**, offers a much more in-depth look at the time on our hosts. Let's look at the current status of NTP on our hosts using the **chronyc** command.

CHAPTER 6   CONTROL YOUR COMPUTER TIME AND DATE WITH SYSTEMD

EXPERIMENT 6-2: CHRONY STATUS AND INFORMATION

Perform this experiment as the root user.

When used with the tracking sub-command, the `chronyc` command provides statistics that tell us how far off the local system is from the reference server.

```
# chronyc tracking
Reference ID    : C0A80034 (yorktown.both.org)
Stratum         : 3
Ref time (UTC)  : Tue Nov 12 18:29:26 2024
System time     : 0.000004870 seconds slow of NTP time
Last offset     : -0.000007259 seconds
RMS offset      : 0.000019674 seconds
Frequency       : 18715.217 ppm fast
Residual freq   : -0.001 ppm
Skew            : 0.087 ppm
Root delay      : 0.030009745 seconds
Root dispersion : 0.002015243 seconds
Update interval : 129.4 seconds
Leap status     : Normal
```

The Reference ID in the first line of the result is the server to which our host is synchronized. The rest of these lines are described in the chronyc(1) man page. The stratum line indicates which stratum our local VM is at, so the yorktown.both.org host—my own NTP server—is at stratum 3.

The other sub-command I find interesting and useful is sources which provides information about the time sources configured in chrony.conf

chronyc sources
```
MS Name/IP address              Stratum Poll Reach LastRx
Last sample
===============================================================
==================
^* yorktown.both.org              2    8    377    55    +418us[
+430us] +/-   18ms
```

This is the sole server provided by my DHCP server. You can see that in the section of dhcpd.conf I've copied below:

```
subnet 192.168.0.0 netmask 255.255.255.0 {

# --- default gateway
        option routers                  192.168.0.254;
        option subnet-mask              255.255.255.0;

#       option nis-domain               "both.org";
        option domain-name              "both.org";
        option domain-search            "both.org";
        option domain-name-servers      192.168.0.52,
                                        8.8.8.8, 8.8.4.4;

        option time-offset              -18000; # Eastern
                                                Standard Time
        option ntp-servers              192.168.0.52;
```

Obviously, the NTP sources will be different on your hosts. For most users, it will be provided by the DHCP server in the router provided by your ISP or the DHCP server on your organization's network.

Now let's modify the chrony.conf on our host. We'll add some servers from the Fedora pool[5] of NTP servers. We need to look these up.

---

[5] The chrony.conf file used to provide the list of Fedora pool servers, but no longer does.

The revised chrony.conf file looks like this:

```
# These servers were defined in the installation:
server yorktown.both.org iburst

# Use public servers from the pool.ntp.org project.
# Please consider joining the pool (https://www.pool.ntp.
org/join.html).

server 0.fedora.pool.ntp.org
server 1.fedora.pool.ntp.org
server 2.fedora.pool.ntp.org
server 3.fedora.pool.ntp.org
server 192.168.0.52 iburst prefer
<SNIP>
```

This shows a couple things of interest. First, the NTP server on my network is shown twice, on line 2, by fully qualified domain name (FQDN) and, second, by IP address, 192.168.0.52. Either form is acceptable.

The "iburst" argument is used to speed synchronization of the local system clock with the specified server. The "prefer" argument tells chrony to use this server if it's available, even if others might have faster response times.

Restart the chronyd service to activate the additional NTP servers.

```
# systemctl restart chronyd
```

Now look at the list of servers.

```
# chronyc sources
```

CHAPTER 6   CONTROL YOUR COMPUTER TIME AND DATE WITH SYSTEMD

```
MS Name/IP address             Stratum Poll Reach LastRx
Last sample
===============================================================
==================
^- triton.ellipse.net             2    10    377
933     +11ms[   +11ms] +/-    51ms
^- dutch.arpnet.net               2    10    377    489    +593us[
+598us] +/-    58ms
^- 167-248-62-201.oa02.lnk0>      3    10    377    942
+990us[+1040us] +/-    96ms
^- 23.155.40.38                   1    10    377    41m   +1198us[
+989us] +/-    21ms
^* yorktown.both.org              2    6     377    34    +109us[
+110us] +/-    16ms
```

Even though I have my local NTP server, yorktown, set as "prefer," it would have been selected anyway because it has the fastest response times.

These four new servers were provided by the NTP pool. The "S" column—Source State—indicates that the server with an asterisk (*) in that line is the one to which our host is currently synchronized. This is consistent with the data from the tracking sub-command.

```
# chronyc tracking
Reference ID    : C0A80034 (yorktown.both.org)
Stratum         : 3
Ref time (UTC)  : Tue Nov 12 22:06:40 2024
System time     : 0.000000119 seconds fast of NTP time
Last offset     : -0.000107550 seconds
RMS offset      : 0.000045720 seconds
Frequency       : 18714.738 ppm fast
Residual freq   : -0.045 ppm
Skew            : 0.134 ppm
```

Root delay   : 0.029763760 seconds
Root dispersion : 0.003469882 seconds
Update interval : 259.3 seconds
Leap status   : Normal

Note that the -v option for the sources sub-command provides a nice description of the fields in this output.

chronyc sources -v
  .-- Source mode '^' = server, '=' = peer, '#' = local clock.
 / .- Source state '*' = current best, '+' = combined, '-' = not combined,
| /   'x' = may be in error, '~' = too variable, '?' = unusable.
|| .- xxxx [yyyy] +/- zzzz
|| Reachability register (octal) -. | xxxx = adjusted offset,
|| Log2(Polling interval) --. | | yyyy = measured offset,
|| \ | | zzzz = estimated error.
|| | | \
MS Name/IP address   Stratum Poll Reach LastRx Last sample
===
^- triton.ellipse.net   2   10   377   400 +9226us[+9247us] +/-   51ms
^- dutch.arpnet.net   2   10   377 1000 +1230us[+1238us] +/-   47ms

```
^- 167-248-62-201.oa02.lnk0>      3  10   377   416   +159us[
  +181us] +/-   71ms
^- 23.155.40.38                    1  10   377   908   -357us[
  -371us] +/-   22ms
^* yorktown.both.org               2   6   377    26
   -19us[  -21us] +/-   17ms
```

This shows the list of servers, their stratum, and their response times. The asterisk (splat) in column 2 indicates the time source in use.

Type quit to exit from chronyc.

When we want a particular server to be the preferred time source for a host, even though it may have a slower response time, we could add the argument "prefer" to the end of the desired line. This configuration file is not sequence-sensitive, so server lines can be placed anywhere.

The host will always be synchronized with the preferred reference source so long as it is available. You could also use the fully qualified hostname for a remote reference server or the hostname only without the domain name for a local reference time source so long as the search statement is set in the /etc/resolv.conf file. I prefer the IP address to ensure that the time source is accessible even if DNS is not working. In most environments, the server name is probably the better option because NTP will continue to work even if the IP address of the server is changed.

You may not have a specific reference source with which you want to synchronize, so it is fine to use the defaults.

Chronyc As an Interactive Tool

I mentioned near the beginning of this section that chronyc can be used as an interactive command tool. I use this interface less frequently than I do directly on the command line, but it can be very useful.

CHAPTER 6   CONTROL YOUR COMPUTER TIME AND DATE WITH SYSTEMD

EXPERIMENT 6-3: USING CHRONYC INTERACTIVELY

Perform this experiment as root. Let's look at the `chronyc` command in more detail. Simply run the command without a sub-command, and you get a chronyc command prompt.

chronyc
chrony version 4.6.1
Copyright (C) 1997-2003, 2007, 2009-2024 Richard P. Curnow and others chrony comes with ABSOLUTELY NO WARRANTY. This is free software, and you are welcome to redistribute it under certain conditions. See the GNU General Public License version 2 for details.

chronyc> **tracking**
Reference ID   : C0A80034 (yorktown.both.org)
Stratum   : 3
Ref time (UTC) : Wed Nov 13 12:37:06 2024
System time   : 0.000003438 seconds slow of NTP time
Last offset   : -0.000007458 seconds
RMS offset   : 0.000018563 seconds
Frequency   : 18715.752 ppm fast
Residual freq   : -0.041 ppm
Skew   : 0.122 ppm
Root delay   : 0.028430695 seconds
Root dispersion : 0.001395065 seconds
Update interval : 64.4 seconds
Leap status   : Normal
chronyc>

Now you can enter just the sub-commands. Try using the **tracking**, **ntpdata**, and **sources** sub-commands. The chronyc command line allows command recall and editing for chronyc sub-commands. You can use the help sub-command to get a list of possible commands and their syntax.

One thing I like to do after my client computers have synchronized with the NTP server is to set the system hardware clock from the system (OS) time using the following system command. Note that it is not a chronyc command, so enter this command as root in a separate terminal session.

[root@studentvm1 ~]# **/sbin/hwclock --systohc**

This command can be added as a cron job, as a script in cron.daily, or as a systemd timer to keep the hardware clock synced with the system time.

Chrony is a powerful tool for synchronizing the times of client hosts whether they are all on the local network or scattered around the globe. It is easy to configure because, despite the large number of configuration options available, only a few are required in most circumstances.

systemd-timesync

The systemd-timesync service is intended to be a replacement for chrony as a tool for managing NTP services. It uses a new command, timedatectl, to manage NTP.

The systemd-timesync daemon provides an NTP implementation that is easy to manage within a systemd context. It is installed by default in Fedora and Ubuntu and started by default in Ubuntu and related distributions but not in Fedora.

CHAPTER 6   CONTROL YOUR COMPUTER TIME AND DATE WITH SYSTEMD

EXPERIMENT 6-4: PREPARATION

We've been using the default chronyd, so we need to stop and disable it.

systemctl disable --now chronyd
Removed /etc/systemd/system/multi-user.target.wants/chronyd.service.

Verify that it is both stopped and disabled.

systemctl status chronyd
* chronyd.service - NTP client/server
     Loaded: loaded (/usr/lib/systemd/system/chronyd.
             service; disabled; vendor preset: enabled)
     Active: inactive (dead)
       Docs: man:chronyd(8)
             man:chrony.conf(5)

Now that the chronyd daemon is disabled, we can begin working with systemd-timesync. We'll begin using the timedatectl command in this experiment.

EXPERIMENT 6-5: TRYING SYSTEMD-TIMESYNC

Check the status of timesyncd before starting. The systemd-timesync's status indicates whether systemd has initiated an NTP service. Because you have not yet started systemd NTP, the timesync-status command returns no data.

timedatectl timesync-status
Failed to query server: Could not activate remote peer 'org.freedesktop.timesync1': activation request failed: unknown unit

But a more simple status request provides some important information. For example, the timedatectl command without an argument or options implies the status sub-command as default.

```
# timedatectl timesync-status
Failed to query server: Could not activate remote peer
'org.freedesktop.timesync1': activation request failed:
unknown unit
# timedatectl status
               Local time: Wed 2024-11-13 13:25:41 EST
           Universal time: Wed 2024-11-13 18:25:41 UTC
                 RTC time: Wed 2024-11-13 13:25:41
                Time zone: America/New_York (EST, -0500)
System clock synchronized: no
              NTP service: active
          RTC in local TZ: yes

Warning: The system is configured to read the RTC time in
the local time zone. This mode cannot be fully supported.
It will create various problems with time zone changes and
daylight saving time adjustments. The RTC time is never
updated, it relies on external facilities to maintain it. If
at all possible, use RTC in UTC by calling 'timedatectl set-
local-rtc 0'.
```

This command returns the local time for your host, the UTC time, and the RTC time. It shows that the system time is set to the America/New_York time zone (TZ), the RTC is set to the time in the local time zone, and the NTP service is not active. The RTC time may start to drift a bit from the system time. This is normal with systems whose clocks have not been synchronized. The amount of drift on a host depends upon the amount of time since the system was last synced and the speed of the drift per unit of time.

CHAPTER 6   CONTROL YOUR COMPUTER TIME AND DATE WITH SYSTEMD

There is also a warning message about using local time for the RTC—this relates to time zone changes and daylight saving time adjustments. If the computer is off when changes need to be made, the RTC time will not change. This is not an issue in servers or other hosts that are powered on 24/7. Also, any service that provides NTP time synchronization will ensure the host is set to the proper time early in the startup process, so it will be correct before it is fully up and running.

Start the systemd-timesyncd daemon.

```
# systemctl enable --now systemd-timesyncd
Created symlink '/etc/systemd/system/dbus-org.freedesktop.timesync1.service' → '/usr/lib/systemd/system/systemd-timesyncd.service'.
Created symlink '/etc/systemd/system/sysinit.target.wants/systemd-timesyncd.service' → '/usr/lib/systemd/system/systemd-timesyncd.service'.
```

Set the time zone for the computer. Usually, you set a computer's time zone during the installation procedure and never need to change it. However, there are times it is necessary to change the time zone, and there are a couple of tools to help. Linux uses time zone files to define the local time zone in use by the host. These binary files are located in the /usr/share/zoneinfo directory. The default for my time zone is defined by the link /etc/localtime -> ../usr/share/zoneinfo/America/New_York. But you don't need to know that to change the time zone.

You need to know the official time zone name for your location. Suppose you want to change the time zone to America, Los Angeles, you can list all time zones. You can then search the data stream for the one you want.

CHAPTER 6 CONTROL YOUR COMPUTER TIME AND DATE WITH SYSTEMD

```
# timedatectl list-timezones | column
<SNIP>
America/La_Paz           Atlantic/St_Helena         Pacific/Guam
America/Lima             Atlantic/Stanley           Pacific/Honolulu
America/Los_Angeles      Australia/ACT              Pacific/Johnston
America/Louisville       Australia/Adelaide         Pacific/Kanton
America/Lower_Princes    Australia/Brisbane         Pacific/Kiritimati
<SNIP>
```

Note that "America" refers to North, Central, and South America.

If you know a bit of the name of the time zone you want, you could narrow it down like this:

```
# timedatectl list-timezones | grep -i los
America/Los_Angeles
```

or this:

```
# timedatectl list-timezones | grep -i angeles
America/Los_Angeles
```

Now you can set the time zone. I used the date command to verify the change, but you could also use timedatectl.

```
root@f41vm:~# date
Sun Nov 17 01:51:06 PM EST 2024
root@f41vm:~# timedatectl set-timezone America/Los_Angeles
root@f41vm:~# date
Sun Nov 17 10:51:52 AM PST 2024
```

Now change your host's time zone back to your local one.

CHAPTER 6   CONTROL YOUR COMPUTER TIME AND DATE WITH SYSTEMD

Configure systemd-timesyncd

The configuration file for systemd-timesyncd is /etc/systemd/timesyncd. conf. It's a simple file with fewer options included than chronyd.

EXPERIMENT 6-6: CONFIGURING SYSTEMD-TIMESYNCD

Let's look at the configuration file for systemd-timesyncd, /usr/lib/systemd/timesyncd.conf.

Here are the complete contents of the default version of this file on my Fedora VM:

```
#  This file is part of systemd.
#
#  systemd is free software; you can redistribute it and/or modify it under the
#  terms of the GNU Lesser General Public License as published by the Free
#  Software Foundation; either version 2.1 of the License, or (at your option)
#  any later version.
#
# Entries in this file show the compile time defaults. Local configuration
# should be created by either modifying this file (or a copy of it placed in
# /etc/ if the original file is shipped in /usr/), or by creating "drop-ins" in
# the /etc/systemd/timesyncd.conf.d/ directory. The latter is generally
```

CHAPTER 6   CONTROL YOUR COMPUTER TIME AND DATE WITH SYSTEMD

```
# recommended. Defaults can be restored by simply deleting
  the main
# configuration file and all drop-ins located in /etc/.
#
# Use 'systemd-analyze cat-config systemd/timesyncd.conf' to
  display the full config.
#
# See timesyncd.conf(5) for details.

[Time]
#NTP=
#FallbackNTP=0.fedora.pool.ntp.org 1.fedora.pool.ntp.org
2.fedora.pool.ntp.org 3.fedora.pool.ntp.org
#RootDistanceMaxSec=5
#PollIntervalMinSec=32
#PollIntervalMaxSec=2048
#ConnectionRetrySec=30
#SaveIntervalSec=60
```

The only section it contains besides comments is [Time], and all the lines are commented out. These are the default values and do not need to be changed or uncommented (unless you have some reason to do so). If you do not have a specific NTP time server defined in the NTP= line, Fedora's default is to fall back on the Fedora pool of time servers. I like to add the time server on my network to this line and uncomment it. If that server's not available, one is selected from the fallback list.

```
NTP=myntpserver
```

Start timesyncd

Starting and enabling systemd-timesyncd is just like any other service. So let's do that now.

> **EXPERIMENT 6-7: STARTING SYSTEMD-TIMESYNCD**

Enable systemd-timesync and start it at the same time.

systemctl enable systemd-timesyncd.service
Created symlink '/etc/systemd/system/dbus-org.freedesktop.timesync1.service' → '/usr/lib/systemd/system/systemd-timesyncd.service'.
Created symlink '/etc/systemd/system/sysinit.target.wants/systemd-timesyncd.service' → '/usr/lib/systemd/system/systemd-timesyncd.service'.

Now check its status.

systemctl status systemd-timesyncd.service
* systemd-timesyncd.service - Network Time Synchronization
     Loaded: loaded (/usr/lib/systemd/system/systemd-timesyncd.service; enabled; preset: disabled)
    Drop-In: /usr/lib/systemd/system/service.d
             └─10-timeout-abort.conf, 50-keep-warm.conf
     Active: active (running) since Mon 2024-11-18 16:12:23 EST; 4min 18s ago
 Invocation: 7be78fc9f690442ca2ef540db009e663
       Docs: man:systemd-timesyncd.service(8)
   Main PID: 1774 (systemd-timesyn)
     Status: "Contacted time server 137.190.2.4:123 (0.fedora.pool.ntp.org)."

```
        Tasks: 2 (limit: 19131)
       Memory: 1.4M (peak: 1.9M)
          CPU: 93ms
       CGroup: /system.slice/systemd-timesyncd.
               serviceExercise Head8
               └─1774 /usr/lib/systemd/systemd-timesyncd

Nov 18 16:12:23 f41vm.both.oreg systemd[1]: Starting
systemd-timesyncd.service - Network Time Synchronization...
Nov 18 16:12:23 f41vm.both.oreg systemd-timesyncd[1774]:
The system is configured to read the RTC time in the local
time zone.>
Nov 18 16:12:23 f41vm.both.oreg systemd[1]: Started systemd-
timesyncd.service - Network Time Synchronization.
```

Set the Hardware Clock

Maintaining accurate time on the system hardware clock is as important as the Linux operating system clock. The hardware clock is also known as the real-time clock (RTC) and the CMOS clock.

The primary reason for this—in my experience—is that from the moment the system is booted, through much of the Linux startup sequence until the network is up and running, the hardware clock is the one being used for journal and log timestamps. If those are far from correct, it becomes difficult to trace the time sequence of boot problems.

I've worked on computers that had a dead CMOS battery and the hardware time always started at 00:00:00 UTC on January 1, 1970.[6] All Unix and Linux computers count the time in seconds from that date. So all logs and journal entries started in 1970 and, when the network became available to sync with an NTP server, switched to the true current time.

---

[6] Wikipedia, "Unix Time," https://en.wikipedia.org/wiki/Unix_time

CHAPTER 6   CONTROL YOUR COMPUTER TIME AND DATE WITH SYSTEMD

EXPERIMENT 6-8: SETTING THE HARDWARE CLOCK

Let's start by using timedatectl to view the system's current time status. Here's what one of my systems looked like after starting timesyncd:

```
# timedatectl
               Local time: Mon 2024-11-18 16:36:44 EST
           Universal time: Mon 2024-11-18 21:36:44 UTC
                 RTC time: Mon 2024-11-18 16:36:43
                Time zone: America/New_York (EST, -0500)
System clock synchronized: yes
              NTP service: active
          RTC in local TZ: yes

Warning: The system is configured to read the RTC time in
the local time zone. This mode cannot be fully supported.
It will create various problems with time zone changes and
daylight saving time adjustments. The RTC time is never
updated, it relies on external facilities to maintain it.
If at all possible, use RTC in UTC by calling 'timedatectl
set-local-rtc 0'.
```

The RTC time is around a second off from local time (EDT), and the discrepancy grew by a couple more seconds over the next few days. This growing discrepancy was due to the fact that I had no process in place to synchronize the RTC.

Because RTC does not have the concept of time zones, the timedatectl command must do a comparison to determine which time zone is a match. If the RTC time does not match local time exactly, it is not considered to be in the local time zone.

CHAPTER 6   CONTROL YOUR COMPUTER TIME AND DATE WITH SYSTEMD

In search of a bit more information, I checked the status of systemd-timesync.service.[7]

systemctl status systemd-timesyncd.service
* systemd-timesyncd.service - Network Time Synchronization
     Loaded: loaded (/usr/lib/systemd/system/systemd-
             timesyncd.service; enabled; vendor preset:
             disabled)
     Active: active (running) since Sat 2020-05-16 13:56:53
             EDT; 18h ago
       Docs: man:systemd-timesyncd.service(8)
   Main PID: 822 (systemd-timesyn)
     Status: "Initial synchronization to time server
             163.237.218.19:123 (2.fedora.pool.ntp.org)."
      Tasks: 2 (limit: 10365)
     Memory: 2.8M
        CPU: 476ms
     CGroup: /system.slice/systemd-timesyncd.service
             └─822 /usr/lib/systemd/systemd-timesyncd

May 16 09:57:24 testvm2.both.org systemd[1]: Starting
Network Time Synchronization...
May 16 09:57:24 testvm2.both.org systemd-timesyncd[822]:
System clock time unset or jumped backwards, restoring from
recorded timestamp: Sat 2020-05-16 13:56:53 EDT
May 16 13:56:53 testvm2.both.org systemd[1]: Started Network
Time Synchronization.
May 16 13:57:56 testvm2.both.org systemd-timesyncd[822]:
Initial synchronization to time server 163.237.218.19:123
(2.fedora.pool.ntp.org).

---

[7] Note that I couldn't reproduce this when writing this book, so I used original data from an article I wrote in 2020.

Notice the log message that says the system clock time was unset or jumped backward. The timesyncd service sets the system time from a timestamp. Timestamps are maintained by the timesyncd daemon and are created at each successful time synchronization.

The timedatectl command does not have the ability to set the value of the hardware clock from the system clock; it can only set the time and date from a value entered on the command line. However, you can set the RTC to the same value as the system time by using the hwclock command.

```
# /sbin/hwclock --systohc --localtime
# timedatectl
               Local time: Mon 2020-05-18 13:56:46 EDT
           Universal time: Mon 2020-05-18 17:56:46 UTC
                 RTC time: Mon 2020-05-18 13:56:46
                Time zone: America/New_York (EDT, -0400)
System clock synchronized: yes
              NTP service: active
          RTC in local TZ: yes
```

The --localtime option ensures that the hardware clock is set to local time, not UTC.

Do You Really Need RTC?

Any NTP implementation will set the system clock during the startup sequence, so is RTC necessary? Not really, so long as you have a network connection to a time server. However, many systems do not have full-time access to a network connection and the hardware clock is useful so that Linux can read it and set the system time. This is a better solution than having to set the time by hand, even if it might drift away from the actual time.

Summary

This chapter explored the use of some systemd tools for managing date, time, and time zones. The systemd-timesyncd tool provides a decent NTP client that can keep time on a local host synchronized with an NTP server. However, systemd-timesyncd does not provide a server service, so if you need an NTP server on your network, you must use something else, such as chrony, to act as a server.

I prefer to have a single implementation for any service in my network, so I use chrony on all my hosts. If you do not need a local NTP server, or if you do not mind dealing with chrony for the server and systemd-timesyncd for the client and you do not need chrony's additional capabilities, then systemd-timesyncd is a serviceable choice for an NTP client.

There is another point I want to make: you do not have to use systemd tools for NTP implementation. You can use chrony or some other NTP implementation. systemd is composed of a large number of services; many of them are optional, so they can be disabled and something else used in its place. It is not the huge, monolithic monster that some make it out to be. It is OK to not like systemd or parts of it, but you should make an informed decision.

I don't dislike systemd's implementation of NTP, but I much prefer chrony because it better meets my needs. And that is what Linux is all about.

Exercises

Perform these exercises to complete this chapter:

1. List at least four reasons why it's important for modern computers to maintain the correct time.

2. Describe the function of the RTC?

3. What is NTP?

4. Describe how NTP works.

5. What NTP server is your host using to synchronize?

6. What stratum is that server?

7. Which NTP implementation provides the most status information for the SysAdmin?

8. Which do you prefer: chrony or systemd-timesyncd?

9. Why?

CHAPTER 7

Analyzing systemd Calendar and Time Spans

Objectives

In this chapter, you will learn

- To analyze systemd calendar and time spans
- To properly understand and interpret timestamps
- To describe the level of accuracy obtainable when using calendar event times for event triggers
- To create calendar event expressions that trigger events at the required times and define time spans when searching the systemd journal for events
- To analyze systemd timestamps

Overview

In our past encounters with systemd, we have seen that it uses calendar time, specifying one or more moments in time to trigger events such as a backup program, and the manner in which entries in the journal are timestamped. systemd can also use time spans which define the amount of time between two events but which are not directly tied to specific calendar times.

In this chapter, we will look in more detail at the way in which time and date are used and specified. Because two slightly different, noncompatible formats can be used, it is important to identify these and how and when they can be used. We will also use time and the systemd journals to explore and manage Linux startup in detail. All of this is very dependent upon time and our understanding of how to read and specify it in the commands we use. So that's where we will start.

Definitions

Time-related commands in systemd use some terms that we need to understand more fully, so let's start with some definitions. The systemd.time(7) man page has a complete description of time and date expressions that can be used in timers and other systemd tools.

Absolute Timestamp

An absolute timestamp is a single unambiguous and unique point in time as defined in the format YYYY-MM-DD HH:MM:SS. The timestamp format is used to specify points in time at which events are triggered by timers. An absolute timestamp can represent only a single point in time, such as 2025-04-15 13:21:05.

Accuracy

Accuracy is the quality of closeness to the true time. It refers to how close to the specified calendar time an event is triggered by a timer. The default accuracy for systemd timers is defined as the one-minute time span starting at the defined calendar time. An event specified to occur at the OnCalendar time of 09:52:17 might actually be triggered at any time between that and 09:53:17.

Calendar Event

Calendar events are one or more specific times specified by a systemd timestamp format, YYYY-MM-DD HH:MM:SS. These can be a single point in time or at a series of points that are well-defined and for which the exact times can be calculated. Timestamps are also used by the systemd journals to mark each event with the exact time it occurred.

An exact moment in time as specified in systemd in the timestamp format, YYYY-MM-DD HH:MM:SS. When only the YYYY-MM-DD portion is specified, the time defaults to 00:00:00. When only the HH:MM:SS portion is specified, the date is arbitrarily defined to be that of the next calendar instance of that time. If the time specified is before the current time today, the next instance will be tomorrow, and if the specified time is later than the current time, the next instance will be today. This is the format used for expression of the OnCalendar times in a systemd timer.

Recurring calendar events can be specified using special characters and formats to represent fields that have multiple value matches. For example, 2026-08-15..25 12:15:00 represents 12:15PM of the 15th through the 25th of August 2026 and would trigger eleven matches. Calendar events can also be specified with an absolute timestamp.

CHAPTER 7   ANALYZING SYSTEMD CALENDAR AND TIME SPANS

Time Span

Time span is the amount of time between two events; it is the duration of something such as an event or the time between two events. Time spans can be used in specifying the desired accuracy with which an event should be triggered by a timer as well as in defining the time to elapse between events. The following units are recognized:

- usec, us, μs
- msec, ms
- seconds, second, sec, s
- minutes, minute, min, m
- hours, hour, hr, h
- days, day, d
- weeks, week, w
- months, month, M (defined as 30.44 days)
- years, year, y (defined as 365.25 days)

Calendar Event Expressions

Calendar event expressions are a key component of tasks such as specifying time ranges for journal searches and triggering timers at desired repetitive times. systemd itself and its timers use a different style for time and date expressions than the format used in crontab. It is more flexible than crontab and allows fuzzy dates and times in the manner of the at command. It should also be familiar enough that it will be easy to understand.

The format for calendar event expressions using OnCalendar= is DOW YYYY-MM-DD HH:MM:SS. The DOW (day of week) is optional and other fields can use an asterisk (*) to match any value for that position. If the time is not specified, it is assumed to be 00:00:00. If the date is not specified but the time is, the next match may be today or tomorrow depending upon the current time. All of the various calendar time expression formats are converted to a normalized form for use. The systemd-analyze calendar command shows the normalized form of the time expression.

systemd provides us with an excellent tool for validating and examining calendar events that are to be used in an expression. The systemd-analyze calendar tool will parse a calendar time event expression and provide the normalized form as well as other interesting information such as the date and time of the next "elapse," that is, match, and the approximate amount of time before the trigger time is reached.

The commands used in this section can be performed by non-root users, but the data displayed for some commands will not be as complete as for the root user. So I suggest you perform all of the experiments in this chapter as the root user.

Exploring systemd Time Syntax

There are two different modes of time syntax. This seems confusing at first, but the two modes are used in different manners.

systemd uses calendar time syntax to specify times to trigger events using timers and to describe the time span between two events. The second mode is used for timestamps in the systemd journals.

Calendar Events

The correct systemd time syntax is important when used to trigger events with timers. It's significantly different from the crontab syntax so needs some explanation and experimentation.

The systemd-analyze calendar command provides a tool for exploring the systemd time syntax and verifying that the times we specify are correct.

EXPERIMENT 7-1: SYSTEMD CALENDAR TIME SYNTAX

This experiment introduces the systemd time syntax. While it can appear complex at first, it makes sense when you've experimented with it.

Perform this experiment as a non-root user.

Let's start with a date in the future without a time. Because all of the date unit fields are explicitly specified, this is a one-time event. In this case, the time is not specified, so the event timer would trigger at 00:00:00 hours on the specified date.

```
$ systemd-analyze calendar 2030-06-17
  Original form: 2030-06-17
Normalized form: 2030-06-17 00:00:00
    Next elapse: Mon 2030-06-17 00:00:00 EDT
       (in UTC): Mon 2030-06-17 04:00:00 UTC
       From now: 5 years 6 months left
```

Tip The times for "Next elapse" and "UTC" will differ based on your local time zone.

Now let's add a time. In this example, the date and time are analyzed separately as non-related entities.

```
$ systemd-analyze calendar 2030-06-17 15:21:16
  Original form: 2030-06-17
Normalized form: 2030-06-17 00:00:00
    Next elapse: Mon 2030-06-17 00:00:00 EDT
       (in UTC): Mon 2030-06-17 04:00:00 UTC
       From now: 5 years 6 months left
```

CHAPTER 7 ANALYZING SYSTEMD CALENDAR AND TIME SPANS

```
  Original form: 15:21:16
Normalized form: *-*-* 15:21:16
    Next elapse: Mon 2024-11-25 15:21:16 EST
       (in UTC): Mon 2024-11-25 20:21:16 UTC
       From now: 1h 33min left
```

To analyze the date and time as a single entity, enclose them together in quotes.

$ systemd-analyze calendar "2030-06-17 15:21:16"
```
Normalized form: 2030-06-17 15:21:16
    Next elapse: Mon 2030-06-17 15:21:16 EDT
       (in UTC): Mon 2030-06-17 19:21:16 UTC
       From now: 5 years 6 months left
```

Now specify a time earlier than the current time and one later. In this case, the current time was approximately 13:50 on 2024-11-25.

$ systemd-analyze calendar 05:21:16 22:15
```
  Original form: 05:21:16
Normalized form: *-*-* 05:21:16
    Next elapse: Tue 2024-11-26 05:21:16 EST
       (in UTC): Tue 2024-11-26 10:21:16 UTC
       From now: 15h left

  Original form: 22:15
Normalized form: *-*-* 22:15:00
    Next elapse: Mon 2024-11-25 22:15:00 EST
       (in UTC): Tue 2024-11-26 03:15:00 UTC
       From now: 8h left
```

CHAPTER 7   ANALYZING SYSTEMD CALENDAR AND TIME SPANS

The `systemd-analyze calendar` tool does not work on timestamps. So things like "tomorrow" or "today" will cause errors when used with the calendar sub-command because they are timestamps rather than OnCalendar time formats.

```
$ systemd-analyze calendar "tomorrow"
Failed to parse calendar expression 'tomorrow': Invalid argument
Hint: this expression is a valid timestamp. Use 'systemd-analyze timestamp "tomorrow"' instead?
```

When used as a timestamp, the term "tomorrow" will always resolve to tomorrow's date and a time of 00:00:00. You must use the normalized expression format, "YYYY-MM-DD HH:MM:SS," for this tool to work in calendar mode. Despite this, the `systemd-analyze calendar` tool can still help you to understand the structure of the calendar time expressions used by systemd timers. I recommend reading the systemd.time(7) man page for a more complete understanding of the time formats that can be used with systemd timers.

Timestamps

Whereas calendar times can be used to match single or multiple points in time, timestamps unambiguously represent a single point in time. For example, timestamps in the systemd journal refer to a precise moment in time when each logged event occurred.

EXPERIMENT 7-2: EXPLORING SYSTEMD TIMESTAMPS

The systemd journal uses timestamps, so let's look at a few of those from today, as I write this. The -S option to the journalctl command specifies the start time we want to begin with. The "S" officially stands for the term "since," which can also be used

journalctl -S today
```
Dec 03 00:00:37 testvm1.both.org systemd[1]: Starting
sysstat-collect.service - system activity accounting tool...
Dec 03 00:00:37 testvm1.both.org systemd[1]: Starting
sysstat-rotate.service - system activity accounting tool...
Dec 03 00:00:37 testvm1.both.org systemd[1]: Starting
unbound-anchor.service - update of the root trust anchor
for DNSSE>
Dec 03 00:00:37 testvm1.both.org systemd[1]: sysstat-collect.
service: Deactivated successfully.
Dec 03 00:00:37 testvm1.both.org systemd[1]: Finished
sysstat-collect.service - system activity accounting tool.
Dec 03 00:00:37 testvm1.both.org audit[1]: SERVICE_
START pid=1 uid=0 auid=4294967295 ses=4294967295
msg='unit=sysstat-co>
Dec 03 00:00:37 testvm1.both.org audit[1]: SERVICE_STOP pid=1
uid=0 auid=4294967295 ses=4294967295 msg='unit=sysstat-col>
Dec 03 00:00:37 testvm1.both.org systemd[1]: sysstat-rotate.
service: Deactivated successfully.
Dec 03 00:00:37 testvm1.both.org systemd[1]: Finished
sysstat-rotate.service - system activity accounting tool.
Dec 03 00:00:37 testvm1.both.org audit[1]: SERVICE_
START pid=1 uid=0 auid=4294967295 ses=4294967295
msg='unit=sysstat-ro>
```

CHAPTER 7   ANALYZING SYSTEMD CALENDAR AND TIME SPANS

Dec 03 00:00:37 testvm1.both.org audit[1]: SERVICE_STOP pid=1 uid=0 auid=4294967295 ses=4294967295 msg='unit=sysstat-rot>
<SNIP>
Dec 03 00:01:00 testvm1.both.org CROND[133534]: (root) CMDEND (run-parts /etc/cron.hourly)
Dec 03 00:07:37 testvm1.both.org systemd[1]: Starting sysstat-summary.service - Generate a daily summary of process acco>
Dec 03 00:07:37 testvm1.both.org systemd[1]: sysstat-summary. service: Deactivated successfully.
Dec 03 00:07:37 testvm1.both.org systemd[1]: Finished sysstat-summary.service - Generate a daily summary of procesDec 03 00:00:37 testvm1.both.org systemd[1]: Starting sysstat-collect.service - system activity accounting tool...
Dec 03 00:00:37 testvm1.both.org systemd[1]: Starting sysstat-rotate.service - system activity accounting tool...
Dec 03 00:00:37 testvm1.both.org systemd[1]: Starting unbound-anchor.service - update of the root trust anchor for DNSSE>
Dec 03 00:00:37 testvm1.both.org systemd[1]: sysstat-collect. service: Deactivated successfully.
Dec 03 00:00:37 testvm1.both.org systemd[1]: Finished sysstat-collect.service - system activity accounting tool.
Dec 03 00:00:37 testvm1.both.org audit[1]: SERVICE_START pid=1 uid=0 auid=4294967295 ses=4294967295 msg='unit=sysstat-co>
Dec 03 00:00:37 testvm1.both.org audit[1]: SERVICE_STOP pid=1 uid=0 auid=4294967295 ses=4294967295 msg='unit=sysstat-col>
Dec 03 00:00:37 testvm1.both.org systemd[1]: sysstat-rotate. service: Deactivated successfully.

CHAPTER 7   ANALYZING SYSTEMD CALENDAR AND TIME SPANS

```
Dec 03 00:00:37 testvm1.both.org systemd[1]: Finished
sysstat-rotate.service - system activity accounting tool.
<SNIP>
```

The `systemd-analyze timestamp` command can be used to analyze timestamp expressions in the same manner that we analyzed calendar expressions. Let's look at one of these times from the journal data stream and one from a couple years in the past.

```
$ systemd-analyze timestamp "Dec 03 11:28:07"
  Original form: Dec 03 11:28:07
Normalized form: Tue 2024-12-03 11:28:07 EST
     (in UTC): Tue 2024-12-03 16:28:07 UTC
  UNIX seconds: @1733243287
      From now: 9min ago
$ systemd-analyze timestamp "Wed 2020-06-17 10:08:41"
  Original form: Wed 2020-06-17 10:08:41
Normalized form: Wed 2020-06-17 10:08:41 EDT
     (in UTC): Wed 2020-06-17 14:08:41 UTC
  UNIX seconds: @1592402921
      From now: 4 years 5 months ago
```

These two timestamps are formatted differently, but any unambiguously expressed time, such as "2020-06-17 10:08:41," is a timestamp because it can only occur once. A timestamp that will occur in the future can also be used in a systemd timer, and that timer will only trigger its defined action once.

A time expressed somewhat more ambiguously, such as "2025-*-* 22:15:00," can only be a calendar time to be used in the OnCalendar statement in a timer unit file. This expression will trigger an event every day in the year 2025 at 22:15:00 (10:15:00PM).

CHAPTER 7   ANALYZING SYSTEMD CALENDAR AND TIME SPANS

The journalctl command tool has some options that can display the timestamps in format that we can easily use with the systemd-analyze tool.

$ **journalctl -o short-full**
Tue 2024-12-03 10:20:06 EST testvm1.both.org systemd[1]: Starting sysstat-collect.service - system activity accounting t>
Tue 2024-12-03 10:20:06 EST testvm1.both.org systemd[1]: sysstat-collect.service: Deactivated successfully.
Tue 2024-12-03 10:20:06 EST testvm1.both.org systemd[1]: Finished sysstat-collect.service - system activity accounting t>
Tue 2024-12-03 10:20:06 EST testvm1.both.org audit[1]: SERVICE_START pid=1 uid=0 auid=4294967295 ses=4294967295 msg='uni>
Tue 2024-12-03 10:20:06 EST testvm1.both.org audit[1]: SERVICE_STOP pid=1 uid=0 auid=4294967295 ses=4294967295 msg='unit>
Tue 2024-12-03 10:30:06 EST testvm1.both.org systemd[1]: Starting sysstat-collect.service - system activity accounting t>
Tue 2024-12-03 10:30:06 EST testvm1.both.org systemd[1]: sysstat-collect.service: Deactivated successfully.
Tue 2024-12-03 10:30:06 EST testvm1.both.org systemd[1]: Finished sysstat-collect.service - system activity accounting t>
<SNIP>

We can also display the journal timestamps in a monotonic format which shows the number of seconds since startup.

$ **journalctl -S today -o short-monotonic**

CHAPTER 7   ANALYZING SYSTEMD CALENDAR AND TIME SPANS

```
[ 6269.847404] testvm1.both.org systemd[1]: Finished
sysstat-collect.service - system activity accounting tool.
[ 6269.846450] testvm1.both.org audit[1]: SERVICE_START pid=1
uid=0 auid=4294967295 ses=4294967295 msg='unit=sysstat-col>
[ 6269.847449] testvm1.both.org audit[1]: SERVICE_STOP pid=1
uid=0 auid=4294967295 ses=4294967295 msg='unit=sysstat-coll>
[ 6869.775575] testvm1.both.org systemd[1]: Starting
sysstat-collect.service - system activity accounting tool...
[ 6869.871332] testvm1.both.org systemd[1]: sysstat-collect.
service: Deactivated successfully.
[ 6869.871678] testvm1.both.org systemd[1]: Finished
sysstat-collect.service - system activity accounting tool.
<SNIP>
```

Be sure to read the journalctl man page for, among other things, a complete list of the timestamp format options.

Time Spans

Time spans are primarily used in systemd timers to define a specific span of time between events. This could be used to trigger events so that they occur a specified amount of time after system startup or after a previous instance of the same event. A sample expression to trigger an event 32 minutes after system startup would look like this in the timer unit file.

OnStartupSec=32m

The default accuracy for triggering systemd timers is a time window starting at the specified time and lasting for one minute. You can specify a narrower trigger time span accuracy to within a microsecond by adding a statement like the following one to the Timer section of the timer unit file:

AccuracySec=1us

CHAPTER 7 ANALYZING SYSTEMD CALENDAR AND TIME SPANS

EXPERIMENT 7-3: EXPLORING TIME SPANS

The `systemd-analyze timespan` command can help ensure that you are using a valid time span in the unit file. The following samples will get you started:

systemd-analyze timespan 15days
Original: 15days
        μs: 1296000000000
    Human: 2w 1d
systemd-analyze timespan "15days 6h 32m"
Original: 15days 6h 32m
        μs: 1319520000000
    Human: 2w 1d 6h 32min

Experiment with these and some of your own:

- "255days 6h 31m"
- "255days 6h 31m 24.568ms"

Time spans are used to schedule timer events a specified interval after a defined event such as startup. Calendar timestamps can be used to schedule timer events on specific calendar days and times either as one-offs or repeating. Timestamps are also used on systemd journal entries although not in a default format that can be used directly in tools like systemd-analyze.

CHAPTER 7   ANALYZING SYSTEMD CALENDAR AND TIME SPANS

Summary

This was all more than just a little confusing to me when I first started working with systemd timers and creating calendar and timestamp expressions that would trigger events. That was partly because of the similar but not quite identical formats used for specifying timestamps and calendar event trigger times.

This chapter covered creating and analyzing calendar, timestamp, and time span expressions. We'll use these in the following chapters.

Exercises

Perform these exercises to complete this chapter:

1. Create an expression that could be used by a timer to schedule an event at 1:45AM on January 1 every year.

2. Create an expression that would be used to perform a daily backup at 1:00AM.

3. Why might you want to schedule a timer for a specific amount of time after a system boots?

4. How can you determine the amount of time in human-readable format since a system booted that an event occurred?

CHAPTER 8

Using systemd Timers

Objectives

In this chapter, you will learn

- More about using the systemctl command
- How to view the existing systemd maintenance timers
- To test calendar event expressions
- To create a Bash program that will be used by a timer
- To create a timer
- To describe and create the different types of timers

Overview

Every one of my physical computers and VMs has at least nine active timers. Each of those timers triggers a program—usually a Bash script—that performs a specific maintenance task. systemd timers provide a more fine-grained control of events than cronjobs and offer more interesting and flexible scheduling possibilities.

CHAPTER 8   USING SYSTEMD TIMERS

A couple years ago, I converted most of my cron jobs to systemd timers. I had used timers for a few years, but usually, I learned just enough to perform the specific task I was working on. While doing research on systemd, I learned that systemd timers have some very interesting capabilities.

Like cron jobs, systemd timers can trigger events—shell scripts and compiled programs—at specified time intervals, such as once a day, on a specific day of the month (perhaps only if it is a Monday), or every 15 minutes during business hours from 8AM to 6PM.

But timers can do some things that cron jobs cannot. For example, a timer can trigger a program to run a specific amount of time after an event such as boot, startup, completion of a previous task, or even the previous completion of the service unit called by the timer.

Some timers that are active by default may not be required, so we'll look at those and how to disable them. There is some overlap of cron jobs and systemd timers that we'll also investigate.

System Maintenance Timers

When Fedora or any systemd-based distribution is installed on a new system, it creates several timers that are part of the system maintenance procedures that happen in the background of any Linux host. These timers trigger events necessary for common maintenance tasks, such as updating system databases, cleaning temporary directories, rotating log files, and more.

As an example, let's look at the timers on my VM.

CHAPTER 8   USING SYSTEMD TIMERS

EXPERIMENT 8-1: LOOKING AT SYSTEMD TIMERS

Let's examine the timers. This experiment should be performed as a non-root user.

First, we'll just do a simple list. I know the font is small for the result, but it gives a better sense of what you should see while still being somewhat legible.

```
$ systemctl -t timer
  UNIT                          LOAD   ACTIVE SUB
    DESCRIPTION
  fstrim.timer                  loaded active waiting
    Discard unused filesystem blocks once a week
  logrotate.timer               loaded active waiting
    Daily rotation of log files
  plocate-updatedb.timer        loaded active waiting
    Update the plocate database daily
  raid-check.timer              loaded active waiting
    Weekly RAID setup health check
  sysstat-collect.timer         loaded active waiting
    Run system activity accounting tool every 10 minutes
  sysstat-rotate.timer          loaded active waiting
    Rotate daily system activity data file at midnight
  sysstat-summary.timer         loaded active waiting
    Generate summary of yesterday's process accounting
  systemd-tmpfiles-clean.timer loaded active waiting
    Daily Cleanup of Temporary Directories
  unbound-anchor.timer          loaded active waiting
    daily update of the root trust anchor for DNSSEC
```

CHAPTER 8   USING SYSTEMD TIMERS

```
Legend: LOAD   → Reflects whether the unit definition was
                 properly loaded.
        ACTIVE → The high-level unit activation state, i.e.
                 generalization of SUB.
        SUB    → The low-level unit activation state, values
                 depend on unit type.
```
```
9 loaded units listed. Pass --all to see loaded but inactive
units, too.
To show all installed unit files use 'systemctl list-
unit-files'.
```

This list contains only the timers that are loaded and active. As the text at the end of the data stream says, you can use the --all option to also list the units that are inactive.

$ systemctl --all -t timer
```
<SNIP>
```

In this case, there are no inactive timer units, but the active ones are still displayed.

Now let's display more detail about the active timers. The asterisk symbol works the same as it does for file globbing, so this command lists all systemd timer units. I've truncated this data stream for brevity, and I've once again used a smaller font size, but not quite so small as last time.

$ systemctl status *timer
```
<SNIP>
● sysstat-summary.timer - Generate summary of yesterday's
process accounting
     Loaded: loaded (/usr/lib/systemd/system/sysstat-
             summary.timer; enabled; preset: enabled)
     Active: active (waiting) since Tue 2024-12-03 21:14:13
             EST; 18h ago
```

CHAPTER 8   USING SYSTEMD TIMERS

   Invocation: f446503972c54200b9da56898b404b8f
      Trigger: Thu 2024-12-05 00:07:00 EST; 7h left
     Triggers: • sysstat-summary.service

Dec 03 21:14:13 testvm1.both.org systemd[1]: Started sysstat-summary.timer - Generate summary of yesterday's process accounting.

• systemd-tmpfiles-clean.timer - Daily Cleanup of Temporary Directories
       Loaded: loaded (/usr/lib/systemd/system/systemd-
               tmpfiles-clean.timer; static)
       Active: active (waiting) since Tue 2024-12-03 21:14:13
               EST; 18h ago
   Invocation: c82023d1e0844d04886965dae75f2c1d
      Trigger: Wed 2024-12-04 21:29:44 EST; 5h 18min
               leftmimedefang-filter
     Triggers: • systemd-tmpfiles-clean.service
         Docs: man:tmpfiles.d(5)
               man:systemd-tmpfiles(8)

Dec 03 21:14:13 testvm1.both.org systemd[1]: Started systemd-tmpfiles-clean.timer - Daily Cleanup of Temporary Directories.

• fstrim.timer - Discard unused filesystem blocks once a week
       Loaded: loaded (/usr/lib/systemd/system/fstrim.timer;
               enabled; preset: enabled)
       Active: active (waiting) since Tue 2024-12-03 21:14:13
               EST; 18h ago

```
   Invocation: 45c67bf52dc64dd889a54ce59d569ba2
      Trigger: Mon 2024-12-09 00:21:50 EST; 4 days left
     Triggers: ● fstrim.service
         Docs: man:fstrim

Dec 03 21:14:13 testvm1.both.org systemd[1]: Started fstrim.
timer - Discard unused filesystem blocks once a week.

● sysstat-collect.timer - Run system activity accounting
tool every 10 minutes
       Loaded: loaded (/usr/lib/systemd/system/sysstat-
               collect.timer; enabled; preset: enabled)
       Active: active (waiting) since Tue 2024-12-03 21:14:13
               EST; 18h ago
   Invocation: 2b38695d2d3f44e4ba4c5d6d6b069144
      Trigger: Wed 2024-12-04 16:20:00 EST; 8min left
     Triggers: ● sysstat-collect.service

Dec 03 21:14:13 testvm1.both.org systemd[1]: Started
sysstat-collect.timer - Run system activity accounting tool
every 10 minutes.
<SNIP>
```

Each timer has at least six lines of information associated with it in this listing:

- The first line has the timer's filename and a short description of its purpose.

- The second line displays the timer's status, whether it is loaded, the full path to the timer unit file, and the vendor preset.

- The third line indicates its active status, which includes the $ systemctl --all -t timer.

- The fourth line contains the date and time the timer will be triggered next and an approximate time until the trigger occurs.

CHAPTER 8   USING SYSTEMD TIMERS

- The fifth line shows the name of the event or the service that is triggered by the timer.

- Some (but not all) systemd unit files have pointers to the relevant documentation. Three of the timers in my virtual machine's output have pointers to documentation. This is a nice (but optional) bit of data.

- The final line is the journal entry for the most recent instance of the service triggered by the timer.

Here's another way to look at the list of timers. The results of this command are too wide to show here even with a reduced font. However, it shows a timestamp indicating the next time the timer will activate, how much time remains before the next activation, a timestamp of the most recent previous activation, the amount of time passed since then, the timer unit, and the service unit activated by the timer.

`systemctl list-timers`

Depending upon your host, you may have some different timers, but these are the ones you'll be most likely to see.

You can see in Experiment 8-1 that these timers trigger events that are critical to the maintenance of your Linux host.

The fstrim.timer activates once a week and cleans up discarded file blocks in SSD storage devices. This is important because SSDs don't release the space allocated to deleted files until fstrim is run. If your computer complains because your SSD doesn't have enough space, you might try running the fstrim.timer more frequently than once a week. You might also consider using a larger SSD.

201

The three timers for sysstat manage all the processes required to collect and process the data used by the **sar** command. The **sar** command uses that collected data to report all of the system performance data in one place that you can view separately in the many other SysAdmin tools. Use **man sar** to read about this powerful command.

Creating a Timer

Although we could deconstruct one or more of the existing timers to learn how they work, let's create our own service unit and a timer unit to trigger it. We'll use a fairly trivial example in order to keep this simple. After we have finished this, it will be easier to understand how the other timers work and to determine what they are doing.

> **EXPERIMENT 8-2: CREATING A TIMER**
>
> Perform this experiment as root user.
>
> First, create a simple service that will run something basic, such as the **free** command. For example, you may want to monitor free memory at regular intervals. Create the following unit file in the /usr/local/lib/systemd/system directory.[1] Name it myMonitor.timer. It does not need to be executable.
>
> ```
> # This service unit is for testing timer units
> # Copyright David Both, 2025
> # GNU All-Permissive License:
> # Copying and distribution of this file, with or without
> # modification, are permitted in any medium without royalty
> ```

---

[1] The /usr/local/lib/systemd/system directory is the proper location for this file based on the Linux Filesystem Hierarchical Standard (LFHS) and systemd best practice.

CHAPTER 8   USING SYSTEMD TIMERS

```
# provided the copyright notice and this notice are
preserved.
# This file is offered as-is, without any warranty.
#

[Unit]
Description=Logs system statistics to the systemd journal
Wants=myMonitor.timer

[Service]
Type=oneshot
ExecStart=/usr/bin/free

[Install]
WantedBy=multi-user.target
```

Now let's look at the status and test our service unit to ensure that it works as we expect it to.

```
# systemctl status myMonitor.service
○ myMonitor.service - Logs system statistics to the
systemd journal
     Loaded: loaded (/usr/local/lib/systemd/system/myMonitor.
             service; disabled; preset: disabled)
    Drop-In: /usr/lib/systemd/system/service.d
             └─10-timeout-abort.conf, 50-keep-warm.conf
     Active: inactive (dead)
```

Now test the new service by starting it. Note that the service will run only once when we start it or it's triggered by a timer, and it won't run on a reboot because we haven't enabled it.

 # systemctl start myMonitor.service

But where's the output?

203

CHAPTER 8 USING SYSTEMD TIMERS

By default, the standard output (STDOUT) from programs run by systemd service units is sent to the systemd journal, which leaves a record you can view now or later—up to a point. Look at the journal specifically for your service unit and for today only. The -S option, which is the short version of --since, allows you to specify the time period that the journalctl tool should search for entries. This isn't because you don't care about previous results—in this case, there won't be any—it is to shorten the search time if your host has been running for a long time and has accumulated a large number of entries in the journal. The -u option allows us to specify the systemd unit that we want to see, excluding all the rest which we don't care about.

journalctl -S today -u myMonitor.service

A task triggered by a service can be a single program, a series of programs, or a script written in any scripting language. Add another task to the service by adding the following line to the end of the [Service] section of the myMonitor.service unit file:

ExecStart=/usr/bin/lsblk

Start the service again and check the journal for the results, which should look like this. You should see the results from both commands in the journal.

journalctl -S today -u myMonitor.service
```
Dec 05 10:47:40 testvm1.both.org systemd[1]: Starting
myMonitor.service - Log>
Dec 05 10:47:40 testvm1.both.org
free[266776]:                    total         us>
Dec 05 10:47:40 testvm1.both.org free[266776]:
Mem:          8122904      6467>
Dec 05 10:47:40 testvm1.both.org free[266776]:
Swap:         8122364            >
```

Dec 05 10:47:40 testvm1.both.org systemd[1]: myMonitor.
service: Deactivated s>
Dec 05 10:47:40 testvm1.both.org systemd[1]: Finished
myMonitor.service - Log>
Dec 05 10:49:12 testvm1.both.org systemd[1]: Starting
myMonitor.service - Log>
Dec 05 10:49:12 testvm1.both.org
free[266786]:   total   us>
Dec 05 10:49:12 testvm1.both.org free[266786]:
Mem: 8122904   6461>
Dec 05 10:49:12 testvm1.both.org free[266786]:
Swap: 8122364   >
Dec 05 10:49:13 testvm1.both.org lsblk[266788]:
NAME   MAJ:MIN RM S>
Dec 05 10:49:13 testvm1.both.org lsblk[266788]:
sda   8:0   0 1>
Dec 05 10:49:13 testvm1.both.org lsblk[266788]:
├─sda1   8:1   0   >
Dec 05 10:49:13 testvm1.both.org lsblk[266788]:
├─sda2   8:2   0   >
Dec 05 10:49:13 testvm1.both.org lsblk[266788]:
└─sda3   8:3   0 1>
Dec 05 10:49:13 testvm1.both.org lsblk[266788]:   ├─vg01-
root   253:0   0   >
Dec 05 10:49:13 testvm1.both.org lsblk[266788]:   ├─vg01-
usr   253:1   0   >
Dec 05 10:49:13 testvm1.both.org lsblk[266788]:   ├─vg01-
var   253:2   0   >
Dec 05 10:49:13 testvm1.both.org lsblk[266788]:   ├─vg01-
home   253:3   0   >

CHAPTER 8   USING SYSTEMD TIMERS

```
Dec 05 10:49:13 testvm1.both.org lsblk[266788]:    ├─vg01-
tmp     253:4     0   >
Dec 05 10:49:13 testvm1.both.org lsblk[266788]:    └─vg01-
TestFS 253:5     0   >
Dec 05 10:49:13 testvm1.both.org lsblk[266788]:
sr0               11:0    1 10>
Dec 05 10:49:13 testvm1.both.org lsblk[266788]:
zram0             252:0    0  7>
Dec 05 10:49:13 testvm1.both.org systemd[1]: myMonitor.
service: Deactivated s>
Dec 05 10:49:13 testvm1.both.org systemd[1]: Finished
myMonitor.service - Log
```

Now that you know your service works as expected, create the timer unit file, myMonitor.timer, in /etc/systemd/system, and add the following:

```
# This timer unit is for testing
# # Copyright David Both, 2025

# GNU All-Permissive License:
# Copying and distribution of this file, with or without
# modification, are permitted in any medium without royalty
# provided the copyright notice and this notice are
preserved.
# This file is offered as-is, without any warranty.
#

[Unit]
Description=Logs some system statistics to the
systemd journal
Requires=myMonitor.service

[Timer]
Unit=myMonitor.service
OnCalendar=*-*-* *:*:00
```

```
[Install]
WantedBy=timers.target
```

The `OnCalendar` time expression, `*-*-* *:*:00`, should trigger the timer to execute the `myMonitor.service` unit every minute. We'll explore `OnCalendar` settings a bit later in this chapter even though we looked at them in the previous chapter.

For now, observe any journal entries pertaining to running your service when it is triggered by the timer. You could also follow the timer, but following the service allows you to see the results in near real time. Run `journalctl` with the `-f` (follow) option:

`journalctl -S today -f -u myMonitor.service`

In another terminal session, start but do not enable the timer, and see what happens after it runs for a while.

`systemctl start myMonitor.service`

One result shows up right away, and the next ones come at—sort of—one-minute intervals. Watch the journal for a few minutes and see if you notice the same things I did.

Be sure to check the status of both the timer and the service.

Timer Accuracy

You probably noticed at least two things in the journal results for Experiment 8-2. First, you don't need to do anything special to cause the `STDOUT` from the `ExecStart` triggers in the `myMonitor.service` unit to be stored in the journal. That is all part of using systemd for running services. However, it does mean that you might need to be careful about running scripts from a service unit and how much `STDOUT` they generate.

The second thing is that the timer does not trigger exactly on the minute at :00 seconds or even exactly one minute from the previous instance. This is intentional, but it can be overridden if necessary (or if it just offends your SysAdmin sensibilities).

The reason for this behavior is to prevent multiple services from triggering at exactly the same time. For example, you can use time expressions such as Weekly, Daily, and more. These shortcuts are all defined to trigger at 00:00:00 hours on the day they are triggered. When multiple timers are specified this way, there is a strong likelihood that they would attempt to start simultaneously.

systemd timers are intentionally designed to trigger somewhat randomly around the specified time to try to prevent simultaneous triggers. They trigger semi-randomly within a time window that starts at the specified trigger time and ends at the specified time plus one minute. This trigger time is maintained at a stable position with respect to all other defined timer units, according to the `systemd.timer` man page. In my journal entries, the timer triggered immediately when it started and then about 46 or 47 seconds after each minute.

Most of the time, such probabilistic trigger times are fine. When scheduling tasks such as backups to run, so long as they run during off-hours, there will be no problems. A SysAdmin can select a deterministic start time, such as 01:05:00 in a typical cron job expression, to not conflict with other tasks, but there is a large range of time values that will accomplish that. A one-minute bit of randomness in a start time is usually irrelevant.

However, for some tasks, exact trigger times are an absolute requirement. For those, you can specify greater trigger time-span accuracy (to within a microsecond) by adding a statement like this to the `Timer` section of the timer unit file:

`AccuracySec=1us`

CHAPTER 8 USING SYSTEMD TIMERS

Time spans can be used to specify the desired accuracy as well as to define time spans for repeating or one-time events. It recognizes the following units:

- usec, us, μs
- msec, ms
- seconds, second, sec, s
- minutes, minute, min, m
- hours, hour, hr, h
- days, day, d
- weeks, week, w
- months, month, M (defined as 30.44 days)
- years, year, y (defined as 365.25 days)

All the default timers in /usr/lib/systemd/system specify a much larger range for accuracy because exact times are not critical.

EXPERIMENT 8-3: TIMER ACCURACY

Look at some of the expressions in the system-created timers. Perform this experiment as root.

```
# grep Accur /usr/lib/systemd/system/*timer
/usr/lib/systemd/system/fstrim.timer:AccuracySec=1h
/usr/lib/systemd/system/logrotate.timer:AccuracySec=1h
/usr/lib/systemd/system/logwatch.timer:AccuracySec=12h
/usr/lib/systemd/system/mlocate-updatedb.
timer:AccuracySec=24h
/usr/lib/systemd/system/raid-check.timer:AccuracySec=24h
/usr/lib/systemd/system/unbound-anchor.timer:AccuracySec=24h
```

You can see that accuracy for these timers ranges from an hour to as much as 24 hours.

View the complete contents of some of the timer unit files in the `/usr/lib/systemd/system` directory to see how they are constructed.

You do not have to enable the timer in this experiment to activate it at boot time, but the command to do so would be

`systemctl enable myMonitor.timer`

The unit files you created do not need to be executable. You also did not enable the service unit because it is triggered by the timer. You can still trigger the service unit manually from the command line, should you want to. Try that and observe the journal.

See the man pages for `systemd.timer` and `systemd.time` for more information about timer accuracy, event-time expressions, and trigger events.

Timer Types

systemd timers have other capabilities that are not found in cron, which triggers only on specific, repetitive, real-time dates and times. systemd timers can be configured to trigger based on status changes in other systemd units. For example, a timer might be configured to trigger a specific elapsed time after system boot, after startup, or after a defined service unit activates. These are called monotonic timers. Monotonic refers to a count or sequence that continually increases. These timers are not persistent because they reset after each boot.

Table 8-1 lists the monotonic timers along with a short definition of each, as well as the `OnCalendar` timer, which is not monotonic and is used to specify future times that may or may not be repetitive. This information is derived from the `systemd.timer` man page with a few minor changes.

Table 8-1. systemd timer definitions

Timer	Monotonic	Definition
OnActiveSec=	X	This defines a timer relative to the moment the timer is activated.
OnBootSec=	X	This defines a timer relative to when the machine boots up.
OnStartupSec=	X	This defines a timer relative to when the service manager first starts. For system timer units, this is very similar to OnBootSec=, as the system service manager generally starts very early at boot. It's primarily useful when configured in units running in the per-user service manager, as the user service manager generally starts on first login only, not during boot.
OnUnitActiveSec=	X	This defines a timer relative to when the timer that is to be activated was last activated.
OnUnitInactiveSec=	X	This defines a timer relative to when the timer that is to be activated was last deactivated.
OnCalendar=		This defines real-time (i.e., wall clock) timers with calendar event expressions. See systemd.time(7) for more information on the syntax of calendar event expressions. Otherwise, the semantics are similar to OnActiveSec= and related settings. This timer is the one most like those used with the cron service.

The monotonic timers can use the same shortcut names for their time spans as the `AccuracySec` statement mentioned before, but systemd normalizes those names to seconds. For example, you might want to specify a timer that triggers an event one time, five days after the system boots; that might look like `OnBootSec=5d`. If the host booted at 2020-06-15 `09:45:27`, the timer would trigger at 2020-06-20 `09:45:27` or within one minute after.

OnCalendar Event Expressions

OnCalendar event expressions are a key part of triggering timers at desired repetitive times. We did cover this in Chapter 7, but let's review it here, because it's key to understanding and creating OnCalendar expressions for timers that will trigger events at the times we need them.

systemd timers use a different style for time and date expressions than the format used in crontab. It is more flexible than crontab and allows fuzzy dates and times in the manner of the `at` command. It should also be familiar enough that it will be easy to understand.

The basic format for systemd timers using `OnCalendar=` is `DOW YYYY-MM-DD HH:MM:SS`. DOW (day of week) is optional, and other fields can use an asterisk (*) to match any value for that position. All calendar time forms are converted to a normalized form. If the time is not specified, it is assumed to be 00:00:00. If the date is not specified but the time is, the next match might be today or tomorrow, depending upon the current time. Names or numbers can be used for the month and day of the week. Comma-separated lists of each unit can be specified. Unit ranges can be specified with two dots "`..`" between the beginning and ending values.

There are a couple interesting options for specifying dates. The tilde (~) can be used to specify the last day of the month or a specified number of days prior to the last day of the month. The "/" can be used to specify a day of the week as a modifier.

CHAPTER 8 USING SYSTEMD TIMERS

Table 8-2 shows some examples of some typical time expressions used in OnCalendar statements.

Table 8-2. Sample OnCalendar event expressions

Calendar Event Expression	Description
DOW YYYY-MM-DD HH:MM:SS	
--* 00:15:30	Every day of every month of every year at 15 minutes and 30 seconds after midnight.
Weekly	Every Monday at 00:00:00.
Mon *-*-* 00:00:00	Same as weekly.
Mon	Same as weekly.
Wed 2020-*-*	Every Wednesday in 2020 at 00:00:00.
Mon..Fri 2021-*-*	Every weekday in 2021 at 00:00:00.
2022-6,7,8-1,15 01:15:00	The 1st and 15th of June, July, and August of 2022 at 01:15:00AM.
Mon *-05~03	The next occurrence of a Monday in May of any year which is also the third day from the end of the month.
Mon..Fri *-08~04	The fourth day preceding the end of August for any years in which it also falls on a weekday.
*-05~03/2	The third day from the end of the month of May and then again two days later. Repeats every year. Note that this expression uses the tilde (~).
*-05-03/2	The third day of the month of May and then every second day for the rest of May. Repeats every year. Note that this expression uses the dash (-).

213

CHAPTER 8   USING SYSTEMD TIMERS

Superfluous Timers

Most of the default timers are useful and necessary, but some may be superfluous. These unnecessary timers can be deactivated in accordance with the Linux philosophy of keeping things simple. Deactivating those timers saves system resources.

> **EXPERIMENT 8-4: DELETING SUPERFLUOUS TIMERS**
>
> When you looked at the list of active timers in Experiment 8-1, you probably saw the same list I did. I've reproduced it here and removed some of the columns so it could be larger and more readable. If you take a minute to consider that list, you'll see some timers that can be deleted if your system doesn't have certain hardware.
>
> ```
> fstrim.timer                  Discard unused filesystem
>                               blocks once a week
> logrotate.timer               Daily rotation of log files
> plocate-updatedb.timer        Update the plocate
>                               database daily
> raid-check.timer              Weekly RAID setup health check
> sysstat-collect.timer         Run system activity accounting
>                               tool every 10 minutes
> sysstat-rotate.timer          Rotate daily system activity
>                               data file at midnight
> sysstat-summary.timer         Generate summary of yesterday's
>                               process accounting
> systemd-tmpfiles-clean.timer  Daily Cleanup of Temporary
>                               Directories
> unbound-anchor.timer          daily update of the root trust
>                               anchor for DNSSEC
> ```

CHAPTER 8   USING SYSTEMD TIMERS

The first one that we see here is the fstrim.timer. The fstrim utility must be run at least weekly to ensure that data blocks on SSD devices are properly freed up and returned to the available pool of storage blocks. If this isn't done, those blocks would never be returned to the pool of free blocks.

If you don't have any SSD devices on your system, this timer can be disabled. Do this on your VM since it doesn't really deal with the hardware directly, and, whether you have SSD hardware or not, this won't affect the physical hardware in any way.

`# systemctl disable --now fstrim.timer`

Removed '/etc/systemd/system/timers.target.wants/fstrim.timer'.

We don't want to touch the logrotate.timer, which prevents the logfiles from becoming excessively large.

Nor do we want to disable the plocate-updatedb.timer because it causes the plocate database to be updated. The plocate database is used by the locate command which allows you to do a very fast search for files on a Linux host.

If you don't have a RAID array, the raid-check.timer can also be disabled. This health check is only needed if a RAID array is present on the system.

Verify for yourself whether any of the other timers are needed or not.

Summary

systemd timers can be used to perform the same kinds of tasks as the cron tool but offer more flexibility in terms of the calendar and monotonic time expressions for triggering events.

CHAPTER 8   USING SYSTEMD TIMERS

Even though the service units you created for this experiment are intended to be triggered by the timer, you can also use the `systemctl start <ServiceName>.service` command to trigger them at any time. Multiple maintenance tasks can be scripted in a single timer; these can be Bash scripts or Linux utility programs. You can run the service triggered by the timer to run all the scripts, or you can run individual scripts as needed.

I have not yet seen any indication that `cron` and `at` will be deprecated. I hope that does not happen because `at`, at least, is much easier to use for one-off task scheduling than systemd timers.

Exercises

Perform these exercises to complete this chapter:

1. Create a shell script that simulates a backup program. All it needs is to print to STDOUT that it's starting, wait for five to ten seconds, then print to STDOUT that the backup is completed.

2. Create a service that runs the backup script. Using the journal, verify that it runs as expected.

3. Create a timer that runs the backup script once every five minutes. Enable the timer and follow the journal entries to verify that the timer works as expected.

4. What type of timer did you use in Exercise 3? Why?

5. Create an OnCalendar expression that would trigger the backup timer every Sunday morning at 01:30AM.

6. Create an OnCalendar expression that would trigger an event the fourth Tuesday of every month.

7. Can you create an event expression that will trigger the last Friday of every month?

CHAPTER 9

Using systemd Journals

Objectives

In this chapter, you will learn

- What the systemd journal is and why it's superior to the old log files
- How to use dmesg to view log entries covering the journal's boot gap
- How to use systemd journals for exploring and problem-solving
- How to configure the systemd journal service
- How to add journal entries from scripts and the command line

Overview

Problem determination of computer system failures can be as much an art as it can a science. Sometimes it seems even a little magic can be useful. We've all encountered situations where a reported failure could not be reproduced, and that is always frustrating for the user as well as the system administrator. Even home appliances and automobiles can be obstinate and refuse to fail when the service person shows up.

Anthropomorphism aside, SysAdmins have some tools that can show us what has been happening in our Linux computers with varying degrees of granularity. We have tools like top, htop, btop, glances, sar, iotop, tcpdump, traceroute, mtr, iptraf-ng, df, du, and many more, all of which can display the current state of a host and several of which can produce logs of various levels of detail.

While these tools can be used to locate ongoing problems, they are not particularly helpful for transient problems and those that have no symptoms that are directly observable by the user—at least until some major and possibly catastrophic problem occurs.

One important tool I have used for problem determination is the system logs—and now with systemd—the systemd journals. Logs and journals are persistent files that are used by the system to store and maintain a complete record of system events. This can provide critical information about a system and what was taking place when an error occurred—even long after the fact.

Many historical style log files are still maintained along with the systemd journals. All log and journal files are stored in the /var/log directory.

The systemd journal is always one of my first tools when solving a problem, especially those that don't seem to happen when I am watching. It took me a long time at the beginning of my SysAdmin career to realize the wealth of information in the log files, and it improved the speed at which I could resolve problems once I finally did.

You have already seen some uses of the **journalctl** command in previous chapters. Let's explore some of the details of the systemd journal and how it works as well as some additional ways for SysAdmins to use journalctl to use the resulting journals to locate and identify problems.

CHAPTER 9   USING SYSTEMD JOURNALS

The Journal

The objective of any log or journal is to maintain a time-sequenced history of the normal activities of the various services and programs that run on a host and to record any errors and warning messages that might occur. The log messages used to be maintained in separate files in /var/log, usually one for the kernel and separate ones for most of the services running on the host. Unfortunately, the large number of log files could delay discovery of the root cause of the problem by spreading out needed information. This could be especially time-consuming while trying to determine what was taking place in the system when the error occurred.

The old /var/log/dmesg file was usually for the kernel, but that file was discontinued several years ago in favor of using the **dmesg** command to display the same information—although only that from the current boot—and integrating those messages and more into the /var/log/messages file. This merger of other logs into the messages file did help to speed up problem determination by keeping much of the data in one file, but there were still many services that had not integrated their logs into the more central messages file.

The systemd journal is designed to collect all messages into a single, unified database that can show a complete picture of everything that happened in a system at and around a specific time or event.

Journaling becomes active very early in the Linux boot process, while systemd itself is initializing. The exact amount of time will depend upon the speed of the host. For my fastest system, this was 1.38 seconds, and my slowest was 6.31 seconds.

Because all of the events, regardless of the source, are in one place in time sequence order, it is possible to see at a glance everything that was happening at a specific point or range of times. This is one of the main benefits of systemd journaling when problem-solving.

The **dmesg** command can also be used to discover the first moments of the kernel startup sequence. The kernel ring buffer is a space in memory that is used to store kernel messages. This data is not persistent, so dmesg can't reveal kernel logs from previous boots. Nor does it contain anything other than kernel messages.

The systemd journal also contains the kernel messages in addition to everything else it records.

Let's explore those first few moments in system initialization.

EXPERIMENT 9-1: EXPLORING SYSTEM INITIALIZATION

Let's start by looking at the earliest portion of the journal during a Linux boot. We'll use monotonic times, so we can see the time since the kernel started its initialization sequence. Enter the following command as a non-root user:

```
$ journalctl -b -o short-monotonic
[    4.023826] testvm1.both.org kernel: Linux version 6.11.8-300.fc41.x86_64 (mockbuild@6a5de21fe85b4b2584ad846216415107) (gcc (G>
[    4.023878] testvm1.both.org kernel: Command line: BOOT_IMAGE=(hd0,gpt2)/vmlinuz-6.11.8-300.fc41.x86_64 root=/dev/mapper/vg01->
[    4.023909] testvm1.both.org kernel: BIOS-provided physical RAM map:
[    4.023931] testvm1.both.org kernel: BIOS-e820: [mem 0x0000000000000000-0x000000000009fbff] usable
[    4.023951] testvm1.both.org kernel: BIOS-e820: [mem 0x000000000009fc00-0x000000000009ffff] reserved
[    4.023973] testvm1.both.org kernel: BIOS-e820: [mem 0x00000000000f0000-0x00000000000fffff] reserved
[    4.024000] testvm1.both.org kernel: BIOS-e820: [mem 0x0000000000100000-0x00000000dffeffff] usable
[    4.024021] testvm1.both.org kernel: BIOS-e820: [mem 0x00000000dfff0000-0x00000000dfffffff] ACPI data
```

[4.024042] testvm1.both.org kernel: BIOS-e820: [mem 0x00000000fec00000-0x00000000fec00fff] reserved
[4.024062] testvm1.both.org kernel: BIOS-e820: [mem 0x00000000fee00000-0x00000000fee00fff] reserved

On my VM, the first entry is at a little over four seconds into the boot. Non-root users can't use the dmesg command, so we'll do that as root.

dmesg | less
[0.000000] Linux version 6.11.8-300.fc41.x86_64 (mock build@6a5de21fe85b4b2584ad846216415107) (gcc (GCC) 14.2.1 20240912 (Red Hat 14.2.1-3), GNU ld version 2.43.1-2.fc41) #1 SMP PREEMPT_DYNAMIC Thu Nov 14 20:37:39 UTC 2024
[0.000000] Command line: BOOT_IMAGE=(hd0,gpt2)/vmlinuz-6.11.8-300.fc41.x86_64 root=/dev/mapper/vg01-root ro rd.lvm.lv=vg01/root rd.lvm.lv=vg01/usr selinux=0
[0.000000] BIOS-provided physical RAM map:
[0.000000] BIOS-e820: [mem 0x0000000000000000-0x000000000009fbff] usable
[0.000000] BIOS-e820: [mem 0x000000000009fc00-<SNIP>
[0.000000] NX (Execute Disable) protection: active
[0.000000] APIC: Static calls initialized
[0.000000] SMBIOS 2.5 present.
[0.000000] DMI: innotek GmbH VirtualBox/VirtualBox, BIOS VirtualBox 12/01/2006
[0.000000] DMI: Memory slots populated: 0/0
[0.000000] Hypervisor detected: KVMThe kernel ring buffer is a space in memory that is used to store kernel messages. This data is not persistent so can't reveal kernel logs from previous boots. In the past, and until recently, the data for previous boots was stored with that from the current boot in the file /var/log/dmesg.

CHAPTER 9   USING SYSTEMD JOURNALS

```
[    0.000000] kvm-clock: Using msrs 4b564d01 and 4b564d00
[    0.000003] kvm-clock: using sched offset of
5815639627 cycles
<SNIP>
```

I expect you've noticed the anomaly here. We'll explore that a little later in this chapter.

As a SysAdmin, the only time I typically use dmesg is to discover the device filename of newly inserted USB storage devices. That's only when I'm working on an chapter or a book and need to be absolutely sure I'm using the correct device and won't delete everything in my root directory. I rely far more on the systemd journal when doing system maintenance and problem determination.

The systemd Journal Service

The systemd journaling service is implemented by the systemd-journald daemon. According to the man page:

> *systemd-journald is a system service that collects and stores logging data. It creates and maintains structured, indexed journals based on logging information that is received from a variety of sources:*
>
> - *Kernel log messages*
> - *Simple system log messages*
> - *Structured system log messages*
> - *Standard output and standard error of service units.*
> - *Audit records, originating from the kernel audit subsystem*

The daemon will implicitly collect numerous metadata fields for each log messages in a secure manner that can't be faked. See systemd.journal-fields(7) for more information about the collected metadata.

Log data collected by the journal is primarily text-based but can also include binary data where necessary. Individual fields making up a log record stored in the journal may be up to 2^{64}-1 bytes in size.

The capability to add entries to the journal in a manner that's both secure and can't be faked is important. One of the ways that some rootkits hide their presence is to enter fake entries into the logs.

Configuration

The systemd journal daemon can be configured using the journald.conf file located in the /etc/systemd/ directory. For many hosts, this file needs no changes because the defaults are quite reasonable. You should look at the journald.conf file now if you have not already.

The most common configuration changes you might encounter are those that specify the maximum journal file size, number of older journal files, and the maximum file retention times. The primary reason for making those changes would be to reduce the storage space used by the journal if you have a small storage device. In a mission-critical environment, you may also want to reduce the amount of time between syncing journal data stored in RAM memory to the storage device.

The journald.conf man page has more details.

CHAPTER 9   USING SYSTEMD JOURNALS

About that Binary Data Format…

One of the controversies surrounding systemd is the binary format in which the journal contents are stored. Some arguments against systemd are based on the systemd journal being stored in a binary format. This would seem to be contrary to the Unix/Linux philosophy to use ASCII text for data. Those who dislike systemd use arguments like the following to support their viewpoints.

Doug McIlroy, the inventor of pipes, says this:

> *This is the Unix Philosophy: Write programs that do one thing well. Write programs to work together. Write programs to handle text steams, because that is a universal interface.*
>
> —Doug McIlroy, in Eric S. Raymond's *The Art of Unix Programming*

However, these arguments seem to be based on at least a partial misconception because the man page clearly states that the data "is primarily text-based" although it does allow for binary data forms. So are the journal files binary or not? Let's explore that question.

EXPERIMENT 9-2: ARE THE JOURNAL FILES IN BINARY?

The systemd journal files are stored in one or more subdirectories of /var/log/journal. Log in to a test system or VM for which you have root access and make /var/log/journal the PWD. List the subdirectories here, choose one, and make it the PWD. I looked at these files in a number of ways. I started with the stat command. The journal filenames on your host will be different from the ones on mine.

CHAPTER 9   USING SYSTEMD JOURNALS

stat system@0f3b8b<snip>a128e.journal
File: system@0f3b8b<snip>a128e.journal
Size: 16777216   Blocks: 30448   IO Block: 4096   regular file
Device: 253,2   Inode: 1573036   Links: 1
Access: (0640/-rw-r-----) Uid: (0/ root) Gid: (190/ systemd-journal)
Access: 2025-01-02 15:45:17.742103482 -0500
Modify: 2024-11-19 12:54:53.673100769 -0500
Change: 2024-11-19 12:54:53.673100769 -0500
Birth: 2024-11-19 12:28:55.266965814 -0500

The journal file is identified as a "regular" file which is not especially helpful. The **file** command identifies it as a "journal" file, but we already know that. But let's look a little inside the file with the dd command. The command below sends the output data stream to STDOUT; you may want to pipe it through the less pager:

dd if=system@0f3b8bac<snip>a128e.journal | less
<SNIP>
@^@^@^@^@^@^@^@_SOURCE_MONOTONIC_TIMESTAMP=41028^@^@^@^@^@
^@^@^A^@^@^@^@^@^@^@n^@^@^@^@^@^@^@
X.^],<83>B^Y^@^@^@^@^@^@^@^@<B8>a9^@^@^@^@^@<88>c9^@^@
^@^@^@^@^@^@^@^@^@^@^@^@^A^@^@^@^@^@^@^@^@^@^@^@^@^@^@^@
^@MESSAGE=ACPI: PM-Timer IO Port: 0x4008^@^@^C^@^@^@
^@^@^@^@h^@^@^@^@^@^@^@<DD>$^B^@^@^@^@^@^U^V<CA>,C'
^F^@Y<A1>H^@^@^@^@^@_<83><88>[5@M <87>Ti^S<E4><B4>
4lJ1<A5><D9>|Oy:O<FA>8^@P<FB>8^@<E8><FB>8^@<E0><FD>
8^@<88><FE>8^@8<FF>8^@<D8><FF>8^@^@^A9^@<A8>b9^@^Xc9^@
^A^@^@^@^@^@^@^@i^@^@^@^@^@^@^@<AD><@^@^@^@^@^@^@^@^@
^A^@^@^@^@^@^@^@^@^@^@^@^@^@^@_SOURCE_MONOTONIC_TIMEST
AMP=41100^@^@^@^@^@^@^A^@^@^@^@^@^@<8E>^@^@^@^@^@^@^
@<95>~l<DD><E5><C3>u>p^S<AC>^@^@^@^@^@^Xc9^@^@^@^@^@<F0>

227

CHAPTER 9 USING SYSTEMD JOURNALS

```
d9^@^@^@^@^@^@^@^@^@^@^@^@^A^@^@^@^@^@^@^@^@^@^@^@
^@^@^@MESSAGE=IOAPIC[0]: apic_id 6, version 32, address
0xfec00000, GSI 0-23^@^@^C^@^@^@^@^@^@^@h^@^@^@^@^@^@^@<
DE>$^B^@^@^@^@^@$^V<CA>,C'^F^@g<A1>H^@^@^@^@^@_<83><88>
[5@M<87>Ti^S<E4><B4>4l<B9><B3>3<83>@^@^@^@^@
^A^@^@^@^@^@^@^@^@^@^@^@^@^@_SOURCE_MONOTONIC_TIMEST
AMP=41104^@^@^@^@^@^@^@^A^@^@^@^@^@^@^@<88>^@^@^@^@^@^@^
@^]<D2>I<A7><F6>J9^V^@^@^@^@^@^@^@^@`d9^@^@^@^@^@Pf9^@^
@^@^@^@^@^@^@^@^@^@^@^@^A^@^@^@^@^@^@^@^@^@^@^@^@^@^@^@
MESSAGE=ACPI: INT_SRC_OVR (bus 0 bus_irq 0 global_irq 2
dfl dfl)^C^@^@^@^@^@^@h^@^@^@^@^@^@^@
<SNIP>
```

The data stream from the **dd** command, of which I only reproduced a minuscule amount, shows an interesting mixture of ASCII text and binary data. Another useful tool is the strings command which simply displays all of the ASCII text strings contained in a file and ignores the binary data.

strings system@34a336<snip>1afdc92.journal | less

This data can be interpreted by humans, and this particular segment looks very similar to the output data stream from the dmesg command.

I leave you on your own for further exploration, but my conclusion is that the journal files are clearly a mix of binary and ASCII text. That mixture makes it cumbersome at best to use the traditional text-based Linux tools to extract usable data. The systemd **journalctl** command provides us a better method with many possibilities for extracting and viewing journal data.

The journalctl Command

The systemd journaling system collects and stores huge amounts of data, and the oldest could be weeks or months ago. This amounted to about three months' worth of data for my primary workstation.

The journalctl command is designed to extract usable information from the systemd journals using powerful and flexible criteria for identifying the desired data. This is the tool we use to explore the content of system journals.

Let's explore this powerful command in more detail.

EXPERIMENT 9-3: USING JOURNALCTL

You can use the journalctl command without any options or arguments to view the entire systemd journal which contains all journal and log information. As we proceed through this experiment, I'll show you various ways to select only the data in which you are interested.

```
# journalctl
```

I'm not even going to try to reproduce the data stream here because there is so much. Scroll through this data using the pager's movement keys.

You can also explicitly show the same data as the **dmesg** command. Open two terminal sessions, place them next to each other, and issue the **dmesg** command in one and the following command in the other:

```
# journalctl --dmesg
```

The only difference you should find is the time format. The dmesg command is in a monotonic format that shows the number of seconds since the system boot. The journalctl output is in a date and time format. The short-monotonic option displays the time since boot, starting with the first boot.

```
# journalctl --dmesg -o short-monotonic
```

CHAPTER 9   USING SYSTEMD JOURNALS

The journalctl command has many options including the -o (output) option with several sub-options that allow you to select from several time and date formats that meet different sets of requirements. Table 9-1 lists most of these, along with a short description of each that I have expanded upon or modified a bit from the journalctl man page. Note that the primary difference between most of these is the format of the date and time, while the other information remains the same.

Table 9-1. journalctl time and date formats

Format Name	Description
short	This is the default format and generates an output that most closely resembles the formatting of classic syslog files, showing one line per journal entry. This option shows journal metadata including the date and time, the fully qualified hostname, and the unit name, such as the kernel, DHCP, etc. `Jul 20 08:43:01 testvm1.both.org kernel: Inode-cache hash table entries: 1048576 (order: 11, 8388608 bytes, linear)`
short-full	This format is very similar to the default, but shows timestamps in the format that the --since= and --until= options accept. Unlike the timestamp information shown in short output mode, this mode includes weekday, year, and time zone information in the output and is locale independent. `Mon 2020-06-08 07:47:20 EDT testvm1.both.org kernel: x86/fpu: Supporting XSAVE feature 0x004: 'AVX registers'`

(continued)

CHAPTER 9   USING SYSTEMD JOURNALS

Table 9-1. (*continued*)

Format Name	Description
short-iso	The short-iso format is very similar to the default, but shows ISO 8601 wallclock timestamps. `2020-06-08T07:47:20-0400 testvm1.both.org kernel: kvm-clock: Using msrs 4b564d01 and 4b564d00`
short-iso-precise	This format is the same as short-iso above, but includes full microsecond precision. `2020-06-08T07:47:20.223738-0400 testvm1.both.org kernel: Booting paravirtualized kernel on KVM`
short-monotonic	Very similar to the default, short-full, but shows monotonic timestamps instead of wallclock timestamps. I find this most useful for `[    2.091107] testvm1.both.org kernel: ata1.00: ATA-6: VBOX HARDDISK, 1.0, max UDMA/133`
short-precise	This format is also similar to the default, but shows classic syslog timestamps with full microsecond precision. `Jun 08 07:47:20.223052 testvm1.both.org kernel: BIOS-e820: [mem 0x000000000009fc00-0x000000000009ffff] reserved`
short-unix	Like the default but shows seconds passed since January 1, 1970, UTC, instead of wallclock timestamps ("UNIX time"). The time is shown with microsecond accuracy. `1591616840.232165 testvm1.both.org kernel: tcp_listen_portaddr_hash hash table entries: 8192`

(*continued*)

231

CHAPTER 9   USING SYSTEMD JOURNALS

Table 9-1. (*continued*)

Format Name	Description
cat	Generates a very terse output, only showing the actual message of each journal entry with no metadata, not even a timestamp. `ohci-pci 0000:00:06.0: irq 22, io mem 0xf0804000`

verbose	This format shows the full data structure for all of the entry items with all fields. This is the format option that is most different from all of the others.
	`Mon 2020-06-08 07:47:20.222969 EDT [s=d52ddc9f3e8f43 4b9b9411be2ea50b1e;i=1;b=dcb6dcc0658e4a8d8c781c21a2c 6360d;m=242d7f;t=5a7912c6148f9;x=8f>`
	　`_SOURCE_MONOTONIC_TIMESTAMP=0`
	　`_TRANSPORT=kernel`
	　`PRIORITY=5`
	　`SYSLOG_FACILITY=0`
	　`SYSLOG_IDENTIFIER=kernel`
	　`MESSAGE=Linux version 5.6.6-300.fc32.x86_64 (mockbuild@bkernel03.phx2.fedoraproject.org) (gcc version 10.0.1 20200328 (Red Hat 10.0.1-0>`
	　`_BOOT_ID=dcb6dcc0658e4a8d8c781c21a2c6360d`
	　`_MACHINE_ID=3bccd1140fca488187f8a1439c832f07`
	　`_HOSTNAME=testvm1.both.org`

CHAPTER 9   USING SYSTEMD JOURNALS

There are other choices available with the -o option that provide for exporting the data in various formats such as binary or JSON. I also find the -x option illuminating because it can show additional explanatory messages for some journal entries. If you try this option, be aware that it can greatly increase the volume of the output data stream. For one useful example, the additional information for an entry like the following:

journalctl -x -S today -o short-monotonic
[121206.308026] studentvm1 systemd[1]: Starting unbound-anchor.service - update of the root trust anchor for DNSSEC validation in unbound...
░░ Subject: A start job for unit unbound-anchor.service
   has begun execution
░░ Defined-By: systemd
░░ Support: https://lists.freedesktop.org/mailman/
   listinfo/systemd-devel
░░
░░ A start job for unit unbound-anchor.service has begun
   execution.
░░
░░ The job identifier is 39813.
[121206.308374] studentvm1 rsyslogd[975]: [origin software="rsyslogd" swVersion="8.2204.0-3.fc37" x-pid="975" x-info="https://www.rsyslog.com"] rsyslogd w>
[121206.308919] studentvm1 systemd[1]: Starting logrotate.service - Rotate log files...
░░ Subject: A start job for unit logrotate.service has
   begun execution
░░ Defined-By: systemd
░░ Support: https://lists.freedesktop.org/mailman/
   listinfo/systemd-devel
░░

233

CHAPTER 9   USING SYSTEMD JOURNALS

```
    A start job for unit logrotate.service has begun
    execution.

    The job identifier is 39491.
<SNIP>
```

There is some new information here, but I think the main benefit is that the available information is contextualized to provide some clarification of the original terse messages. The URL provided by the Support line for each entry points to a mailing list that you can join for active support.

Narrowing the Search

Most of the time, it is not necessary or desirable to list all of the journal entries and manually search through them. Sometimes I look for entries related to a specific service and sometimes entries that took place at specific times. The journalctl command provides powerful options that allow us to see only those data in which we have an interest.

Tip   Be sure to use boot offsets and UIDs, as well as dates and times for your situation as the ones shown here are for my time and date.

Let's start with the --list-boots option which lists all of the boots that took place during the time period for which journal entries exist. Note that the journalctl.conf file may specify that journal entries be discarded after they reach a certain age or after the storage device (HDD/SSD) space taken by the journals reaches a specified maximum amount.

CHAPTER 9   USING SYSTEMD JOURNALS

`journalctl --list-boots`

```
IDX BOOT ID
    FIRST ENTRY                     LAST ENTRY
-79 93b506c4ef654d6c85da03a9e3436894
    Tue 2023-01-17 02:53:26 EST Wed 2023-01-18 07:55:16 EST
-78 85bacafb6f11433089b0036374865ad9
    Fri 2023-01-20 06:11:11 EST Fri 2023-01-20 11:15:44 EST
-77 39ac25ab4bfa43a8ae3de0c6fe8c1987
    Fri 2023-01-20 11:18:40 EST Fri 2023-01-20 11:21:13 EST
-76 61b9a620bfaa4e39ba1151ea87702360
    Fri 2023-01-20 11:25:15 EST Fri 2023-01-20 11:30:57 EST
<SNIP>
 -3 2624601ee2464c68abc633fe432876e5
    Tue 2023-04-25 09:20:47 EDT Tue 2023-04-25 10:27:57 EDT
 -2 74796c22509344849f4cacb57278151d
    Tue 2023-04-25 10:28:28 EDT Wed 2023-04-26 07:40:51 EDT
 -1 a60f595794bf4789b04bbe50371147a8
    Thu 2023-04-27 02:13:49 EDT Fri 2023-04-28 05:49:54 EDT
  0 920a397a6fc742899bb4e0576cfe7a70
    Fri 2023-04-28 10:20:14 EDT Fri 2023-04-28 20:50:16 EDT
```

The most recent boot ID appears at the bottom and is the long, random Hex number. Now we can use this data to view the journals for a specific boot. This can be specified using the boot offset number in the left-most column or the UUID in the second column. This command displays the journal for the boot instance with the offset of -2—the second previous boot from the current one.

`journalctl -b -2`

```
Apr 25 10:28:28 studentvm1 kernel: Linux version
6.1.18-200.fc37.x86_64 (mockbuild@bkernel01.iad2.
fedoraproject.org) (gcc (GCC) 12.2.1 20221121 (Red Hat 1>
```

CHAPTER 9   USING SYSTEMD JOURNALS

```
Apr 25 10:28:28 studentvm1 kernel: Command line: BOOT_
IMAGE=(hd0,gpt2)/vmlinuz-6.1.18-200.fc37.x86_64 root=/dev/
mapper/fedora_studentvm1-root ro rd.lvm.lv>
Apr 25 10:28:28 studentvm1 kernel: x86/fpu: Supporting
XSAVE feature 0x001: 'x87 floating point registers'
Apr 25 10:28:28 studentvm1 kernel: x86/fpu: Supporting
XSAVE feature 0x002: 'SSE registers'
<SNIP>
```

Or you could use the UUID for the desired boot. The offset numbers change after each boot, but the UUID does not. In this example, I am using the UID for the 76th previous boot. The UUIDs for the boots on your VM will be different, but choose one and use it in the following command:

journalctl -b 61b9a620bfaa4e39ba1151ea87702360

The -u option allows selection of specific units to examine. You can use a unit name or a pattern for matching and can use this option multiple times to match multiple units or patterns. In this example, I used it in combination with -b to show chronyd journal entries for the current boot.

journalctl -u chronyd -b
```
Apr 28 10:20:41 studentvm1 systemd[1]: Starting chronyd.
service - NTP client/server...
Apr 28 10:20:43 studentvm1 chronyd[1045]: chronyd version
4.3 starting (+CMDMON +NTP +REFCLOCK +RTC +PRIVDROP
+SCFILTER +SIGND +ASYNCDNS +NTS +SECHASH +IP>
Apr 28 10:20:43 studentvm1 chronyd[1045]: Frequency
15369.953 +/- 0.034 ppm read from /var/lib/chrony/drift
Apr 28 10:20:43 studentvm1 chronyd[1045]: Using right/UTC
timezone to obtain leap second data
Apr 28 10:20:43 studentvm1 chronyd[1045]: Loaded seccomp
filter (level 2)
```

CHAPTER 9   USING SYSTEMD JOURNALS

Apr 28 10:20:43 studentvm1 systemd[1]: Started chronyd.service - NTP client/server.
Apr 28 14:20:58 studentvm1 chronyd[1045]: Forward time jump detected!
Apr 28 14:21:16 studentvm1 chronyd[1045]: Selected source 192.168.0.52
Apr 28 14:21:16 studentvm1 chronyd[1045]: System clock TAI offset set to 37 seconds
Apr 28 14:24:32 studentvm1 chronyd[1045]: Selected source 138.236.128.36 (2.fedora.pool.ntp.org)

Suppose we want to look at events that were recorded between two arbitrary times. We can use -S (--since) and -U (--until) to specify the beginning and ending times as well. The following command displays journal entries starting at 15:36:00 on March 24, 2023, up through the current time:

journalctl -S "2023-03-24 15:36:00"

And this command displays all journal entries starting at 15:36:00 on March 24, 2023, and up until 16:00:00 on March 30.

journalctl -S "2023-03-24 15:36:00" -U "2023-03-30 16:00:00"

The next command combines -S, -U, and -u to give us the journal entries for the NetworkManager service unit starting at 15:36:00 on July 24, 2020, and up until 16:00:00 on July 20, 2029.

journalctl -S "2023-03-24 15:36:00" -U "2029-07-20 16:00:00" -u NetworkManager

If the full range of dates doesn't exist, journalctl will display the range that does exist.

237

CHAPTER 9   USING SYSTEMD JOURNALS

Determine the range of dates contained in the journals for your system and reduce the date range in the journalctl command to display only a portion of those dates that actually exist.

Some syslog facilities such as cron, auth, mail, daemon, user, and more can be viewed with the --facility option. You can use --facility=help to list the available facilities. In this example, the mail facility is not the sendmail service that would be used for an email service but the local client used by Linux to send email to root as event notifications. Sendmail actually has two parts, the server which, for Fedora and related distributions, is not installed by default and the client which is always installed so that it can be used to deliver system emails to local recipients, especially root.

```
# journalctl --facility=help
Available facilities:
kern
user
mail
<SNIP>
# journalctl --facility=kern
```

This data should look familiar.

Commonly Used Options

Table 9-2 summarizes some of the options that I use most frequently. Most of these options can be used in various combinations to further narrow down the search. Be sure to refer to Chapter 7, "Analyzing systemd Calendar and Time Spans," for details on creating and testing timestamps as well as important tips like using quotes around timestamps.

Table 9-2. Some options used to narrow searches of the journal

Option	Description
--list-boots	Displays a list of boots. That information can be used to specify that only journal entries for a selected boot be shown.
-b [offset|boot ID]	Used to specify which boot to display information for. This includes all journal entries from that boot through shutdown or reboot.
--facility=[facility name]	Used to specify the facility names as known to syslog. Use --facility=help to list the valid facility names.
-k, --dmesg	Displays only kernel messages. This is equivalent to using the dmesg command.
-S, --since [timestamp]	Shows all journal entries since (after) the specified time. Can be used with --until to display an arbitrary range of time. Fuzzy times such as "yesterday" and "2 hours ago"—with quotes—are also allowed.
-u [unit name]	The -u option allows selection of specific units to examine. You can use a unit name or a pattern for matching. This option can be used multiple times to match multiple units or patterns.
-U, --until [timestamp]	Shows all journal entries until (prior to) the specified time. Can be used with --since to display an arbitrary range of time. Fuzzy times such as "yesterday" and "2 hours ago"—with quotes—are also allowed.

The journalctl man page lists all of the options that can be used to narrow searches to the specific data we need.

CHAPTER 9   USING SYSTEMD JOURNALS

Other Interesting Options

The `journalctl` program offers other interesting options, some of which are listed in Table 9-3. These options are useful for refining the data search, how the journal data is displayed, and managing the journal files themselves.

Table 9-3. Some additional interesting journalctl options

Option	Description
`-f, --follow`	This **journalctl** option is similar to using the **tail -f** command. It shows the most recent entries in the journal that match whatever other options have been specified and also displays new entries as they occur. This can be useful when watching for events and when testing changes.
`-e, --pager-end`	The -e option displays the end of the data stream instead of the beginning. This does not reverse the order of the data stream; rather, it causes the pager to jump to the end.
`--file [journal filename]`	Specify the name of a specific journal file in /var/log/journal/<journal subdirectory>.
`-r, --reverse`	This option reverses the order of the journal entries in the pager so that the newest are at the top rather than the bottom.
`-n, --lines=[X]`	Shows the most recent X number lines from the journal.
`--utc`	Displays the times in UTC rather than local time.

(continued)

CHAPTER 9   USING SYSTEMD JOURNALS

Table 9-3. (*continued*)

Option	Description
-g, --grep=[REGEX]	I like the -g option because it enables me to search for specific patterns in the journal data stream. This is just like piping a text data stream through the **grep** command. This option uses Perl-compatible regular expressions.
--disk-usage	This option displays the amount of disk storage used by the current and archived journals. It might not be as much as you think.
--flush	Journal data stored in the virtual filesystem /run/log/journal/ which is volatile storage is written to /var/log/journal/ which is persistent storage.
--sync	Writes all unwritten journal entries (still in RAM but apparently not in /run/log/journal) to the persistent filesystem. All journal entries known to the journaling system at the time the command is entered are moved to persistent storage.
--vacuum-size= --vacuum-time= --vacuum-files=	These can be used singly or in combination to remove the oldest archived journal files until the specified condition is met. These options only consider the archived files and not active files, so the result might not be exactly what was specified.

More options can be found in the journalctl man page. We explore some of the entries from Table 9-3 in the next sections.

241

CHAPTER 9   USING SYSTEMD JOURNALS

Journal Files

> **EXPERIMENT 9-4: EXPLORING THE JOURNAL FILES**

If you've not already done so, be sure to list the files in the journal directory on your host. Remember that the directory containing the journal files has a long random number as a name. This directory contains multiple active and archived journal files including some for users.

```
# cd /var/log/journal/
# ll
total 8
drwxr-sr-x+ 2 root systemd-journal 4096 Apr 25 13:40 d1fbbe41229942289e5ed31a256200fb
# cd d1fbbe41229942289e5ed31a256200fb
# ll
<SNIP>
-rw-r-----+ 1 root systemd-journal   4360720 Mar 14 10:15 user-1000@81e2499fc0df4505b251bf3c342e2d88-000000000000cfe6-0005f6b5daebaab2.journal
-rw-r-----+ 1 root systemd-journal   4246952 Apr 25 09:17 user-1000@81e2499fc0df4505b251bf3c342e2d88-00000000000f148-0005f74376644013.journal
-rw-r-----+ 1 root systemd-journal   8388608 Apr 28 05:49 user-1000.journal
-rw-r-----+ 1 root systemd-journal   3692360 Mar 12 11:43 user-1001@1c165b49f11f42399380c5d449c7e7e1-0000000000005151-0005f4fc6561390c.journal
```

You can see the user files in this listing for the UID 1000, which is our Linux login account. The --files option allows us to see the content of specified files including the user files.

CHAPTER 9   USING SYSTEMD JOURNALS

`journalctl --file user-1000.journal`

This output shows, among other things, the temporary file cleanup for the user with UID 1000. Data relating to individual users may be helpful in locating the root cause of problems originating in user space. I found a number of interesting entries here. Try it on your VM and see what you find.

After experimenting with this for a while, make root's home directory the PWD.

Adding Your Own Journal Entries

It can be useful to add your own entries to the journal. For example, you may want to record checkpoints reached by a program in the journal. This can assist with problem-solving. Adding entries to the journal is accomplished with the **systemd-cat** program which allows us to pipe the STDOUT of a command or program to the journal.

EXPERIMENT 9-5: ADDING ENTRIES TO THE JOURNAL

This command can be used as part of a pipeline on the command line or in a script.

`echo "Hello world" | systemd-cat -p info -t myprog`

The -p option specifies a priority, "emerg," "alert," "crit," "err," "warning," "notice," "info," "debug," or a value between 0 and 7 that represents each of those named levels. These priority values are the same as defined by syslog(3). The default is "info." The -t option is an identifier which can be any arbitrary short string such as a program or script name. This string can be used for searches by the journalctl command.

List the five most recent entries in the journal.

Chapter 9 Using Systemd Journals

```
# journalctl -n 5
```
Jan 06 07:20:58 testvm1.both.org systemd[1]: sysstat-collect.service: Deactivated successfully.
Jan 06 07:20:58 testvm1.both.org systemd[1]: Finished sysstat-collect.service - system activity accounting tool.
Jan 06 07:20:58 testvm1.both.org audit[1]: SERVICE_START pid=1 uid=0 auid=4294967295 ses=4294967295 msg='unit=sysstat-collect comm="systemd" exe=">
Jan 06 07:20:58 testvm1.both.org audit[1]: SERVICE_STOP pid=1 uid=0 auid=4294967295 ses=4294967295 msg='unit=sysstat-collect comm="systemd" exe="/>
Jan 06 07:28:14 testvm1.both.org myprog[132792]: Hello world
lines 1-5/5 (END)

There is not a lot happening on our VMs, so the last line is the journal entry we created. We can also use the string "myprog" to search for the entry.

```
# journalctl -t myprog
```
Jan 06 07:28:14 testvm1.both.org myprog[132792]: Hello world

This can be a powerful tool to embed in the Bash programs we use for automation. We can use it to create records of when and what our programs do in case problems occur.

Journal Storage Usage

Journal files take up storage space, so it is necessary to monitor them. That way, we can rotate them and delete old ones when necessary in order to free up storage space. In this context, rotation means to stop adding data

CHAPTER 9   USING SYSTEMD JOURNALS

to the currently active journal (or log) file and to start a new file and add all future data to that one. Old, inactive files are maintained for some arbitrary time span and deleted when that time expires.

The journalctl command provides methods for us to see how much storage space is being used by the journals as well as configuration of the parameters used to trigger rotation. It also allows us to initiate rotation manually on demand.

EXPERIMENT 9-6: JOURNAL STORAGE AND ROTATION

Start by determining how much storage space is used by the journals.

```
# journalctl --disk-usage
Archived and active journals take up 551.2M in the file system.
```

The result on my primary workstation is 3.5GB. Journal sizes depend greatly on the use to which a host is put and daily runtime. My physical hosts all run 24x7.

The /etc/systemd/journald.conf file can be used to configure the journal file sizes and rotation and retention times to meet any needs not met by the default settings. You can also configure the journal file directory on the storage device or whether to store everything in RAM—volatile storage. If the journals are stored in RAM, they will not be persistent between boots.

The default time unit in the journald.conf file is seconds, but that can be overridden using the suffixes "year," "month," "week," "day," "h," or "m."

Suppose you want to limit the total amount of storage space allocated to journal files to 1GB, to store all journal entries in persistent storage, keep a maximum of ten files, and delete any journal archive files that are more than one month old. You can configure this in /etc/systemd/journald.conf using the following entries:

```
SystemMaxUse=1G
Storage=persistent
SystemMaxFiles=10
MaxRetentionSec=1month
```

By default, the SystemMaxUse is 10% of available disk space. All of the default settings have been fine for the various systems I work with, and I have had no need to change any of them. The journald.conf man page also states that the time-based settings that can be used to determine the length of time to store journal entries in a single file or to retain older files are normally not necessary. This is because the file number and size configurations usually force rotation and deletion of old files before any time settings might come into effect.

The SystemKeepFree option can be used to ensure that a specific amount of space is kept free for other data. Many databases and application programs use the /var filesystem to store data, so ensuring enough storage space is available can be critical in systems with smaller hard drives and a minimum amount of space allocated to /var.

If you do make changes to this configuration, be sure to monitor the results carefully for an appropriate period of time to ensure that they are performing as expected.

Journal File Rotation

The journal files are typically rotated automatically based upon the configuration in the /etc/systemd/journald.conf file. Files are rotated whenever one of the specified conditions is met. So if, for one example, the amount of space allocated to journal files is exceeded, the oldest file or files are deleted, the active file is made into an archive, and a new active file is created.

CHAPTER 9 USING SYSTEMD JOURNALS

Journal files can also be rotated manually. I suggest using the --flush option first to ensure that all current data is moved to persistent storage to ensure that it is all rotated and the new journal files start empty. This option is listed in Table 9-3 but can also be found in the option section of the journalctl man page.

It is also possible to purge old journal files without performing a file rotation. The vacuum-size=, vacuum-files=, and vacuum-time= commands are tools that can be used to delete old archive files down to a specified total size, number of files, or time prior to the present. The option values consider only the archive files and not the active ones, so the resulting reduction in total file size might be somewhat less than expected unless you flush all data from volatile storage to persistent storage.

EXPERIMENT 9-7: JOURNAL FILE MANAGEMENT

Before starting this experiment, we need to set some conditions to make it work properly. As I discovered when creating this experiment, there is not enough data to cause a rotation even when performed manually.

There were 39 files that took up about 497M on my VM.

Open a terminal session and escalate your privileges to root. Make /var/log/journal/<Your-Journal-Directory> the PWD and look at the files in the journal directory. I have only a single journal directory on my VM, but the files it contains go back about three months.

```
# cd   /var/log/journal/d1fbbe41229942289e5ed31a256200fb
[root@studentvm1 d1fbbe41229942289e5ed31a256200fb]# ls
system@0005f2b035b5ec5c-a8d2b8b6d3f7b880.journal~
system@0005f2b04d5b1e40-350154cf9aedf8d0.journal~
system@0005f2b0d952b50f-9a23264d3adef5f5.journal~
system@0005f2b0fa23a6f4-376b000f611d8ac3.journal~
system@0005f2b13b66495c-2888d80cf01e1793.journal~
```

247

CHAPTER 9   USING SYSTEMD JOURNALS

```
system@0005f2b8d01f6b1b-36122a575e54d385.journal~
system@0005f2b8eaf61ac9-3071861fcecbcb11.journal~
system@0005f2b90329031c-bd4bef8a7bdce927.journal~
system@0005f2ff9e4c5cdc-e1f2ef3a72fc7675.journal~
system@0005f301c088fb9c-789178eb0f4ea0fd.journal~
system@0005f32735d4452f-4f5917137c44c9fd.journal~
system@0005f404e4026118-048976ba41c03dc2.journal~
system@0005f41ea1668b3d-cc6c81aed5f935f1.journal~
system@0005f42ea3e53fc5-ce69998ea6a38a3f.journal~
system@0005f431322b92b4-831c6756317a6dd1.journal~
system@0005f453110b09e4-6c80463d876ae956.journal~
system@0005f4d7e9ca1d4a-80c25a84c8aec6d1.journal~
system@0005f56bd926461d-f89a91e4425992ef.journal~
system@0005f5b08a161a8f-309c9fceb66b753c.journal~
system@0005f5b3b6ea5881-a8dc0539c4ab3197.journal~
system@0005f5fe836012c6-d6ce03272713f47b.journal~
system@0005f637ce5e849a-330fd866eb58a62e.journal~
system@0005f69cf2da4392-3e38a13f8e0bc669.journal~
system@0005f6c9e94576a2-f314d048307ac935.journal~
system@0005f6ca18260e8b-8c793b1d198593b6.journal~
system@0005f6ca2587111d-ea8996c255b04c5f.journal~
system@0005f7401797df22-5ecb9901d0977a51.journal~
system@0005f764896fe3c2-672a972fa95262ce.journal~
system@0005f8071a1af6a7-97ce48062602e8ed.journal~
system@34a3369229c84735810ef3687e3ea888-0000000000000001-
0005f69cf1afdc92.journal
system@a4c3fe82821e4894a5b2155fe84a1bb0-0000000000000001-
0005f6ca2400d3f8.journal
system@cd7e3b29fb8e45bdb65d728e1b69e29e-0000000000000001-
0005f80719125411.journal
system.journal
user-1000@0005f43566ce0a41-96c83a31073b4c54.journal~
```

CHAPTER 9   USING SYSTEMD JOURNALS

```
user-1000@81e2499fc0df4505b251bf3c342e2d88-000000000000068a-
0005f43566ce084c.journal
user-1000@81e2499fc0df4505b251bf3c342e2d88-000000000000cfe6-
0005f6b5daebaab2.journal
user-1000@81e2499fc0df4505b251bf3c342e2d88-000000000000f148-
0005f74376644013.journal
user-1001@1c165b49f11f42399380c5d449c7e7e1-0000000000005151-
0005f4fc6561390c.journal
# journalctl --disk-usage
Archived and active journals take up 496.8M in the
file system.
# ll | wc -l
39
[root@studentvm1 d1fbbe41229942289e5ed31a256200fb]#
```

Do a long listing of the files in this directory, so you will have something to compare with the results of the commands we are going to be experimenting with.

Power off the VM and take a new snapshot of your StudentVM1. Add the following text in the "Description" field:

"Taken at the beginning of Experiment 9-7: Journal File Management. This allows restoring this snapshot in order to see the different effects of journal rotation and vacuum on the same set of starting journal data."

You will restore this snapshot multiple times during this experiment. Then boot the VM.

The most simple approach to journal file management is a simple rotation.

```
# journalctl --rotate
```

List the files in the journal directory. They haven't changed much—not at all, really. I don't know why as the journalctl man page indicates that this

249

command should stop adding data to the existing files and start new ones. Because this did not work as the man page said it should, I reported the failure on Red Hat's Bugzilla web page.

The following command does work, and it purges old archive files so that only ones that are less than one month old are left. You can use the "s," "m," "h," "days," "months," "weeks," and "years" suffixes.

```
# journalctl --vacuum-time=1month
Deleted archived journal /var/log/journal/
d1fbbe41229942289e5ed31a256200fb/system@0005f2b035b5ec5c-
a8d2b8b6d3f7b880.journal~ (16.0M).
Deleted archived journal /var/log/journal/d1fbbe41229942289
e5ed31a256200fb/user-1000@0005f43566ce0a41-96c83a31073b4c54.
journal~ (8.0M).
Deleted archived journal /var/log/journal/
d1fbbe41229942289e5ed31a256200fb/system@0005f2b04d5b1e40-
350154cf9aedf8d0.journal~ (8.0M).
<SNIP>
Vacuuming done, freed 488.8M of archived journals from /
var/log/journal/d1fbbe41229942289e5ed31a256200fb.
Vacuuming done, freed 0B of archived journals from /run/
log/journal.
Vacuuming done, freed 0B of archived journals from /var/
log/journal.
```

Check the disk usage.

Power off the VM and restore the last snapshot. You did create that snapshot, right? Verify that the expected number of files and data are present.

This command deletes all archive files except for the four most recent ones. If there are fewer than four archive files, nothing will be done, and the original number of files will remain.

CHAPTER 9   USING SYSTEMD JOURNALS

`journalctl --vacuum-files=4`
\<SNIP\>
Deleted archived journal /var/log/journal/79c9dac7c584478196d4cd8c6243884d/system@0f3b8bac99bd4559a61f08fbae3fd4da-000000000002b80c-000627bf01a840c9.journal (11.2M).
Deleted archived journal /var/log/journal/79c9dac7c584478196d4cd8c6243884d/user-1000@0f3b8bac99bd4559a61f08fbae3fd4da-000000000002d8a2-0006284f5ee8080e.journal (3.9M).
Deleted archived journal /var/log/journal/79c9dac7c584478196d4cd8c6243884d/system@0f3b8bac99bd4559a61f08fbae3fd4da-000000000002df97-00062859b09f35c5.journal (5.2M).
Deleted archived journal /var/log/journal/79c9dac7c584478196d4cd8c6243884d/system@0f3b8bac99bd4559a61f08fbae3fd4da-000000000002ea61-0006286424c3b24e.journal (15M).
Deleted archived journal /var/log/journal/79c9dac7c584478196d4cd8c6243884d/user-1000@0f3b8bac99bd4559a61f08fbae3fd4da-0000000000033ba3-00062abf3d69e051.journal (3.6M).
Deleted archived journal /var/log/journal/79c9dac7c584478196d4cd8c6243884d/system@0f3b8bac99bd4559a61f08fbae3fd4da-0000000000033d59-00062ac889ba8f22.journal (5.9M).
Deleted archived journal /var/log/journal/79c9dac7c584478196d4cd8c6243884d/system@0f3b8bac99bd4559a61f08fbae3fd4da-0000000000034cd3-00062ae84ff9825a.journal (6M).
Vacuuming done, freed 363.1M of archived journals from /var/log/journal/79c9dac7c584478196d4cd8c6243884d.

Check the disk usage after this vacuum and list the files in the journal directory. This reduced the number of files in my journal directory from about 35 to 4.

Power off and restore the last snapshot again. Verify that the expected number of files and data are present.

This last vacuum command deletes archive files until only 200MB or less of archived files are left.

```
# journalctl --vacuum-size=200M
Vacuuming done, freed 0B of archived journals from /var/log/journal.
Vacuuming done, freed 0B of archived journals from /run/log/journal.
Deleted archived journal /var/log/journal/d1fbbe41229942289e5ed31a256200fb/system@0005f2b035b5ec5c-a8d2b8b6d3f7b880.journal~ (16.0M).
Deleted archived journal /var/log/journal/d1fbbe41229942289e5ed31a256200fb/user-1000@0005f43566ce0a41-96c83a31073b4c54.journal~ (8.0M).
<snip>
Deleted archived journal /var/log/journal/d1fbbe41229942289e5ed31a256200fb/system@0005f4d7e9ca1d4a-80c25a84c8aec6d1.journal~ (24.0M).
Deleted archived journal /var/log/journal/d1fbbe41229942289e5ed31a256200fb/system@0005f56bd926461d-f89a91e4425992ef.journal~ (24.0M).
Deleted archived journal /var/log/journal/d1fbbe41229942289e5ed31a256200fb/user-1001@1c165b49f1
1f42399380c5d449c7e7e1-0000000000005151-0005f4fc6561390c.journal (3.5M).
Deleted archived journal /var/log/journal/d1fbbe41229942289e5ed31a256200fb/system@0005f5b08a161a8f-309c9fceb66b753c.journal~ (16.0M).
```

```
Vacuuming done, freed 305.5M of archived journals from
/var/log/journal/d1fbbe41229942289e5ed31a256200fb.
```

Check the disk usage again.

Only complete files are deleted. The vacuum commands do not truncate archive files to meet the specification. They also only work on archive files, not active ones. But they do work and do what they are supposed to.

Summary

The systemd journals provide a complete, time-sequenced record of Linux system activity. We've looked at how to use the journal with the journalctl command to extract and use that data.

We discussed some ways to configure journal retention and rotation. We determined that the systemd journals are a hybrid of ASCII text and binary data, thus making use of standard Linux tools that work with ASCII problematic at best. However, the journalctl command is a powerful tool that we can use to extract data from the systemd journals with great precision and finesse.

Adding our own entries into the journal is easy and can be used in scripts and on the command line.

We also learned how to manage disk space by manually rotating and vacuuming journals.

Exercises

Perform these exercises to complete this chapter.

If possible, use a noncritical, physical Linux host that has been in service for some time to perform these exercises. Otherwise, continue to use the VM.

1. Determine the full date range of the journals for the host.
2. View the dmesg data for the last two boots using three different methods—but not the dmesg command.
3. Are there any critical entries in the journals?
4. If so, explore them and see if you can determine the cause.
5. Are there any alert or warning messages?
6. If so, explore them and see if you can determine the cause.

CHAPTER 10

Managing the Firewall with firewalld

Objectives

In this chapter, you will learn to

- Describe the function of a firewall
- Define and describe the term "port"
- Use firewalld zones for firewall management under different sets of circumstances
- Set a default zone
- Assign network interfaces to a zone
- Modify existing zones
- Create a new zone to meet a set of specifications
- Integrate Fail2Ban dynamic firewall software with firewalld to automate protection against specific Internet attacks

CHAPTER 10   MANAGING THE FIREWALL WITH FIREWALLD

Introduction

Firewalls are a vital part of network security, so it's important for a SysAdmin to be familiar with how they work. If you understand firewalls, you can keep your network secure by making intelligent choices about the traffic you allow in and out.

Because "firewall" is such an exciting name, people often imagine an intricate Tron-style[1] neon battle happening on the outskirts of a network, with packets of rogue data being set alight by the defenses to protect your users' techno-fortress. In reality, a firewall is just a piece of software controlling incoming and outgoing network traffic.

> **Note** firewalld is not part of systemd. However, it is an important part of security and system administration. It has also adopted the systemd command structure's use of multiple sub-commands and is the default firewall interface on many distributions, so I've decided to include it here.

Ports

A firewall is able to manage network traffic by monitoring network ports. In the world of firewalls, the term port doesn't refer to a physical connection like a USB, VGA, or HDMI port. For the purpose of firewalls, a port is an artificial construct created by the operating system to represent a pathway for a specific type of data. This system could have been called anything, like "contacts," "connections," or even "penguins," but the creators used

---

[1] Wikipedia, "Tron," https://en.wikipedia.org/wiki/Tron

CHAPTER 10 MANAGING THE FIREWALL WITH FIREWALLD

"ports," and that's the name that we still use today. The point is there's nothing special about any port; they are just a way to designate an address where data transference happens.

There are a number of ports that are well-known, but even these are only conventions. For instance, you may know that HTTP traffic occurs on port 80, HTTPS traffic uses port 443, FTP uses port 21, and SSH uses port 22. When your computer transmits data to another computer, it adds a prefix to the data to indicate which port it wants to access. If the port on the receiving end is accepting data of the same protocol as the data you are sending, then the data is successfully exchanged as seen in Figure 10-1.

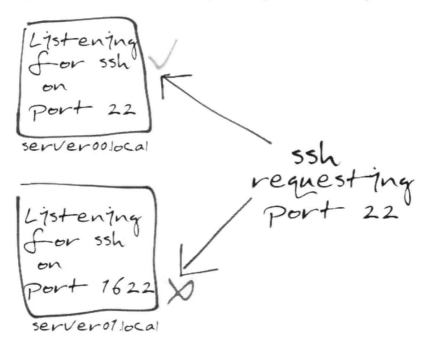

Figure 10-1. *An SSH—or any other—connection can only be made if the server is listening on the correct port*

CHAPTER 10   MANAGING THE FIREWALL WITH FIREWALLD

You can see this process in action by going to any website. Open a web browser and navigate to example.com:80, which causes your computer to send an HTTP request to port 80 of the computer serving the example. com website. You receive a web page in return. Web browsers don't require you to enter the port you want to access every time you navigate to a URL, however, because it's assumed that HTTP traffic accesses port 80 or 443.

EXPERIMENT 10-1: TESTING PORTS

You can test this process using a terminal-based web browser. The curl command also returns some statistics that are displayed before the HTTP code that makes up the first four lines of the web server's response.

```
[root@testvm1:~]# curl --connect-timeout 3 "http://example.com:80" | head -n4
  % Total    % Received % Xferd  Average Speed   Time    Time     Time  Current
                                 Dload  Upload   Total   Spent    Left  Speed
100  1256  100  1256     0       0      12337    0  --:--:-- --:--:-- --:--:-- 12435
<!doctype html>
<html>
<head>
    <title>Example Domain</title>
[root@testvm1:~]#
```

Tip   The example.com domain is a valid site that has been created for use by anyone who needs to test some basic network functions such as simple pings, traceroute, HTTP connections, and more. The sites example.org and example.net are also available for testing.

Using the same notation, you can force rejection by navigating to a website using a nonstandard port. Navigate to an arbitrary port, example.com:79, for instance. Your request for a web page is declined.

258

```
[root@testvm1:~]# curl --connect-timeout 3 "http://
example.com:79"
curl: (28) Failed to connect to example.com port 79 after
1703 ms: Connection timed out
[root@testvm1:~]#
```

The correlation between ports and protocols are merely conventions mutually agreed upon by a standards group and a user base. These settings can be changed on individual computers. In fact, back in the pioneer days of computing, many people thought that just changing the port number of popular services would prevent an attack. Attacks are a lot more sophisticated now so there's little value in surprising an automated port scanner by changing which port a service listens on.

Instead, a firewall governs what activity is permitted in or out on any given port.

Firewall Rules

By default, most firewalls have rule sets that block all incoming packets unless explicitly allowed. Certainly, this is true for Fedora and other Red Hat–based distributions that use firewalld or iptables. This, plus the fact that most server services are not needed so are not installed or not enabled, means that Linux is very secure right from the initial installation. Outbound packets are not blocked by the firewall so that we don't need to add rules for protocols like email, SSH, and web browsers just to access remote hosts using these services from our client hosts.

The flow of packets as they enter the Linux host is generally from start to finish through the rule set. If a packet matches one of the rules, the action defined in the rule is taken. Ultimately, each packet will be accepted, rejected, or dropped. When a packet matches a rule that has

CHAPTER 10   MANAGING THE FIREWALL WITH FIREWALLD

one of these three actions, that action is taken and the packet travels no further through the rules. The three possible actions require just a bit of explanation:

- **Accept**: The packet is accepted and passed to the designated TCP port and a server such as a web server, Telnet, or SSH, to which it is addressed.

- **Reject**: The packet is rejected and sent back to the originator with a message. This message allows the host on the other end to know what happened and try again if need be or to terminate the connection.

- **Drop**: The packet is dropped and proceeds no further through the rules. No message is sent back to the originator. This action maintains the connection for the timeout period specified on the sender's end. This is useful when blocking IP addresses of known spammers so that when they attempt a connection their sending host must wait through the timeout to try again, thus slowing down their attacks significantly.

All Linux firewalls are based on a kernel protocol called netfilter[2] which interprets and enforces the rules. Netfilter.org[3] is the organization responsible for netfilter and its functions. The administrative tools we use, like firewalld and IPTables, simply allow us to add, modify, and remove netfilter rules that examine each data packet and determine how to handle it.

---

[2] Wikipedia, "netfilter," https://en.wikipedia.org/wiki/netfilter
[3] Netfilter.org, https://www.netfilter.org/index.html

CHAPTER 10   MANAGING THE FIREWALL WITH FIREWALLD

Firewall Tools

There are three primary tools that are commonly used to manage Netfilter firewall rules, iptables, nftables, and firewalld. All are intended to make firewall management a bit easier for SysAdmins, but they differ in how they approach that task, and the use cases at hand can determine which tool is best. Fedora installs all three tools by default.

Red Hat's online documentation, *Configuring and managing networking*,[4] contains recommendations for using these tools.

> **When to use firewalld, nftables, or iptables**
>
> *The following is a brief overview in which scenario you should use one of the following utilities:*
>
> - ***firewalld:*** *Use the firewalld utility for simple firewall use cases. The utility is easy to use and covers the typical use cases for these scenarios.*
>
> - ***nftables:*** *Use the nftables utility to set up complex and performance-critical firewalls, such as for a whole network.*
>
> - ***iptables:*** *The iptables utility on Red Hat Enterprise Linux uses the nf_tables kernel API instead of the legacy back end. The nf_tables API provides backward compatibility so that scripts that use iptables commands still work on Red Hat Enterprise Linux. For new firewall scripts, Red Hat recommends to use nftables.*
>
> —*Configuring and managing networking*, Chapter 46

---

[4] Red Hat, "Configuring and managing networking," `https://access.redhat.com/documentation/en-us/red_hat_enterprise_linux/8/html/configuring_and_managing_networking/index`

These tools use different user interfaces and store their data in different formats. We will cover firewalld in some depth in this chapter.

My reading indicates that iptables on Linux is more or less obsolete and will probably be discontinued. I have already converted most of my hosts to firewalld and will be completing the rest soon. I like firewalld and it appears to meet my needs, including the ability to manage a true DMZ. The use of nftables, because it is designed for very complex rule sets, is outside the scope of this book.

Block (Almost) Everything

Common advice when configuring a firewall is to first block everything and then open the ports you know you actually need. That means you have to know what you need, though, and sometimes figuring that out is an afternoon's job all its own.

If your organization runs its own DNS or DNS caching service, for instance, then you must remember to unblock the port (usually 53) handling DNS communication. If you rely on SSH to configure your servers remotely, then you must not block that port. You must account for every service running on your infrastructure, and you must understand whether that service is internal-only or whether it needs to interact with the outside world.

In the case of proprietary software, there may be calls made to the outside world that you're not even aware of. If some applications react poorly to a strict firewall recently put in place, you may have to reverse engineer (or talk to the application's support line) to discover what kind of traffic it's trying to create and why. In the open source world, this issue is less common, but it's not outside the realm of possibility, especially in the case of complex software stacks (e.g., today even media players make calls out to the Internet, if only to fetch album art or a track listing).

Crunchy on the Outside

I have encountered many networks in my career that SysAdmins say are "crunchy on the outside, soft and gooey on the inside."[5] This refers to some types of candy that have a hard shell but are quite soft in the middle. Networks can be like that. When the firewall on the edge of the network is cracked, no matter how hard that was, the rest of the network is laid open to plunder.

As a result, Linux distributions all ensure that they are installed with an active firewall that allows access only by a small number of necessary services.

As you will see in this chapter, I have experimented with reducing the number of open ports even smaller because I like to ensure the maximum level of security on all Linux hosts in my network. This includes an active firewall on every one.

firewalld

firewalld is the default firewall management daemon used by current releases of Fedora and many other distributions. It has superseded but not replaced iptables which has been around for many years. firewalld provides some interesting features such as runtime rules in addition to permanent rules. Runtime rules can be used to meet temporary conditions and can be left active until a reboot, or they can be manually removed, or they can be set to expire after a predefined period of time. Permanent rules—as their name suggests—are persistent through reboots.

---

[5] Extreme Networks Blog, `https://academy.extremenetworks.com/extreme-networks-blog/networks-hard-crunchy-on-the-outside-soft-gooey-on-the-inside/`, 2019.

firewall-cmd uses preconfigured zones as presets, giving you sane defaults to choose from. Doing this saves you from having to build a firewall from scratch. Zones apply to a network interface, so on a server with two Ethernet interfaces, you may have one zone governing one Ethernet interface and a different zone governing the other.

Standard systemctl commands are used to start, stop, enable, and disable firewalld. All other interactions with firewalld are through its own set of tools.

Changes made to firewalld are instant. The firewalld.service does not need to be restarted. There are a couple circumstances that require you to reload the firewalld configuration. I will point those out.

The firewalld.org website has excellent documentation you can use.[6]

firewalld Zones

The firewalld service can provide a complex and intricate set of rules for a firewall. It uses the concept of zones to collect related rules in such a way as to create levels of trust. Each zone represents a level of trust that can be independently modified without affecting other zones. firewalld has several predefined zones.

Each network interface is assigned a zone and all network traffic to that interface is filtered by the rules in that zone. Network interfaces can be easily switched from one zone to another if necessary, thus making preconfigured changes easy. These zones are arbitrary constructs developed to meet a specific set of needs in a firewall. For example, a network interface that is connected to the internal network would be placed in the trusted zone, while an interface that connects to the Internet would be placed in the external or dmz zones, depending upon the logical and physical structure of the network.

---

[6] firewalld.org, Documentation, `https://firewalld.org/documentation/concepts.html`

CHAPTER 10 ■ MANAGING THE FIREWALL WITH FIREWALLD

firewalld has nine predefined zones that can be used as is or modified to meet local needs. Table 10-1 lists the predefined firewalld zones and a short description of each.

Table 10-1. *The default firewalld zones*

Zone	Description
drop	Any incoming network packets are dropped; there is no reply. Only outgoing network connections are possible.
block	Any incoming network connections are rejected with an icmp-host-prohibited message for IPv4 and icmp6-adm-prohibited for IPv6. Only network connections initiated within this system are possible.
public	For use in public areas. You do not trust the other computers on networks to not harm your computer. Only selected incoming connections are accepted.
external	For use on external networks with IPv4 masquerading enabled especially for routers. You do not trust the other computers on networks to not harm your computer. Only selected incoming connections are accepted.
dmz	For computers in your demilitarized zone that are publicly accessible with limited access to your internal network. Only selected incoming connections are accepted.
work	For computers in your demilitarized zone that are publicly accessible with limited access to your internal network. Only selected incoming connections are accepted.
home	For use in home areas. You mostly trust the other computers on networks to not harm your computer. Only selected incoming connections are accepted.
internal	For use on internal networks. You mostly trust the other computers on the networks to not harm your computer. Only selected incoming connections are accepted.
trusted	All incoming network connections are accepted.

CHAPTER 10   MANAGING THE FIREWALL WITH FIREWALLD

Exploring the Firewall

Your work infrastructure may have a server in a rack with the sole purpose of running a firewall, or you may have a firewall embedded in the router—or modem—acting as your primary gateway to the Internet. You probably also have a firewall running on your personal workstation or laptop. All of these firewalls have their own configuration interface.

firewall-cmd is a front-end tool for managing the firewalld daemon, which interfaces with the Linux kernel's netfilter framework. This stack probably isn't present on the embedded modems common in small- to medium-sized businesses, but it's on or available for any Linux distribution that uses systemd.

Let's do some initial exploration of firewalld. In Experiment 10-2, we'll poke around a bit and make a simple change.

> **EXPERIMENT 10-2: INITIAL EXPLORATION OF FIREWALLD**
>
> Without an active firewall, firewall-cmd has nothing to control, so the first step is to ensure that firewalld is running:
>
> [root@testvm1:~]# **systemctl enable --now firewalld**
>
> This command starts the firewall daemon and sets it to auto-load upon reboot.
>
> View the status of the firewalld.service. This does not show anything about the firewalld configuration such as which ports are open or which zones are in use.
>
> [root@testvm1:~]# **systemctl status firewalld.service**
> ● firewalld.service - firewalld - dynamic firewall daemon
>   Loaded: loaded (/usr/lib/systemd/system/firewalld.service;
>   enabled; preset: enabled)
>   Drop-In: /usr/lib/systemd/system/service.d
>   └─10-timeout-abort.conf, 50-keep-warm.conf

CHAPTER 10   MANAGING THE FIREWALL WITH FIREWALLD

```
Active: active (running) since Sun 2025-01-12 16:03:25
EST; 17h ago
Invocation: bd91633a8da24f7a8ee6aa1122b737e5
Docs: man:firewalld(1)
Main PID: 1210 (firewalld)
Tasks: 2 (limit: 9472)
Memory: 48.8M (peak: 49M)
CPU: 898ms
CGroup: /system.slice/firewalld.service
    └─1210 /usr/bin/python3 -sP /usr/sbin/firewalld
--nofork --nopid

Jan 12 16:03:24 testvm1.both.org systemd[1]: Starting
firewalld.service - firewalld - dynamic firewall daemon...
Jan 12 16:03:25 testvm1.both.org systemd[1]: Started
firewalld.service - firewalld - dynamic firewall daemon.
Jan 13 09:29:59 testvm1.both.org systemd[1]: Started
firewalld.service - firewalld - dynamic firewall daemon.
```

The firewalld command-line tool can show whether it is running, but that is all so it is not especially helpful. This command is useful when used in a script used to automate firewall and network actions.

```
[root@testvm1:~]# firewall-cmd --state
running
```

This next command shows all of the supported zones in sorted order with uppercase first.

```
[root@testvm1:~]# firewall-cmd --get-zones
FedoraServer FedoraWorkstation block dmz drop external home
internal nm-shared public trusted work
```

267

CHAPTER 10 MANAGING THE FIREWALL WITH FIREWALLD

One important bit of data to know is what the default zones are for the running systems.

```
[root@testvm1:~]# firewall-cmd --get-default-zone
public
```

This shows that the default setting is one of the most restricted zones. However, this command does not show the currently assigned zones for the installed network interfaces. For that we do the following which lists each zone and displays the interfaces assigned to that zone:

```
[root@testvm1:~]# firewall-cmd --get-active-zones
public (default)
interfaces: enp0s3 enp0s8
```

We now know that both interfaces on my VM are in the public zone. Your VM will probably only have a single interface, enp0s3. If you're using a physical Linux host, the interfaces will depend upon the physical hardware and where it's installed on the PCI-e or USB bus.

This leads us to determining the actual configuration for the public zone. This command displays the configuration for the active zones. Only the public zone is active. It also shows the interfaces assigned to this zone.

```
[root@testvm1:~]# firewall-cmd --zone=public --list-all
public (default, active)
  target: default
  ingress-priority: 0
  egress-priority: 0
  icmp-block-inversion: no
  interfaces: enp0s3 enp0s8
  sources:
  services: dhcpv6-client mdns ssh
  ports:
  protocols:
```

```
forward: yes
masquerade: no
forward-ports:
source-ports:
icmp-blocks:
rich rules:
```

You can see the services listed in the Services field for the public zone. Look at the permanent settings for the public zone.

```
[root@testvm1:~]# firewall-cmd --zone=public --list-all
--permanent
public
  target: default
  icmp-block-inversion: no
  interfaces:
  sources:
  services: dhcpv6-client mdns ssh
  protocols:
  forward: yes
  masquerade: no
  forward-ports:
  source-ports:
  icmp-blocks:
  rich rules:
```

Do you see the difference? There are no interfaces assigned because this is only a configuration and the actual assignments are performed when firewalld is activated at boot time or is restarted.

CHAPTER 10   MANAGING THE FIREWALL WITH FIREWALLD

Adding a New Zone

Although the preexisting zones may meet our needs, sooner than later there will be a need that none of them can meet. We could simply modify one of these original zones, but I think it wise to create a new zone and leave the originals intact.

EXPERIMENT 10-3: ADDING A NEW ZONE

To create a new zone, use the --new-zone option. This creates a zone file that rejects everything because it contains no rules to open any specific ports such as SSH. All firewall-cmd actions persist only until the firewall or the computer running it restarts. Anything you want to be permanent must be accompanied by the --permanent flag. But you must do both in order to make it permanent and activate it immediately.

Create a new permanent zone called corp and then do it again without the --permanent flag to activate the zone immediately.

```
# firewall-cmd --new-zone corp --permanent
success
# ll /etc/firewalld/zones
total 12
-rw-r--r--  1 root root  54 May 17 13:34 corp.xml
-rw-rw-r--. 1 root root 353 May 17 09:05 public.xml
# firewall-cmd --reload
success
```

Before assigning any network interface to this new zone, add the ssh service so you can access it remotely. Make /etc/firewalld/zones the PWD. Then look at the resulting file.

```
[root@testvm1 zones]# firewall-cmd --zone corp --add-service ssh --permanent
```

CHAPTER 10 MANAGING THE FIREWALL WITH FIREWALLD

```
success
[root@testvm1 zones]# firewall-cmd --zone corp --add-
service ssh
success
[root@testvm1 zones]# cat corp.xml
<?xml version="1.0" encoding="utf-8"?>
<zone>
  <service name="ssh"/>
</zone>
```

Your new zone, called corp, is now active, rejects all but SSH traffic, and is assigned to no specific network interface. We'll look at zone files in more detail in another experiment in this chapter.

To make corp the active and the default zone for the network interface you want to protect (enp0s3 in this example), use the --change-interface option.

```
[root@testvm1 zones]# firewall-cmd --change-interface enp0s3
--zone corp --permanent
success
[root@testvm1 zones]# firewall-cmd --change-interface enp0s3
--zone corp
success
```

By making corp the default zone, all future commands are applied to corp unless the --zone option specifies a different zone. Whether you want to set corp as the default depends on whether you plan to make this zone as your new primary zone. If so, the following does the job.

```
[root@testvm1 zones]# firewall-cmd --set-default corp ;
firewall-cmd --set-default corp --permanent
```

271

To view the zones currently assigned to each interface, use the --get-active-zones option.

```
[root@testvm1 zones]# firewall-cmd --get-active-zones
corp
  interfaces: enp0s3
public
  interfaces: enp0s8
```

This shows that each of the two interfaces I have on my VM is assigned to a different zone.

Zones in a Complex Environment

Adding a new zone seems to be simple at first glance. In a host where there is only one NIC that has not been explicitly assigned a zone, it is quite simple. Just create your new zone and set that as the default zone. There is no need to assign the interface to a zone. Without any zone assignment, all interfaces are protected by the default zone, no matter which one that might be.

Changing the assignment of an interface to a different zone, it is actually quite simple. The real problem is that everything I've read seems to overcomplicate the process.

EXPERIMENT 10-4: REASSIGN A NIC TO A DIFFERENT ZONE

Start with a reboot and then verify the current status of the network interfaces. It is always good to verify the beginning state of things—anything—before you change it.

```
[root@testvm1:~]# firewall-cmd --get-zone-of-interface=enp0s3
corp
[root@testvm1:~]# firewall-cmd --get-active-zones
```

CHAPTER 10 MANAGING THE FIREWALL WITH FIREWALLD

```
corp
  interfaces: enp0s3
public (default)
  interfaces: enp0s8
```

You can reassign the enp0s3 interface to the dmz zone by removing it from the current zone. This action reverts the interface to the default zone.

```
[root@testvm1:~]# firewall-cmd --remove-interface=enp0s3
--zone=corp --permanent
success
[root@testvm1:~]# firewall-cmd --remove-interface=enp0s3
--zone=corp
success
[root@testvm1:~]# firewall-cmd --get-active-zones
public
  interfaces: enp0s8 enp0s3
[root@testvm1:~]#
```

This is part of what had me confused at first. Now assign the interface to the dmz zone and verify the change.

```
[root@testvm1:~]# firewall-cmd --change-interface=enp0s3
--zone=dmz --permanent
success
[root@testvm1:~]# firewall-cmd --change-interface=enp0s3
--zone=dmz
success
@testvm1:~]# firewall-cmd --get-active-zones
dmz
  interfaces: enp0s3
public
  interfaces: enp0s8
[root@testvm1:~]#
```

Reboot one more time and again verify that enp0s3 is assigned to the dmz zone. What services are allowed by the dmz zone?

```
[root@testvm1:~]# firewall-cmd --list-services --zone=dmz
ssh
[root@testvm1:~]# firewall-cmd --info-zone=dmz
dmz (active)
  target: default
  icmp-block-inversion: no
  interfaces: enp0s3
  sources:
  services: ssh
  ports:
  protocols:
  forward: yes
  masquerade: no
  forward-ports:
  source-ports:
  icmp-blocks:
  rich rules:
[root@testvm1:~]#
```

The dmz zone is the least trusted of any zone that actually allows any inbound connections. It allows only SSH as an inbound connection. The two zones that have no trust at all are drop and block. You can read the differences in Table 10-1.

Note that changing the runtime zone is not necessary. Neither is reloading nor using the runtime-to-permanent sub-command. The reboots we did were not necessary to complete the task; they were only for us to verify that the changes were verifiable and persistent through a reboot.

CHAPTER 10　MANAGING THE FIREWALL WITH FIREWALLD

We have seen that it's important to understand exactly how adding services—and ports—to a zone works. This set of guidelines is based on my experiments and describes how it can be expected to work:

1. **The public zone is the default by—ummm—default.** The default zone can be changed. A different zone can be designated as the default, or the configuration of the default zone can be altered to allow a different set of services and ports.

2. **All interfaces that are not specifically assigned to any zone use the designated default zone.** In this event, all interfaces, whether there is only one as in our VMs or ten or fifty in a complex router environment, use the default zone whatever that may be. Typically in Fedora, that is the public zone. If the default zone is changed, for example, from the public zone to the work zone, all of these interfaces immediately start using the work zone.

3. **All interfaces are explicitly assigned to a zone.** This use case is the least likely to cause unexpected problems and confusion. Changing the default zone does not affect any interface in any manner. Interfaces can be reassigned to different zones, and the zone configuration can be changed.

4. **Some interfaces are explicitly assigned to a zone, while other interfaces are not.** In this use case, changing the default zone affects only those interfaces that are not explicitly assigned to a zone. All of the unassigned zones begin using the new default zone.

5. **Deleting the zone assignment for an interface.** The interface is unassigned and reverts to using the default zone.

6. **Changing the configuration of the default zone.** All interfaces using the default zone, whether by explicit assignment to that zone or by having no assignment, immediately reflect the configuration change.

Adding and Deleting Services

As an old—um, mature—SysAdmin, I tend to think in terms of ports when working with firewalls and network services. Sometimes I need to look up a port number associated with a particular service, but that is no big deal because they are all defined in /etc/services, which has been around long before firewalld.

EXPERIMENT 10-5: LISTING SERVICES

Look at the list of services in the /etc/services file.

```
[root@testvm1:~]# less /etc/services
# /etc/services:
# $Id: services,v 1.49 2017/08/18 12:43:23 ovasik Exp $
#
# Network services, Internet style
# IANA services version: last updated 2021-01-19
#
# Note that it is presently the policy of IANA to assign a
  single well-known
# port number for both TCP and UDP; hence, most entries here
  have two entries
```

```
# even if the protocol doesn't support UDP operations.
# Updated from RFC 1700, ``Assigned Numbers'' (October
  1994).  Not all ports
# are included, only the more common ones.
#
# The latest IANA port assignments can be gotten from
#       http://www.iana.org/assignments/port-numbers
# The Well Known Ports are those from 0 through 1023.
# The Registered Ports are those from 1024 through 49151
# The Dynamic and/or Private Ports are those from 49152
  through 65535
#
# Each line describes one service, and is of the form:
#
# service-name   port/protocol   [aliases ...]   [# comment]
tcpmux           1/tcp                           # TCP port service
                                                   multiplexer
tcpmux           1/udp                           # TCP port service
                                                   multiplexer
rje              5/tcp                           # Remote Job Entry
rje              5/udp                           # Remote Job Entry
echo             7/tcp
echo             7/udp
discard          9/tcp           sink null
discard          9/udp           sink null
systat           11/tcp          users
systat           11/udp          users
daytime          13/tcp
daytime          13/udp
qotd             17/tcp          quote
qotd             17/udp          quote
```

```
chargen          19/tcp          ttytst source
chargen          19/udp          ttytst source
ftp-data         20/tcp
ftp-data         20/udp
# 21 is registered to ftp, but also used by fsp
ftp              21/tcp
ftp              21/udp          fsp fspd
ssh              22/tcp                     # The Secure Shell
                                              (SSH) Protocol
ssh              22/udp                     # The Secure Shell
                                              (SSH) Protocol
telnet           23/tcp
telnet           23/udp
<SNIP>
```

This command eliminates the comment lines and counts the remaining lines. Notice that Telnet is on port 23.

```
[root@testvm1:~]# grep -v ^# /etc/services | wc -l
11472
[root@testvm1:~]#
```

The services file contains 11,472 entries. Many ports are listed for both TCP and UDP protocols.

We can also list the services explicitly understood by firewalld.

```
[root@testvm1:~]# firewall-cmd --get-services
```

The output of this command is a simple space-separated list of 209 services. These are the services that can be added to a zone by name. Any services not listed here must be added to a zone by port.

The firewalld firewall works perfectly well with services, but for those that are not defined, it also supports the use of port numbers. In Experiment 10-6, we first add a port to a zone and then remove it. Working with ports like this requires the use of both the port number and the protocol specification of either TCP or UDP.

> **EXPERIMENT 10-6: ADDING/REMOVING A PORT**
>
> I have arbitrarily selected the Telnet[7] service from this list so that we can use to add to and delete from our dmz zone. First, install and enable the Telnet server and client so we can test our work.
>
> [root@testvm1:~]# **dnf -y install telnet telnet-server**
>
> Start Telnet. The command to do so does not start the server itself. It starts a socket that listens for connections on port 23 and only starts the server when a Telnet connection is initiated on port 23.[8]
>
> [root@testvm1:~]# **systemctl enable --now telnet.socket**
> Created symlink /etc/systemd/system/sockets.target.wants/telnet.socket → /usr/lib/systemd/system/telnet.socket.
> [root@testvm1:~]#

---

[7] Telnet is a very old and vulnerable communications protocol. It provides no means for encrypting data transferred over the network so is completely insecure. SSH has replaced it as a secure choice. I use it here only for illustrative purposes.

[8] This process is very similar to the xinetd service used by the SystemV init system. Xinetd listened for connections for Telnet and other services and only started them when a connection was made.

CHAPTER 10 MANAGING THE FIREWALL WITH FIREWALLD

Now we add the service to the firewall. We won't do this permanently, but only for the current instance.

```
[root@testvm1 zones]# firewall-cmd --add-service=telnet
--zone=dmz
success
[root@testvm1 zones]# firewall-cmd --info-zone=dmz
dmz (active)
  target: default
  icmp-block-inversion: no
  interfaces: enp0s3
  sources:
  services: ssh telnet
  ports:
  protocols:
  forward: yes
  masquerade: no
  forward-ports:
  source-ports:
  icmp-blocks:
  rich rules:
[root@testvm1 zones]#
```

Let's test to ensure that the Telnet service works as expected.

```
[root@testvm1:~]# telnet testvm1
telnet testvm1
Trying 192.168.0.101...
Connected to testvm1.
Escape character is '^]'.
Kernel 6.12.9-200.fc41.x86_64 on an x86_64 (1)
testvm1 login: tuser
Password: <Enter tuser password>
Last login: Sun May 21 15:41:47 on :0
```

CHAPTER 10 MANAGING THE FIREWALL WITH FIREWALLD

Log out of the Telnet connection.

```
[tuser@testvm1:~]$ exit
logout
Connection closed by foreign host.
[root@testvm1:~]#
```

Remove the Telnet service from the dmz zone and verify the result.

```
[root@testvm1 zones]# firewall-cmd --remove-service=telnet --zone=dmz
success
[root@testvm1 zones]# firewall-cmd --info-zone=dmz
dmz (active)
  target: default
  icmp-block-inversion: no
  interfaces: enp0s3
  sources:
  services: ssh
  ports:
  protocols:
  forward: yes
  masquerade: no
  forward-ports:
  source-ports:
  icmp-blocks:
  rich rules:
[root@testvm1 zones]#
```

Of course, we would have used --permanent if we intended to make these changes persistent. We can also do this using the port number rather than the service name.

```
[root@testvm1 zones]# firewall-cmd --add-port=23/tcp --zone=dmz
success
```

CHAPTER 10 MANAGING THE FIREWALL WITH FIREWALLD

```
[root@testvm1 zones]# firewall-cmd --info-zone=dmz
dmz (active)
  target: default
  icmp-block-inversion: no
  interfaces: enp0s3
  sources:
  services: ssh
  ports: 23/tcp
  protocols:
  forward: yes
  masquerade: no
  forward-ports:
  source-ports:
  icmp-blocks:
  rich rules:
[root@testvm1 zones]#
```

Remove port 23.

```
[root@testvm1 zones]# firewall-cmd --remove-port=23/tcp --zone=dmz
success
```

Verify that it has been removed.

When using firewalld for firewall services, it is always a good idea to be consistent and add new rules using the service name rather than the port number. It may be necessary to use the port number for a service that is not predefined although it is also possible to add a new service file to /etc/firewalld/services with a name of the form <servicename>.service. These files are all in XML and should be easily understandable. Most of us will never need to modify or even look at these files. That is, unless you are running a Linux box as a router and play a lot of 1990s games with their own weird and wild takes on how networking should work.

Adding a Service for a Specific Period of Time

I have sometimes needed to open a port in my firewall for a limited period of time for one reason or another. This can be done easily with firewalld using the `--timeout` option in the command to add the service. It's definitely one of the more interesting features of firewalld that's not available in IPTables.

> **EXPERIMENT 10-7: ADD A SERVICE FOR A LIMITED TIME**
>
> We will use Telnet again for this experiment. Add the service, this time using the timeout for ten minutes. Then verify that Telnet was added to the dmz zone.
>
> ```
> [root@testvm1 zones]# firewall-cmd --add-service=telnet
> --zone=dmz --timeout=10m
> success
> [root@testvm1 zones]# firewall-cmd --info-zone=dmz
> dmz (active)
>   target: default
>   icmp-block-inversion: no
>   interfaces: enp0s3
>   sources:
>   services: ssh telnet
>   ports:
>   protocols:
>   forward: yes
>   masquerade: no
>   forward-ports:
>   source-ports:
>   icmp-blocks:
>   rich rules:
> [root@testvm1 zones]#
> ```

CHAPTER 10   MANAGING THE FIREWALL WITH FIREWALLD

Test as we did above to verify that Telnet is listening. After ten minutes, check the zone information again to verify that the Telnet service has been removed.

```
[root@testvm1:~]# firewall-cmd --info-zone=dmz
dmz (active)
  target: default
  icmp-block-inversion: no
  interfaces: enp0s3
  sources:
  services: ssh
  ports:
  protocols:
  forward: yes
  masquerade: no
  forward-ports:
  source-ports:
  icmp-blocks:
  rich rules:
[root@testvm1:~]#
```

The timeout= option takes its arguments as a plain number, which is interpreted as seconds. It also recognizes three trailing characters, where *s* is seconds, *m* is minutes, and *h* is hours.

So timeout=3m sets the timeout at three minutes, and 4h sets it at four hours.

Timeout mode is incompatible with the --permanent option. It would be counterproductive to use a permanent timeout.

CHAPTER 10   MANAGING THE FIREWALL WITH FIREWALLD

Wireless

Some quick experiments on my laptop systems show that, like wired connections, the default zone is applied to wireless connections unless they are assigned to a specific zone. Since many of the wireless connections we use out in public are completely unprotected, I strongly recommend assigning the drop zone which just ignores all incoming connection attempts. This does not block your outbound connections such as web pages, email, VPN, or others.

Even those public networks that have some level of encryption are usually quite easy to crack into. Many crackers even use their own devices to spoof the public network so that users will log in to the cracker's network device instead. Once logged in, your computer is completely vulnerable unless you have a decent firewall applied to your wireless interface.

In the next experiment, we'll see the complete process of migrating one of my laptops from iptables to firewalld and assigning the wireless interface to the drop zone.

> **Tip**   If you don't have a laptop that's running Linux, you still may be able to do this experiment. There are a number of USB wireless adapters available for under $20. To perform this experiment on your VM, you can insert the USB wireless adapter into the physical host and then connect the adapter to the VM. This will work exactly like it does on a physical laptop.

CHAPTER 10   MANAGING THE FIREWALL WITH FIREWALLD

EXPERIMENT 10-8: ASSIGNING THE WIRELESS INTERFACE TO THE DROP ZONE

First, check the name of the wireless interface. On my laptop, it is wlp113s0. All wireless interface names start with the letter "w."

```
[root@voyager zones]# nmcli
enp111s0: connected to Wired connection 1
        "Realtek RTL8111/8168/8411"
<SNIP>
wlp113s0: connected to LinuxBoy2
        "Intel 8265 / 8275"
        wifi (iwlwifi), 34:E1:2D:DD:BE:27, hw, mtu 1500
        inet4 192.168.25.199/24
        route4 192.168.25.0/24 metric 600
        route4 default via 192.168.25.1 metric 600
        inet6 fe80::44e5:e270:634d:eb20/64
        route6 fe80::/64 metric 1024
<SNIP>
```

View the configuration of the drop zone. All packets are sent directly to the DROP target. This means that they are ignored and no response of any kind is sent back to the originating host.

```
[root@voyager zones]# firewall-cmd --info-zone=drop
drop
  target: DROP
  icmp-block-inversion: no
  interfaces:
  sources:
  services:
  ports:
  protocols:
```

CHAPTER 10   MANAGING THE FIREWALL WITH FIREWALLD

```
  forward: yes
  masquerade: no
  forward-ports:
  source-ports:
  icmp-blocks:
  rich rules:
[root@testvm1:~]#
```

The drop zone is safer than using the block zone which blocks the packets but sends a rejection back to the source. That tells the cracker that there is a responsive computer on that IP address so they may keep attacking, looking for an exploitable vulnerability.

Now we can disable iptables and enable firewalld. I needed to do this to make the conversion, but you won't need to if your host is already running firewalld.

```
[root@voyager ~]# systemctl disable --now iptables
Removed "/etc/systemd/system/multi-user.target.wants/
iptables.service".
[root@voyager ~]# systemctl enable --now firewalld.service
Created symlink /etc/systemd/system/dbus-org.fedoraproject.
FirewallD1.service → /usr/lib/systemd/system/firewalld.
service.
Created symlink /etc/systemd/system/multi-user.target.wants/
firewalld.service → /usr/lib/systemd/system/firewalld.
service.
```

Now that firewalld is running, whether it was to begin with or you had to switch to it as I did, verify the default zone. It is public for both wired and wireless interfaces, which is what should be expected.

```
[root@voyager zones]# firewall-cmd --get-active-zones
public
  interfaces: enp111s0 wlp113s0
```

287

CHAPTER 10   MANAGING THE FIREWALL WITH FIREWALLD

Now we change the wireless interface and add it to the drop zone.

```
[root@voyager zones]# firewall-cmd --change-interface=wlp113s0 --zone=drop --permanent
The interface is under control of NetworkManager, setting zone to 'drop'.
success
[root@voyager zones]# firewall-cmd --get-zone-of-interface=wlp113s0
drop
[root@voyager zones]# firewall-cmd --get-active-zones
public
  interfaces: enp111s0
drop
  interfaces: wlp113s0
```

Setting the zone for the wireless interface works even if the interface is not currently connected to a wireless network.

Using --reload

The experiments I have performed on my VMs and my own physical systems in preparation for writing this chapter have taught me a couple things about managing with firewalld. I have seen a lot of misinformation about using the --reload sub-command, most of which indicates that it should be performed more frequently than I have found to be truly necessary.

The times I have found it necessary to use `firewall-cmd --reload` are twofold. First, do it immediately after creating a new zone whether using the easy command-line technique you did in Experiment 10-3 or when creating a new zone file using an editor or copying a zone file from another

288

host. The second instance is when first starting the firewalld.service after migrating from iptables or another firewall tool. Start firewalld.service and then run `firewall-cmd --reload`.

There may be other times when it is necessary, but I have not definitively identified them yet.

Zone Files

It's time to look at the zone configuration files in more detail. The default zone file is public.xml, and it is located in the /etc/firewalld/zones directory. Other zone files may be there also.

All the predefined default zone files are located in the /usr/lib/firewalld/zones directory. These files are never changed. If you were to reset firewalld to its defaults, the files in the /usr/lib/firewalld/zones directory are used to restore the firewall to that condition. The /etc/firewalld/zones/ directory contains a file called public.xml.old which is a backup created automatically when the zone configuration is changed.

These files are ASCII text files using the XML format for the data, but it is not necessary to be an XML expert to understand their content. XML stands for Extensible Markup Language. It is a markup language for documents using a format that is both human- and machine-readable.

Let's look at a couple zone files and see how they are constructed.

EXPERIMENT 10-9: ZONE CONFIGURATION FILES

Because it is the most commonly used, we will start by examining the default public zone file. It contains enough information for us to understand.
Make /etc/firewall/zone the PWD. Then examine the public.xml file.

```
[root@testvm1 zones]# cat public.xml
<?xml version="1.0" encoding="utf-8"?>
<zone>
```

```
    <short>Public</short>
    <description>For use in public areas. You do not trust the
    other computers on networks to not harm your computer. Only
    selected incoming connections are accepted.</description>
    <service name="ssh"/>
    <service name="mdns"/>
    <service name="dhcpv6-client"/>
    <forward/>
</zone>
[root@testvm1 zones]#
```

The first line specifies the version of XML used by the file and the language encoding. The second line, <zone>, identifies the beginning of a zone file. There is a closing line at the end of the file, </zone>. All other statements are enclosed by these two statements.

The short name is the one displayed when you use commands that show the zone names.

```
[root@testvm1 zones]# firewall-cmd --get-zones
FedoraServer FedoraWorkstation block corp dmz drop external
home internal nm-shared public trusted work
```

The description field is a place to store a longer description of the zone. I have not found a command that displays the description. It appears to be only visible when you edit or `cat` the file.

The next three lines list the services that are allowed to connect to this host, in this case, ssh, mdns, and dhcpv6-client. This seems to be a common set of services in the home, internal, public, and work zone files. The home and internal zones have an additional service.

```
[root@testvm1 zones]# cat internal.xml
<?xml version="1.0" encoding="utf-8"?>
<zone>
```

```
  <short>Internal</short>
  <description>For use on internal networks. You mostly
  trust the other computers on the networks to not harm
  your computer. Only selected incoming connections are
  accepted.</description>
  <service name="ssh"/>
  <service name="mdns"/>
  <service name="samba-client"/>
  <service name="dhcpv6-client"/>
  <forward/>
</zone>
```

The samba client is an open source version of the Microsoft SMB (Server Message Block) protocol and allows Linux hosts and other hosts and devices to participate on Windows networks.

The forward statement in these zones allows TCP/IP packets entering the host on the interface assigned to this zone to be forwarded to other interfaces on the same host computer.

The external zone has an interesting statement.

```
[root@testvm1 zones]# cat external.xml
<?xml version="1.0" encoding="utf-8"?>
<zone>
  <short>External</short>
  <description>For use on external networks. You do not
  trust the other computers on networks to not harm
  your computer. Only selected incoming connections are
  accepted.</description>
  <service name="ssh"/>
  <masquerade/>
  <forward/>
</zone>
```

The masquerade entry is typically used only on the firewall and is for packets that are outbound to the external network—usually the Internet. That entry causes the firewall to change the source IP address of the outbound packet from that of the originating computer on the internal network to that of the firewall computer. The firewall keeps track of the packets using connection IDs. Any inbound packets addressed to the firewall computer with that connection ID will be sent to the computer in your network that originated the request. Thus, a request from a computer inside your network to `www.example.com` on port 80 to retrieve a web page will contain a connection ID. When the packets returned from that website contain that ID, they are sent to the computer in your network that originated the request.

Masquerading is common, and it allows computers inside a network to communicate to the outside world through the firewall. The external computers cannot identify the specific computer inside your network because its IP address is not contained in the data packet—only the IP address of the firewall computer is.

Remember that the zone files provided with firewalld are intended as basic sets of rules that can be modified as required to meet your needs. As I have already mentioned, you should leave the existing zone files intact and create new ones based on the existing one that most closely meets your needs.

Minimum Usable Firewall Configuration

While writing this chapter, I have experimented with various aspects of firewalld in my own environment. One of the issues I was exploring was the question, "What is the minimum set of firewall rules needed on a workstation?" Put another way, "How secure can I make the computers on my network and yet keep them talking to each other?"

I have a fairly simple setup. All of my workstations use DHCP to obtain their network configuration from my one server. That server also provides name services, email, NTP, and multiple websites. I also have a host that serves only as a firewall and router. My primary workstation is also my Ansible hub. All of my administrative interactions with various hosts on my network are handled using SSH, and Ansible uses SSH and nothing else.

So all of my workstations and the server need only SSH for me to manage my network and its hosts.

The server needs incoming SMTP, IMAP, NTP, HTTP, and DNS from the internal network. It also needs SMTP, IMAP, and HTTP from the outside Internet. The firewall uses port forwarding to direct email and web requests from the Internet to the server.

It's not especially complex. Aside from email and the websites on the server and firewall, the only service that is needed on my network is SSH. I do however have one other inbound port open on all of the hosts on my internal network. I won't tell you what it is, but I use it on my primary workstation to remotely manage an application that runs on all of my hosts.

Panic Mode

We now have a well-protected host that is located inside a well-protected network. But vulnerabilities can still be exploited into a full-blown breach by the crackers.

What do you do then?

firewalld has a panic mode that you can set. It blocks all inbound and outbound packets, effectively creating a logical isolation of the host. The caveat is that you must have some level of physical or direct access to the host in order to turn panic mode off. Panic mode is not persistent so does not survive a reboot—so if all else fails…

EXPERIMENT 10-10: PANIC MODE

Panic mode is easy to activate. If you activate it remotely, you get no response and the terminal will freeze. You will need direct access to the host, physical or virtual, to deactivate panic mode.

Perform this experiment from the testvm1 command line in a terminal on the desktop. First, turn panic mode on.

```
[root@testvm1:~]# firewall-cmd --panic-on
success
```

Ping a remote host to verify that you cannot access the outside world. After a short wait, exit from the ping using Ctrl+C.

```
[root@testvm1:~]# ping -c3 example.com
^C
PING 10.0.2.1 (10.0.2.1) 56(84) bytes of data.
^C
--- 10.0.2.1 ping statistics ---
3 packets transmitted, 0 received, 100% packet loss, time 2120ms
[root@testvm1:~]# firewall-cmd --panic-off
success
[root@testvm1:~]# ping -c3 example.com
PING example.com (93.184.216.34) 56(84) bytes of data.
64 bytes from 93.184.216.34 (93.184.216.34): icmp_seq=1 ttl=50 time=13.7 ms
64 bytes from 93.184.216.34 (93.184.216.34): icmp_seq=2 ttl=50 time=13.6 ms
64 bytes from 93.184.216.34 (93.184.216.34): icmp_seq=3 ttl=50 time=13.7 ms
```

```
--- example.com ping statistics ---
3 packets transmitted, 3 received, 0% packet loss,
time 2012ms
rtt min/avg/max/mdev = 13.642/13.711/13.748/0.049 ms
[root@testvm1:~]#
```

When panic mode is on, no communication is allowed, either in or out.

Like other firewalld settings, panic mode can be turned on for a specified period of time. Normal access using your configured firewall zones will resume at the expiration of the timer. However, I recommend against doing so as it's not possible to predict how long it will take to correct the problem that caused us to set panic mode in the first place.

firewall-config GUI

In addition to the command-line tools, firewalld has a well-designed and useful GUI interface. Like many GUI tools, it may not be available on the hosts you will need to administer such as servers and hosts used as firewalls. When it is available, however, it can make firewalld management at least a little easier. We still need to understand what is really happening behind the scenes, and that's why we spend so much time on command-line tools—that and the fact that they will always be available even when the GUI ones are not.

nftables

The nftables rules and the nftables.service, along with the **nft** command-line tool, are a complete firewall solution. However, when using firewalld, the nftables service is disabled.

CHAPTER 10 MANAGING THE FIREWALL WITH FIREWALLD

The zone files we use to define the firewall characteristics for network interfaces are used, along with the other configuration files in /etc/firewalld, to create rule sets using the nftables file formats. firewalld is used to create nftables rules that are used by the appropriate kernel modules to examine every network packet and determine their final disposition.

You can view all of the current nftables rules, but even though they are human-readable, they are not very understandable.

EXPERIMENT 10-11: VIEWING THE NFTABLES RULES

This command displays all of the nftables rules for the currently active zones.

```
[root@testvm1:~]# nft list ruleset | less
table inet firewalld {
        chain mangle_PREROUTING {
                type filter hook prerouting priority mangle
                + 10; policy accept;
                jump mangle_PREROUTING_ZONES
        }
        chain mangle_PREROUTING_POLICIES_pre {
                jump mangle_PRE_policy_allow-host-ipv6
        }
        chain mangle_PREROUTING_ZONES {
                iifname "enp0s8" goto mangle_PRE_public
                iifname "enp0s3" goto mangle_PRE_dmz
                goto mangle_PRE_public
        }
<SNIP>
```

Search on the strings "dmz" to locate the rules pertaining to that zone. You can also search on network interface names like enp0s3.

These rules cannot be accessed and changed directly. You must use one of the command-line tools, `firewall-cmd` for firewalld or `nft` for nftables, to manipulate the firewall as an entity. I find it easier to use `firewall-cmd`, and the strategies and logical structure of firewalls created by firewalld are much easier to understand than nftables.

Outbound Blocking

I mentioned at the beginning of this chapter that outbound network traffic from a given host is not blocked so as to ensure that we as users can access external websites, send email, use SSH to communicate with remote hosts on our own network as well as those that are even more remote, and more. However, there is a use case in which outbound blocking can be appropriate.

In the event that a host becomes infected with certain types of malware, this may be an effective tool to prevent other hosts from being infected. Malware which sends spam email, or which can propagate itself to other computers, or which can participate in coordinated denial of service (DOS) attacks, is a major problem—although primarily on Windows hosts. For example, a firewall can be configured such that the only email allowed to pass through to the Internet can only originate from a known and trusted internal email server. Thus, direct spamming is thwarted.

The most secure networks are also those that prevent internal problems from escaping to the outside world and the internal network as well.

CHAPTER 10　MANAGING THE FIREWALL WITH FIREWALLD

Fail2Ban

A great firewall is one that can adapt as the threats change. I needed something like this to stem the large number of attacks via SSH I had been experiencing a few years ago. After a good bit of exploring and research, I found fail2ban, open source software which automates what I was previously doing by hand and adds repeat offenders to a blocklist in firewalls. The best part is that it integrates nicely with both iptables and firewalld.

Fail2Ban has an extensive series of configurable matching rules and separate actions that can be taken when attempts are made to crack into a system. It has rules for many types of attacks that include web, email, and many other services that might have vulnerabilities. Fail2Ban works by detecting attacks and then adding a rule to the firewall that will block further attempts from that specific, single IP address for a specified and configurable amount of time. After the time has expired, it removes the blocking rule.

Let's install Fail2Ban and see how it works.

EXPERIMENT 10-12: FAIL2BAN

Perform this experiment as the root user. First, install Fail2Ban. This only takes a minute or so and does not require a reboot. The installation includes the firewalld interface to Fail2Ban.

[root@testvm1:~]# **dnf -y install fail2ban**

We need to perform a bit of configuration before enabling Fail2Ban. Make /etc/fail2ban the PWD and list the files there. The jail.conf file is the main configuration file, but it is not used for most configuration because it might get overwritten during an update. We will create a jail.local file in the same directory. Any settings defined in jail.local will override ones set in jail.conf.

Copy jail.conf to jail.local. Edit the jail.local file and ignore the comment near the beginning that tells you not to modify this file. It is, after all, the file we will be modifying.

Find the line **# ignoreself = true** which should be line 87. Remove the comment hash, and change it to **ignoreself = false**. We do this so that Fail2Ban will not ignore failed login attempts from the localhost. It can and should be changed back to true after finishing this chapter.

Scroll down to the line **bantime = 10m** (line 101) and change that to 1 minute (1m). Since we have no other hosts to test from, we will test using the localhost. We do not want the localhost banned for long so that we can resume experiments quickly. In the real world, I would set this to several hours so that the crackers cannot get more attempts for a long time.

Change **maxretry = 5** to 2. This is the maximum number of retries allowed after any type of failed attempt. Two retries is a good number for experimental purposes. I normally set this to three because anyone failing three retries to get into my systems using SSH does not belong there.

We could also change both of these configuration options in the [sshd] filter section which would limit them to sshd, while the global settings we just changed apply to all filters.

Read the comments for the other miscellaneous options in this section of the file, then scroll down to the [sshd] section in JAILS.

Add the highlighted line that enables the sshd jail, **enabled = true**. The documentation is not clear about needing to add this line. In previous versions, the line was **enabled = false**, so it was clear that changing false to true would enable the sshd jail.

```
[sshd]
# To use more aggressive sshd modes set filter parameter
"mode" in jail.local:
# normal (default), ddos, extra or aggressive (combines all).
```

CHAPTER 10   MANAGING THE FIREWALL WITH FIREWALLD

```
# See "tests/files/logs/sshd" or "filter.d/sshd.conf" for
usage example and details.
```
enabled = true
```
#mode    = normal
port     = ssh
logpath  = %(sshd_log)s
backend  = %(sshd_backend)s
```

Do not enable fail2ban, but start it.

[root@testvm1:~]# **systemctl start fail2ban.service**

Now ssh to localhost and log in using a bad user account or password on a good user account. It takes three failed password entries. After the second failed login attempts, the connection is locked, and after a timeout, an error message is displayed.

dboth@testvm1:~$ ssh user@localhost
user@localhost's password:
Permission denied, please try again.
user@localhost's password:
Connection closed by 127.0.0.1 port 22

This means that the sshd jail is working.

Whether you use firewalld or iptables for your firewall front end, you can list the nftables rules and page to the bottom to find the following entries which were added by Fail2Ban:

```
[root@testvm1:~]# nft list ruleset | less
table ip6 filter {
        chain INPUT {
                type filter hook input priority filter;
                policy accept;
                meta l4proto tcp tcp dport 22 counter
                packets 68 bytes 11059 jump f2b-sshd
```

CHAPTER 10   MANAGING THE FIREWALL WITH FIREWALLD

```
        }
        chain f2b-sshd {
                ip6 saddr ::1 counter packets 4 bytes
                320 reject
                counter packets 54 bytes 9939 return
        }
}
table ip filter {
        chain INPUT {
                type filter hook input priority filter;
                policy accept;
                meta l4proto tcp tcp dport 22 counter
                packets 62 bytes 9339 jump f2b-sshd
        }

        chain f2b-sshd {
                ip saddr 127.0.0.1 counter packets 2 bytes
                120 reject
                counter packets 54 bytes 8859 return
        }
}
```

Now look at a couple log files. In /var/log, first look at /var/log/secure. You should see a number of entries indicating failed passwords. These are the log entries checked by Fail2Ban for failures.

Look at the /var/log/fail2ban.log file. This log file shows the times that triggering entries were found in the secure log and the ban and unban actions taken to protect the system.

Be aware that the f2b-sshd chain entries do not appear in the iptables rule set until the first time a ban is triggered. Once there, the first and last lines of the chain are not deleted, but the lines rejecting specific IP addresses are removed as they time out. It took me a bit of work to figure out this bit.

The installation of Fail2Ban installs the configuration files needed for logwatch to report on Fail2Ban activity. It is possible to create your own filters and actions for Fail2Ban, but that is beyond the scope of this course.

Be sure to look at the various jails in the fail2ban.local file. There are many different events that can trigger fail2ban to ban source IP addresses from access to a particular port or service.

Cleanup

We need to do just a bit of cleanup before we continue.

Find the line **ignoreself = false** which should be line 87. This is the line we changed in Experiment 10-12. Remove the comment hash, and change it to # **ignoreself = true**. We do this so that Fail2Ban will again ignore failed login attempts from the localhost.

Scroll down to the line **bantime = 1m** (line 101) and change that to 10 minutes (10m).

Change **maxretry = 2** back to 5.

Finally, stop Fail2Ban. We didn't enable it, so it won't start on the next boot in any event.

Summary

Security is a big part of our job as SysAdmins, and firewalls are a major tool in keeping our networks safe. While Linux is quite secure as initially installed, any device connected to a wired or wireless network is always a target for crackers. A good firewall in the edge of your network where it interfaces with the Internet is a good first step in ensuring that your network is hardened. However, without appropriately configured firewalls present on every host in the network, a cracker who breaches the firewall host also gains immediate access to every host on your network.

The best approach to setting up any firewall is to start by blocking everything. Only then should you start considering the specific services that should be allowed to access your network. firewalld does an excellent job as the default firewall using the public zone because it blocks almost everything. Like I did, you should experiment to see whether an even more restrictive zone configuration might provide all of the access needed into your hosts and network while making them even more secure.

I do recommend that you not change the preinstalled zone files. I suggest that you do what I do and copy the existing zone file that most closely meets your needs and modify it as necessary. firewalld provides some basic yet very secure zone files to start. You may find that one of those is perfect for your needs on some or all of your hosts.

We explored zones as a concept and the reality of how they work and how they can be adapted to better meet your needs. This was done in the context of a workstation rather than a server or designated firewall to protect your entire network.

Exercises

Perform the following exercise to complete this chapter.

This is a single exercise to add a new zone to your firewall. The list below describes the functions required of the zone and some specific instructions and requirements you need to follow to successfully complete this task:

1. Copy an existing zone file to create a new one. *Don't* use the **firewall-cmd --new-zone** command. Name the new zone "telnet".

2. Configure the new zone to block all external access except for SSH and Telnet.

CHAPTER 10   MANAGING THE FIREWALL WITH FIREWALLD

3. Forwarding and masquerading are not required.

4. Do not make this new zone the default. Your default zone should be the public zone. If not, make it so.

5. Explicitly assign the enp0s3 interface to the new zone.

6. Test the new zone to ensure that both SSH and Telnet are listening and accepting connections in this zone.

7. For cleanup, exit from all Telnet and SSH connections and disable telnet.

8. Remove the zone from the network interface and ensure that it has reverted to the public zone default.

CHAPTER 11

Resource Management with cgroups

Objectives

In this chapter, you will learn

- What cgroups are
- Why cgroups are used for resource management
- How to use cgroups to view and understand how Linux manages groups of related processes
- How to use systemd cgroups for resource management

Introduction

There is little more frustrating to me as a SysAdmin than unexpectedly running out of some computing resource. On more than one occasion, I have filled all available disk space in a partition, run out of RAM, and not had enough CPU time to perform the tasks at hand in the necessary period of time. Resource management is one of the most important tasks performed by SysAdmins.

CHAPTER 11　RESOURCE MANAGEMENT WITH CGROUPS

The point of resource management is to ensure that all processes have relatively equal access to the system resources they need. Resource management also involves ensuring that RAM, hard drive space, and CPU capacity are added when necessary or rationed when that is not possible. Users who hog system resources, whether intentionally or accidentally, should also be prevented from doing so.

We have tools that enable us to monitor and manage various system resources. Tools such as top and many similar tools allow us to monitor the use of memory, I/O, storage (disk, SSD, etc.), network, swap space, CPU usage, and more. These tools, particularly those that are CPU-centric, are mostly based on the paradigm that the running process is the unit of control. At best they provide a way to adjust the nice number—and through that the priority—or to kill a running process.

Other tools based on traditional resource management in a SystemV environment are managed by the /etc/security/limits.conf file and the local configuration files located in /etc/security/limits.d directory. Resources can be limited in a fairly crude but useful manner by user or group. Resources that can be managed include various aspects of RAM, total CPU time per day, total amount of data, priority, nice number, number of concurrent logins, number of processes, maximum file size, and more.

Using cgroups for Process Management

One major difference between systemd and SystemV is the way in which they handle processes. SystemV treats each process as an entity unto itself. systemd collects related processes into control groups called cgroups and manages system resources for the cgroup as a whole. This means that resources can be managed per application rather than the individual processes that make up an application.

CHAPTER 11   RESOURCE MANAGEMENT WITH CGROUPS

The control units for cgroups are slice units. Slices are a conceptualization that allows systemd to order processes in a tree format for ease of management. I found the description below in an article[1] by Steve Ovens of Red Hat that provides an excellent example of how cgroups are used by the system itself:

> *As you may or may not know, the Linux kernel is responsible for all of the hardware interacting reliably on a system. That means, aside from just the bits of code (drivers) that enable the operating system (OS) to understand the hardware, it also sets limits on how many resources a particular program can demand from the system. This is most easily understood when talking about the amount of memory (RAM) a system has to divide up amongst all of the applications your computer may execute. In its most basic form, a Linux system is allowed to run most applications without restriction. This can be great for general computing if all applications play nicely together. But what happens if there is a bug in a program, and it starts to consume all of the available memory? The kernel has a facility called the Out Of Memory (OOM) Killer. Its job is to halt applications in order to free up enough RAM so that the OS may continue to function without crashing.*
>
> *That's great, you say, but what does this have to do with cgroups? Well, the OOM process acts as a last line of defense before your system comes crashing down around you. It's useful to a point, but since the kernel can control which processes must survive the OOM, it can also determine which applications cannot consume too much RAM in the first place.*

---

[1] Ovens, Steve, "A Linux SysAdmin's introduction to cgroups," Enable SysAdmin, 2020, `https://www.redhat.com/sysadmin/cgroups-part-one`

CHAPTER 11   RESOURCE MANAGEMENT WITH CGROUPS

Cgroups are, therefore, a facility built into the kernel that allow the administrator to set resource utilization limits on any process on the system. In general, cgroups control:

- *The number of CPU shares per process.*
- *The limits on memory per process.*
- *Block Device I/O per process.*
- *Which network packets are identified as the same type so that another application can enforce network traffic rules.*

There are more facets than just these, but those are the major categories that most administrators care about.

EXPERIMENT 11-1: VIEWING CGROUPS

Let's start with some commands that allow us to view various types of information about cgroups. The systemctl status <service> command displays slice information about a specified service including its slice. This example shows the at daemon.

```
[root@studentvm1 ~]# systemctl status atd.service
• atd.service - Deferred execution scheduler
Loaded: loaded (/usr/lib/systemd/system/atd.service;
enabled; preset: enabled)
Drop-In: /usr/lib/systemd/system/service.d
        └─10-timeout-abort.conf, 50-keep-warm.conf
Active: active (running) since Wed 2025-01-15 13:45:11 EST;
3 days ago
Invocation: 06c10af0a7054e62ba04d3aeb04c7ec4
Docs: man:atd(8)
```

CHAPTER 11   RESOURCE MANAGEMENT WITH CGROUPS

```
Main PID: 1245 (atd)
Tasks: 1 (limit: 9472)
Memory: 336K (peak: 1020K)
CPU: 19ms
CGroup: /system.slice/atd.service
└─1245 /usr/sbin/atd -f

Jan 15 13:45:11 testvm1.both.org systemd[1]: Started atd.
service - Deferred execution scheduler.
Jan 15 13:45:11 testvm1.both.org (atd)[1245]: atd.service:
Referenced but unset environment vari
```

This is an excellent example of one reason that I find systemd more useful than SystemV and the old init program; there is so much more information here that SystemV was able to provide. The cgroup entry includes the hierarchical structure where the system.slice is systemd (PID 1) and the atd.service is one level below and is part of the system.slice. The second line of the cgroup entry also shows the process ID (PID) and the command used to start the daemon.

The systemctl command allows us to see multiple cgroup entries. The --all option shows all slices including those that are not currently active.

```
[root@studentvm1 ~]# systemctl -t slice --all
UNIT                              LOAD   ACTIVE
  SUB     DESCRIPTION
-.slice                           loaded active
  active Root Slice
system-cups.slice                 loaded active
  active CUPS Slice
system-getty.slice                loaded active
  active Slice /system/getty
```

309

```
system-modprobe.slice                    loaded
  active active Slice /system/modprobe
system-sshd\x2dkeygen.slice              loaded
  active active Slice /system/sshd-keygen
system-systemd\x2dfsck.slice             loaded
  active active Slice /system/systemd-fsck
system-systemd\x2dzram\x2dsetup.slice loaded
  active active Slice /system/systemd-zram-setup
system-telnet.slice                      loaded
  active active Slice /system/telnet
system.slice                             loaded
  active active System Slice
user-0.slice                             loaded
  active active User Slice of UID 0
user-1000.slice                          loaded
  active active User Slice of UID 1000
user-983.slice                           loaded
  active active User Slice of UID 983
user.slice                               loaded
  active active User and Session Slice

Legend: LOAD   → Reflects whether the unit definition
was properly loaded.
ACTIVE → The high-level unit activation state, i.e.
generalization of SUB.
SUB    → The low-level unit activation state, values
depend on unit type.

13 loaded units listed.
To show all installed unit files use 'systemctl list-
unit-files'.
```

CHAPTER 11 RESOURCE MANAGEMENT WITH CGROUPS

The first thing to notice about the above data is that it shows user slices for UIDs 0 (root) and 1000, which is my user login. This shows only the slices and not the services that are a part of each slice. So it becomes obvious from this data that a slice is created for each user at the time they log in. This can provide a means to manage all of the tasks for that user as a single cgroup entity.

Exploring the Cgroup Hierarchy

All well and good so far, but cgroups are hierarchical, and all of the service units run as members of one of these cgroups. Viewing that hierarchy is easy and uses one old command and one new one that is part of systemd.

EXPERIMENT 11-2: CGROUPS

The ps command can be used to map the processes and their locations in the cgroup hierarchy. Note that it is necessary to specify the desired data columns when using the ps command. I have significantly reduced the volume of output from this command but have tried to leave enough so that you can get a feel for what you might find on your own systems.

```
[root@studentvm1 ~]# ps xawf -eo pid,user,cgroup,args
  PID USER     CGROUP                      COMMAND
    2 root     -                           [kthreadd]
    3 root     -                            \_ [rcu_gp]
    4 root     -                            \_ [rcu_par_gp]
    5 root     -                            \_ [slub_
                                               flushwq]
<SNIP>
```

CHAPTER 11   RESOURCE MANAGEMENT WITH CGROUPS

```
1154 root      0::/system.slice/gssproxy.s /usr/sbin/
gssproxy -D
1175 root      0::/system.slice/sshd.servi sshd: /usr/
sbin/sshd -D [listener] 0 of<snip>
1442 root      0::/user.slice/user-0.slice  \_ sshd:
                                                root [priv]
1454 root      0::/user.slice/user-0.slice  |  \_ sshd:
                                                   root@pts/0
1455 root      0::/user.slice/user-0.slice  |
 \_ -bash
1489 root      0::/user.slice/user-0.slice  |
    \_ screen
1490 root      0::/user.slice/user-0.slice  |
        \_ SCREEN
1494 root      0::/user.slice/user-0.slice  |
           \_ /bin/bash
4097 root      0::/user.slice/user-0.slice  |
           |  \_ ps xawf -eo pid,<snip>
4098 root      0::/user.slice/user-0.slice  |
           |  \_ less
2359 root      0::/user.slice/user-0.slice  |
           \_ /bin/bash
2454 root      0::/user.slice/user-0.slice
  \_ sshd: root [priv]
2456 root      0::/user.slice/user-0.slice
  |  \_ sshd: root@pts/3
2457 root      0::/user.slice/user-0.slice
  |       \_ -bash
3014 root      0::/user.slice/user-1000.sl
  \_ sshd: student [priv]
3027 student   0::/user.slice/user-1000.sl
      \_ sshd: student@pts/4
```

CHAPTER 11 RESOURCE MANAGEMENT WITH CGROUPS

```
    3028 student   0::/user.slice/user-1000.sl
             \_ -bash
    1195 colord    0::/system.slice/colord.ser /usr/
    libexec/colord
<SNIP>
```

We can view the entire hierarchy with the systemd-cgls command which is a bit simpler because it requires no complex options.

I have shortened this tree view considerably, too. This was done on StudentVM1 and is about 230 lines long; the amount of data from my primary workstation is about 400 lines.

```
[root@studentvm1 ~]# systemd-cgls
Control group /:
-.slice
├─user.slice (#1323)
│ → user.invocation_id: 05085df18c6244679e0a8e31a9d7d6ce
│ → trusted.invocation_id: 05085df18c6244679e0a8e31a9d7d6ce
│ ├─user-0.slice (#6141)
│ │ → user.invocation_id: 6535078b3c70486496ccbca02a735139
│ │ → trusted.invocation_id: 6535078b3c70486496ccbca02a735139
│ │ ├─session-2.scope (#6421)
│ │ │ → user.invocation_id: 4ce76f4810e04e2fa2f166971
│ │ │     241030c
│ │ │ → trusted.invocation_id: 4ce76f4810e04e2fa2f
│ │ │     166971241030c
│ │ │ ├─1442 sshd: root [priv]
│ │ │ ├─1454 sshd: root@pts/0
│ │ │ ├─1455 -bash
│ │ │ ├─1489 screen
│ │ │ ├─1490 SCREEN
│ │ │ ├─1494 /bin/bash
```

313

```
│   │   │   ├─2359 /bin/bash
│   │   │   ├─4119 systemd-cgls
│   │   │   └─4120 less
<SNIP>
│   └─user-1000.slice (#10941)
│     → user.invocation_id: 2b5f1a03abfc4afca295e003494b73b2
│     → trusted.invocation_id: 2b5f1a03abfc4afca295e0034
│       94b73b2
│     ├─user@1000.service … (#11021)
│     │ → user.delegate: 1
│     │ → trusted.delegate: 1
│     │ → user.invocation_id: cfd09d6c3cd641d898ddc23e22
│         916195
│     │ → trusted.invocation_id: cfd09d6c3cd641d898ddc23e229
│         16195
│     │ └─init.scope (#11061)
│     │   ├─3017 /usr/lib/systemd/systemd --user
│     │   └─3019 (sd-pam)
│     └─session-5.scope (#11221)
│       → user.invocation_id: a8749076931f425d851c59fd
│         956c4652
│       → trusted.invocation_id: a8749076931f425d851c59fd
│         956c4652
│       ├─3014 sshd: student [priv]
│       ├─3027 sshd: student@pts/4
<SNIP>
│     ├─session-7.scope (#14461)
│     │ → user.invocation_id: f3e31059e0904df08d6b44856
│         aac639b
│     │ → trusted.invocation_id: f3e31059e0904df08d6b44856
│         aac639b
```

CHAPTER 11   RESOURCE MANAGEMENT WITH CGROUPS

```
│   │   ├─1429 lightdm --session-child 13 20
│   │   ├─4133 /usr/bin/gnome-keyring-daemon --daemonize
│   │       --login
│   │   ├─4136 xfce4-session
│   │   ├─4300 /usr/bin/VBoxClient --clipboard
│   │   ├─4301 /usr/bin/VBoxClient --clipboard
│   │   ├─4315 /usr/bin/VBoxClient --seamless
│   │   ├─4316 /usr/bin/VBoxClient --seamless
│   │   ├─4321 /usr/bin/VBoxClient --draganddrop
│   │   ├─4326 /usr/bin/VBoxClient --draganddrop
│   │   ├─4328 /usr/bin/VBoxClient --vmsvga-session
│   │   ├─4329 /usr/bin/VBoxClient --vmsvga-session
│   │   ├─4340 /usr/bin/ssh-agent /bin/sh -c exec -l /bin/
│   │       bash -c "startxfce4"
│   │   ├─4395 /usr/bin/gpg-agent --sh --daemon
│   │   ├─4396 xfwm4 --display :0.0 --sm-client-id
│   │       2e79712f7-299e-4c6f-a503-2f64940ab467
│   │   ├─4409 xfsettingsd --display :0.0 --sm-client-id
│   │       288d2bcfd-3264-4caf-ac93-2bf552b14688
│   │   ├─4412 xfce4-panel --display :0.0 --sm-client-id
│   │       2f57b404c-e176-4440-9830-4472e6757db0
│   │   ├─4416 Thunar --sm-client-id 21b424243-7aed-4e9e-
│   │       9fc5-c3b1421df3fa –daemon
<SNIP>
```

This tree view shows all of the user and system slices and the services and programs running in each cgroup. Notice that within the user-1000.slice in the listing above, the units called "scope" which group related programs together into a manageable unit. The user-1000.slice/session-7.scope cgroup contains the GUI desktop program hierarchy starting with the LXDM display manager session and all of its subtasks including things like Bash shell and the Thunar GUI file manager.

Scope units are not defined in configuration files but are generated programmatically as the result of starting groups of one or more related programs. Scope units do not create or start the processes running as part of that cgroup. All processes within the scope are equal, and there is no internal hierarchy. The life of a scope begins when the first process is created and ends when the last process is destroyed.

Open several windows on your desktop such as terminal emulators, LibreOffice, or whatever you want, then switch to an available virtual console and start something like top or midnight commander. Run the `systemd-cgls` command on your host and take note of the overall hierarchy and the scope units.

The `systemd-cgls` command provides the most complete representation of the cgroup hierarchy and details of the units that make it up of any other command that I have found. I prefer its cleaner representation of the tree than that provided by the ps command.

Managing cgroups with systemd

I thought about writing this section myself but found a series of four articles by Steve Ovens on Red Hat's Enable SysAdmin website. I have found this information helpful in what I have written already, but since it covers the subject so well and goes beyond the scope of this course, I decided to list the articles here and let you read them for yourself:

1. "A Linux SysAdmin's introduction to cgroups"[2]

---

[2] Ovens, Steve, "A Linux SysAdmin's introduction to cgroups," Enable SysAdmin, 2020, https://www.redhat.com/sysadmin/cgroups-part-one

2. "How to manage cgroups with CPUShares"[3]

3. "Managing cgroups the hard way-manually"[4]

4. "Managing cgroups with systemd"[5]

Although some SysAdmins may need to manage system resources using cgroups, many will not. It may be worth noting here that containers are dependent on cgroups, so with the ubiquity of container platforms like Kubernetes and Podman and Docker, cgroups have become more relevant than ever. If you do, the best way to get started is with the series of articles listed above.

Summary

This chapter introduced cgroups and looked at their use as tools to help manage system resources such as RAM and CPU. We used the systemctl command to identify cgroups in system services. We also took a look at the cgroup hierarchy.

Because actual resource management using cgroups is beyond the scope of this course, I have provided links to some excellent materials by Steve Ovens that provide enough information to get you started. In the first article of that series, Ovens says that adoption of cgroups is very limited because of widespread lack of knowledge of its existence.

---

[3] Ovens, Steve, "How to manage cgroups with CPUShares," Enable SysAdmin, 2020, https://www.redhat.com/sysadmin/cgroups-part-two

[4] Ovens, Steve, "Managing cgroups the hard way-manually," Enable SysAdmin, 2020, https://www.redhat.com/sysadmin/cgroups-part-three

[5] Ovens, Steve, "Managing cgroups with systemd," Enable SysAdmin, 2020, https://www.redhat.com/sysadmin/cgroups-part-four

Exercises

Complete the following exercises to finish this chapter:

1. Why are cgroups important for resource management?

2. Why are cgroups more widely used by SysAdmins?

3. In Experiment 11-1, one slice on my VM was for UID 983. If you have that UID or any other slice belonging to a user, determine which user it is and why it exists.

CHAPTER 12

Using systemd-resolved Name Service

Objectives

After reading this chapter, you will be able to

- Describe how a name search works
- Use the nsswitch file to configure name services
- Use resolv.conf in both historical and contemporary modes
- Use systemd-resolved to provide Domain Name Services
- Describe the three name service strategies
- Identify and describe the problems with systemd-resolved in certain use cases
- Revert a Linux host to use nsswitch and the traditional NSS (Name Service Switch) resolver

CHAPTER 12   USING SYSTEMD-RESOLVED NAME SERVICE

Introduction

The Domain Name Services (DNS)[1] system provides the database used in the translation of Internet locations from human-readable hostnames, such as `www.example.net`, to IP addresses, like 54.204.39.132, so that our Internet-connected computers and other devices can access them. Without these name resolver services, it would be nearly impossible to surf the Web as freely and easily as we do. As humans, we tend to do better with names like opensource.org, while computers do much better with numbers like 104.21.84.214. So we need a translation service to convert the names that are easy for us to the IP addresses that are easy for our computers.

Every computer needs its own resolver service so that it can locate hosts on the local network and the Internet. But it's complicated.

In this chapter, we'll start with an exploration of name services and how they work. Then we'll look at the details of the resolver services and how they work in modern distributions. We'll learn about the historical NSS resolver and the systemd-resolved resolver along with tools and techniques for managing both.

We'll also explore one method for optimizing name services on some hosts by reverting to the traditional NSSwitch resolver.

How a Name Search Works

Let's start with a simplified example of what happens when a name request for a web page is made by a client service on your computer. For this example, I use `www.example.net` as the website I want to view in my browser. I also assume that there is a local name server on the network, as is the case with my own network.

---

[1] Both, David, *Introduction to the Domain Name System (DNS)*, https://www.both.org/?p=4759

Local name resolution will vary a bit depending upon the sequence of entries for the host line in the nsswitch.conf file. External name resolution always works like this regardless of which local resolver is being used.

1. First, I type in the URL or select a bookmark containing that URL. In this case, the URL is www.example.net.

2. The browser client, whether it is Opera, Firefox, Chrome, Min, Lynx, Links, or any other browser, sends the request to the operating system.

3. The operating system first checks the /etc/hosts file to see if the hostname is there. If so, the IP address of that entry is returned to the browser. If not, we proceed to the next step. In this case, we assume that the name is not in /etc/hosts.

4. The hostname is then sent to the first name server specified in /etc/resolv.conf. In this case, the IP address of the first name server is my own internal name server. For this example, my name server does not have the IP address for www.example.net cached and must look further afield. So we go on to the next step.

5. The local name server sends the request to a remote name server. This can be one of two destination types, one type of which is a forwarder. A forwarder is simply another name server such as the ones at your ISP or a public name server such as Google at 8.8.8.8 or 8.8.4.4. The other destination type is that of the top-level root name servers. The root servers don't usually respond with the desired target IP

321

CHAPTER 12   USING SYSTEMD-RESOLVED NAME SERVICE

address or www.example.net; they respond with the authoritative name server for that domain. The authoritative name servers are the only ones that have the authority to maintain and modify the data for a domain.

6. The local name server is configured to use the root name servers so the root name server for the .com top-level domain returns the IP address of the authoritative name server for example.net. That IP address could be for any one of the three (at the time of this writing) name servers, ns1.redhat.com, ns2.redhat.com, or ns3.redhat.com.

7. The local name server then sends the query to the authoritative name server which returns the IP address for www.example.net.

8. The browser uses the IP address for www.example.net to send a request for a web page which is downloaded to the browser.

One of the important side effects of this name search is that the results are cached for a period of time by my local name server. That means that the next time I, or anyone on my network, want to access example.net, the IP address is probably already stored in the local cache which prevents doing another remote lookup.

resolv.conf

We start by exploring the /etc/resolv.conf file because it is the key to determining exactly how the systemd-resolved.service works.

CHAPTER 12　USING SYSTEMD-RESOLVED NAME SERVICE

Historical Usage

This file used to be an ASCII plain-text file that contained a list of up to three domain name servers that would be used to perform hostname resolution into IP addresses. It still can be used that way, but that would bypass systemd-resolved. Of course, that might be a desired outcome as it was for me when NetworkManager took over this service and then when systemd-resolved was first introduced and had a few problems. It all works fine now, so I haven't needed to do that for a few years on most of my hosts.

The resolv.conf file also contains the domain name to search when a fully qualified domain name (FQDN) isn't appended to the hostname. For example, a fully qualified domain name would be host1.example. com. This can be searched without a problem. But suppose I just use a hostname line host1 and not the domain name. In that case, the domain name specified for searches is appended to the hostname.

A typical /etc/resolv.conf file used to look like that in Figure 12-1. It is a link in /etc to the /run/NetworkManager/resolv.conf and contains the search domain as well as the IP addresses of three name servers.

```
[root@david etc]# ll resolv.conf
lrwxrwxrwx 1 root root 31 Jun  1 09:07 resolv.conf ->
/run/NetworkManager/resolv.conf

[root@david etc]# cat resolv.conf
# Generated by NetworkManager
search both.org
nameserver 192.168.0.52
nameserver 8.8.8.8
nameserver 8.8.4.4
[root@david etc]#
```

Figure 12-1. *A typical /etc/resolv.conf file prior to the advent of systemd-resolved*

The first name server in the list is my internal name server. The second and third are fallback external name servers. I use Google name servers because I trust them to be reliable and to have the most up-to-date information in their DNS database—far more than my ISP's. Whichever ISP I have been using at a given time, I have had many disruptions to my Internet service due to nonresponsive, poorly configured, name servers that were not updated in a timely manner. This is one of the reasons I decided to set up my own internal name server. We'll set one up for our virtual network later in this chapter.

Current Usage

The current use of /etc/resolv.conf is as a symbolic link (symlink) to a stub file, /run/systemd/resolve/stub-resolv.conf, or to /run/systemd/resolve/resolv.conf. The file linked determines how systemd-resolved is supposed to deal with name service resolution requests. The default setup is for /etc/resolv.conf to link to /run/systemd/resolve/stub-resolv.conf which enables use of systemd-resolved although the systemd-resolved.service must also be up and running.

EXPERIMENT 12-1: RESOLV.CONF

Let's start by looking at /etc/resolv.conf. As you can see, it is a link that points to /run/systemd/resolve/stub-resolv.conf.

```
[root@testvm1 ~]# cd /etc ; ll resolv.conf ; cat resolv.conf
lrwxrwxrwx. 1 root root 39 Nov  5  2022 resolv.conf -> ../run/systemd/resolve/stub-resolv.conf
# This is /run/systemd/resolve/stub-resolv.conf managed by man:systemd-resolved(8).
# Do not edit.
#
```

CHAPTER 12 USING SYSTEMD-RESOLVED NAME SERVICE

```
# This file might be symlinked as /etc/resolv.conf. If you're looking at
# /etc/resolv.conf and seeing this text, you have followed the symlink.
#
# This is a dynamic resolv.conf file for connecting local clients to the
# internal DNS stub resolver of systemd-resolved. This file lists all
# configured search domains.
#
# Run "resolvectl status" to see details about the uplink DNS servers
# currently in use.
#
# Third party programs should typically not access this file directly, but only
# through the symlink at /etc/resolv.conf. To manage man:resolv.conf(5) in a
# different way, replace this symlink by a static file or a different symlink.
#
# See man:systemd-resolved.service(8) for details about the supported modes of
# operation for /etc/resolv.conf.

nameserver 127.0.0.53
options edns0 trust-ad
search example.com
[root@testvm1 etc]#
```

The nameserver line in this file points to an IP address that has been designated to represent the local hosts resolver. In this address, 127.0.0.53, the last octet, 53, is the same number as the standard DNS port of 53.

CHAPTER 12   USING SYSTEMD-RESOLVED NAME SERVICE

Name Service Strategies

There are currently three strategies available for use in resolving domain names into IP addresses. Each has its own tools, advantages, and best use cases. Two of these tools require work on the part of the SysAdmin.

One of these, mDNS, though requiring almost no administrative work, is quite chatty and creates a significant amount of network traffic. It also has its share of problems.

We'll explore all three strategies in this section, the /etc/hosts file, Multicast DNS (mDNS), and nss-DNS.

The /etc/hosts File

The /etc/hosts[2] file is an ASCII plain-text file that can list the IP addresses of all hosts on the local network and was the first tool used for local network name resolution. It can also be used for non-local hosts.

In small networks, the /etc/hosts file on each host can be used as a simple local name resolver. The SysAdmin can add and manage entries in the hosts file. Maintaining copies of this file on several hosts can become very time-consuming, and errors can cause much confusion and wasted time before they're found. Although the hosts file can have non-local domains such as `www.example.net` added to it, if the IP addresses can be discovered, it is a labor-intensive tool best suited for use in small local networks.

A default hosts file is always present, but it would normally contain only the lines needed to enable internal services and commands to translate the localhost hostname to IPV4 address 127.0.0.1 and IPV6 address ::1—this is an explicitly defined standard to enable Linux services and commands to deal with the local host.

---

[2] Wikipedia, "hosts (file)," `https://en.wikipedia.org/wiki/Hosts_(file)`

EXPERIMENT 12-2: USING /ETC/HOSTS

Perform this experiment as root on your test system. In this experiment, you will see the simple /etc/hosts file on your VM and then add some entries for the local network to make it easier to communicate with other local hosts.

Open the /etc/hosts file in an editor. It will look like this, with only a set of default entries.

```
# Loopback entries; do not change.
# For historical reasons, localhost precedes localhost.
localdomain:
127.0.0.1     localhost localhost.localdomain localhost4 localhost4.localdomain4
::1           localhost localhost.localdomain localhost6 localhost6.localdomain6
# See hosts(5) for proper format and other examples:
# 192.168.1.10 foo.mydomain.org foo
# 192.168.1.13 bar.mydomain.org bar
```

Make a backup copy of the /etc/hosts file and store it in /root. Try to ping a fake remote host before we change anything. I know, but bear with me. We're simulating a situation in which a remote host exists, but has no DNS entry in the DNS database. The example.com domain exists and is intended for use in testing such as we're doing here.

```
[root@testvm1 ~]# ping -c2 badname.example.com
ping: badname.example.com: Name or service not known
```

This result shows that there is no resolution from the given hostname to an IP address. Now edit the /etc/hosts file on testvm1 adding one line to the end so that it looks like this:

```
# Loopback entries; do not change.
# For historical reasons, localhost precedes localhost.
localdomain:
```

CHAPTER 12   USING SYSTEMD-RESOLVED NAME SERVICE

```
127.0.0.1    localhost localhost.localdomain localhost4 localhost4.localdomain4
::1          localhost localhost.localdomain localhost6 localhost6.localdomain6
# See hosts(5) for proper format and other examples:
# 192.168.1.10 foo.example.org foo
# 192.168.1.13 bar.example.org bar
23.192.228.80   badname.example.com
```

Save the revised file. A reboot is not necessary.

Notice that IP addresses can have multiple hostnames associated with them. Only a single host can be assigned a specific address, so these hostnames are aliases and all point to the same host. This can be a way to maintain backward compatibility with previous naming strategies, for example.

Let's test the /etc/hosts file.

```
# ping badname.example.com -c2
PING badname.example.com (23.192.228.80) 56(84) bytes of data.
64 bytes from badname.example.com (23.192.228.80): icmp_seq=1 ttl=44 time=62.1 ms
64 bytes from badname.example.com (23.192.228.80): icmp_seq=2 ttl=44 time=62.1 ms

--- badname.example.com ping statistics ---
2 packets transmitted, 2 received, 0% packet loss, time 1020ms
rtt min/avg/max/mdev = 62.088/62.112/62.136/0.024 ms
```

Comment out or delete the line you added to /etc/hosts and save the file again.

I used the /etc/hosts file to manage name services for my network for several years. It ultimately became too much trouble to maintain even with only the 8–12 physical computers and a similar number of VMs I normally have operational. As a result, I converted to running my own BIND name server to resolve both internal and external hostnames.[3]

Most networks of any size require centralized management with name services software such as BIND. However, smaller local networks can use mDNS for hands-free resolver services.

mDNS

Multicast DNS (mDNS)[4] is a relatively new addition to name service resolution. This name service strategy is that used by systemd-resolved.

Intended to provide name resolution for local networks that have no internal, central name resolver, mDNS requires no user intervention. In addition to automatic discovery of local hosts, it also uses more traditional name services for access to the Internet.

Multicast services like mDNS send out broadcast (multicast) packets[5] that are received and examined by every host on the network. The packet is a request to the computer with the hostname it wants to communicate with, to respond with its IP address so the requesting computer can send further packets directly to that host. Since only one computer (hopefully) has that hostname, only that computer will respond with its IP address and the requesting host enters that hostname/IP address into its local database. Other computers on the network that use mDNS can also add

---

[3] Both, David, *Build your own DNS server on Linux*, https://www.both.org/?p=4918
[4] Wikipedia, "Multicast DNS," https://en.wikipedia.org/wiki/Multicast_DNS
[5] Wikipedia, "IP multicast," https://en.wikipedia.org/wiki/IP_multicast

that data to their own mDNS databases. With mDNS each host keeps its own database. Entries in the database have a TTL (Time to Live), so the entries will expire at the end of their TTL. This means that the host must make another mDNS broadcast request to the network in order to obtain that IP address again.

This hands-off approach means that even users with an internal network consisting of a moderate number of hosts requires no user intervention. It is implemented via the Avahi package which is installed during the initial Fedora installation.

The cost of this level of automation for local host discovery is a significant amount of network traffic from each host that is intended to discover other hosts on the network. This type of chatty protocol sucks up network bandwidth, uses host system resources, and is not fast relative to the more traditional nss-DNS protocols.

How It Works

The mDNS protocols require that the systemd-resolved.service be running on all hosts. The `resolvectl` command can be used to view and provide a little management of the state of the systemd-resolved.service.

EXPERIMENT 12-3: THE RESOLVECTL COMMAND

Perform this experiment as root. This first command starts systemd-resolved on my VM. I'd disabled it so that you can see what it looks like as it starts.

```
# systemctl start systemd-resolved.service
root@testvm1:/etc# systemctl status systemd-resolved.service
• systemd-resolved.service - Network Name Resolution
 Loaded: loaded (/usr/lib/systemd/system/systemd-resolved.
 service; disabled; preset: enabled)
 Drop-In: /usr/lib/systemd/system/service.d
         └─10-timeout-abort.conf, 50-keep-warm.conf
```

CHAPTER 12   USING SYSTEMD-RESOLVED NAME SERVICE

Active: active (running) since Thu 2025-01-23 14:42:47
EST; 1s ago
Invocation: 30dae60d4b9c48fca7b2d736373a31b4
Docs: man:systemd-resolved.service(8)
man:org.freedesktop.resolve1(5)
https://systemd.io/WRITING_NETWORK_CONFIGURATION_MANAGERS
https://systemd.io/WRITING_RESOLVER_CLIENTS
Main PID: 2737 (systemd-resolve)
Status: "Processing requests..."
Tasks: 1 (limit: 9472)
Memory: 3.6M (peak: 4M)
CPU: 121ms
CGroup: /system.slice/systemd-resolved.service
└─2737 /usr/lib/systemd/systemd-resolved

Jan 23 14:42:47 testvm1.both.org systemd[1]: Starting systemd-resolved.service - Network Name Resolution...
Jan 23 14:42:47 testvm1.both.org systemd-resolved[2737]: Positive Trust Anchors:
Jan 23 14:42:47 testvm1.both.org systemd-resolved[2737]: . IN DS 20326 8 2 e06d44b80b8f1d39a95c0b0d7c65d08458e880409bbc683457104237c7f8ec8d
Jan 23 14:42:47 testvm1.both.org systemd-resolved[2737]: Negative trust anchors: home.arpa 10.in-addr.arpa 16.172.in-addr.arpa 17.172.in-addr.arpa 1>
Jan 23 14:42:47 testvm1.both.org systemd-resolved[2737]: Using system hostname 'testvm1.both.org'.
Jan 23 14:42:47 testvm1.both.org systemd[1]: Started systemd-resolved.service - Network Name Resolution.
Jan 23 14:42:47 testvm1.both.org systemd-resolved[2737]: enp0s3: Bus client set search domain list to: both.org
Jan 23 14:42:47 testvm1.both.org systemd-resolved[2737]: enp0s3: Bus client set default route setting: yes

CHAPTER 12   USING SYSTEMD-RESOLVED NAME SERVICE

```
Jan 23 14:42:47 testvm1.both.org systemd-resolved[2737]:
enpOs3: Bus client set DNS server list to: 192.168.0.52,
8.8.8.8, 8.8.4.4
Jan 23 14:42:47 testvm1.both.org systemd-resolved[2737]: enpOs8:
Bus client set default route setting: no
lines 1-28/28 (END)
```

We can see the log entries that indicate setting the system's hostname, the default route, and the list of name servers.

The resolvectl command can be used to display the DNS status of all network interfaces. This result is from my VM.

```
root@testvm1:~# resolvectl status
Global
Protocols: LLMNR=resolve -mDNS -DNSOverTLS DNSSEC=no/unsupported
resolv.conf mode: stub

Link 2 (enpOs3)
Current Scopes: DNS LLMNR/IPv4 LLMNR/IPv6
Protocols: +DefaultRoute LLMNR=resolve -mDNS -DNSOverTLS
DNSSEC=no/unsupported
Current DNS Server: 192.168.0.52
DNS Servers: 192.168.0.52 8.8.8.8 8.8.4.4
DNS Domain: both.org

Link 3 (enpOs8)
Current Scopes: LLMNR/IPv6
Protocols: -DefaultRoute LLMNR=resolve -mDNS -DNSOverTLS
DNSSEC=no/unsupported
```

This command can be used to resolve an FQDN to an IP address. This is similar to the dig and nslookup commands, but it also shows the interface on which it was discovered.

```
+[root@testvm1 etc]# resolvectl query www.example.net
www.example.net: 93.184.216.34                    -- link: enp0s3
                 2606:2800:220:1:248:1893:25c8:1946 --
                 link: enp0s3

-- Information acquired via protocol DNS in 2.2ms.
-- Data is authenticated: no; Data was acquired via local or
encrypted transport: no
-- Data from: network
```

The Details

The /etc/resolv.conf and /etc/nsswitch.conf files are symbolic (soft) links to the created files. Let's look at these files.

> **EXPERIMENT 12-4: EXAMINING THE NSSWITCH AND RESOLV.CONF FILES**

Because the nsswitch.conf and resolv.conf files contain the configuration for name service resolution, let's look at them in some detail.

Although these files are now links to the actual content, they were previously both regular files and not links. systemd-resolved uses the link targets to determine how to handle name resolution.

The links keep the same date and time as when they were originally included in the installation package. The /etc/authselect/nsswitch.conf file was created during system installation. The ../run/systemd/resolve/stub-resolv.conf was created during the most recent boot.

```
# cd /etc/ ; ll resolv.conf nsswitch.conf
lrwxrwxrwx. 1 root root 29 Jan 29 10:16 nsswitch.conf -> /etc/
authselect/nsswitch.conf
lrwxrwxrwx. 1 root root 39 Oct 24 10:53 resolv.conf -> ../run/
systemd/resolve/stub-resolv.conf
```

CHAPTER 12   USING SYSTEMD-RESOLVED NAME SERVICE

Actually, two versions of the resolv.conf file are created in the /run/systemd/resolve/ directory each time the host is booted.

cat resolv.conf
This is /run/systemd/resolve/resolv.conf managed by man:systemd-resolved(8).
Do not edit.
#
This file might be symlinked as /etc/resolv.conf. If you're looking at
/etc/resolv.conf and seeing this text, you have followed the symlink.
#
This is a dynamic resolv.conf file for connecting local clients directly to
all known uplink DNS servers. This file lists all configured search domains.
#
Third party programs should typically not access this file directly, but only
through the symlink at /etc/resolv.conf. To manage man:resolv.conf(5) in a
different way, replace this symlink by a static file or a different symlink.
#
See man:systemd-resolved.service(8) for details about the supported modes of
operation for /etc/resolv.conf.

nameserver 192.168.0.52
nameserver 8.8.8.8
nameserver 8.8.4.4
search both.org

CHAPTER 12   USING SYSTEMD-RESOLVED NAME SERVICE

cat /run/systemd/resolve/stub-resolv.conf
This is /run/systemd/resolve/stub-resolv.conf managed by man:systemd-resolved(8).
Do not edit.cat stub-resolv.conf
#
This file might be symlinkevd as /etc/resolv.conf. If you're looking at
/etc/resolv.conf and seeing this text, you have followed the symlink.
#
This is a dynamic resolv.conf file for connecting local clients to the
internal DNS stub resolver of systemd-resolved. This file lists all
configured search domains.
#
Run "resolvectl status" to see details about the uplink DNS servers
currently in use.
#
Third party programs should typically not access this file directly, but only
through the symlink at /etc/resolv.conf. To manage man:resolv.conf(5) in a
different way, replace this symlink by a static file or a different symlink.
#
See man:systemd-resolved.service(8) for details about the supported modes of
operation for /etc/resolv.conf.

nameserver 127.0.0.53
options edns0 trust-ad
search both.org

The first file is a more traditional resolv.conf file, but it is not being used. It defines three external servers for name resolution. This information can be obtained from the DHCP server for the network or from NetworkManager network connection files for static configurations.

The second file is the systemd-resolved version, stub-resolv.conf, and it is the target of the /etc/resolv.conf symlink. This file defines the local host as the name server for this client host.

mDNS Performance

After several not-very-scientific experiments involving the **time** command, I have found that mDNS is measurably slower than using historical DNS services, especially in comparison to a network that provides its own name servers. My experiments show that mDNS can take as much as five times longer than historical name services. Of course, we're only talking about hundredths of a second difference, but that can be important in some situations.

Delays can be especially noticeable to users accessing websites with a lot of external links that need to be resolved such as found on large, complex, commercial websites. Using ad blockers can help by simply not attempting to load from external addresses that are known advertising sources. However, in the ongoing battle between suppliers of ads and ad blockers, the latest strategy is to pop up a dialog that informs you to unblock ads or subscribe to the service.

nss-DNS

This is the historical name service and resolver combination. The Name Service Switch (NSS)[6] resolver performs the client tasks of requesting IP addresses from the global Domain Name Service distributed database. It has the attributes of being fast, easy to use, mature, and well known.

Originally developed by Sun Microsystems as part of their Solaris operating system, it was rewritten for the GNU utilities and tools. Its code is embedded in the GNU glibc[7] library so is still available.

Top-Level Configuration

Two ASCII plain-text files are used to provide the primary configuration for name services. These files, nsswitch.conf and resolv.conf, have historical origins having been around since the earliest versions of name service resolvers. They're still in use by systemd-resolved, but as we've seen, their usage has taken on additional functionality.

NSS and NSSwitch

As its name implies, the nsswitch—short for Name Service Switch—is used to define the database sources and order in which name-service information is obtained.

Unicast services like nss-DNS use a single server that maintains the entire database. If a host needs the IP address of another host on the network, it sends a unicast packet only to the name server requesting the IP address from it. The name server responds only to the requesting host with a packet containing that IP address.

---

[6] gnu.org documentation, *System Databases and Name Service Switch*, https://www.gnu.org/software/libc/manual/html_node/Name-Service-Switch.html

[7] General C Library. A collection of basic Linux functions that are always present.

CHAPTER 12   USING SYSTEMD-RESOLVED NAME SERVICE

The NSS facility is a tool that is used by a number of services that need name resolver data. Using NSS based on the data in the /etc/nsswitch.conf configuration file, it aids them in locating the appropriate configuration and name resolution sources in a specified sequence.

The sequences listed for each service in this file can be changed, and can differ between distributions. They can also be modified to meet local needs. I have never needed to change anything about this file, but it is a good place to start problem determination if there seems to be a problem with name resolution that can't be otherwise explained.

Let's take a look at it.

EXPERIMENT 12-5: THE NSSWITCH.CONF FILE

As root on your test host, display the nsswitch.conf file. Note that some lines are wrapped in the data stream below:

```
[root@testvm1 etc]# cat nsswitch.conf
# Generated by authselect on Tue Jan 17 21:33:15 2023
# Do not modify this file manually, use authselect instead. Any
user changes will be overwritten.
# You can stop authselect from managing your configuration by
calling 'authselect opt-out'.
# See authselect(8) for more details.

# In order of likelihood of use to accelerate lookup.
passwd:     files sss systemd
shadow:     files
group:      files sss systemd
hosts:      files myhostname mdns4_minimal [NOTFOUND=return]
            resolve [!UNAVAIL=return] dns
services:   files sss
netgroup:   files sss
automount:  files sss
```

CHAPTER 12 USING SYSTEMD-RESOLVED NAME SERVICE

```
aliases:     files
ethers:      files
gshadow:     files
networks:    files dns
protocols:   files
publickey:   files
rpc:         files
```

Look at the hosts database entry in the data stream. The first entry is "files" which means that the resolver is to search first the local database. The database isn't explicitly specified here, but it is the /etc/hosts file that we experimented with above.

If a match is not found, the resolver moves on to the next entry which is "myhostname." This provides name resolution for the locally configured system hostname as contained in the $HOSTNAME environment variable.

The myhostname entry in this line is new and is intended to provide fail-safe resolution of any local hostnames such as localhost and localhost.localdomain. This is built into the resolver code and is not dependent on the entries in the /etc/hosts file.

Because all of these entries are sequence-sensitive, if an entry is found for a hostname in the /etc/hosts database, that takes precedent over any other, later entries.

How can you find the system hostname? There are multiple ways to do that, but the $HOSTNAME environment variable contains the hostname and can be easily used in system administration scripts.

```
[root@testvm1 etc]# echo $HOSTNAME
testvm1.both.org
```

Many tools and applications require a local hostname to function properly, so if the actual hostname is not present in the hosts file, it can be found in this variable. Do you remember setting the hostname during the installation of Fedora or your own preferred distribution?[8] That's where the hostname in this variable comes from. It's hugely important.

The **hostnamectl**[9] utility can be used to change the hostname as well as to display information about the host. I did this on my primary workstation, but you can also do this on the VM, which is, unfortunately, much less interesting.

```
[root@david ~]# hostnamectl status
     Static hostname: testvm1.both.org
           Icon name: computer-vm
             Chassis: vm 🖥
          Machine ID: 679fb335f6e94d87b55e8ad3993245f8
             Boot ID: ab3fa56413c8470e8a6da7ff376c4b5c
        Product UUID: a7b3a47e-d756-6c41-91f5-8ce11f20b152
      Virtualization: oracle
    Operating System: Fedora Linux 41 (Xfce)
         CPE OS Name: cpe:/o:fedoraproject:fedora:41
       OS Support End: Mon 2025-12-15
 OS Support Remaining: 10month 2w 5d
              Kernel: Linux 6.12.10-200.fc41.x86_64
        Architecture: x86-64
     Hardware Vendor: innotek GmbH
      Hardware Model: VirtualBox
     Hardware Serial: 0
    Firmware Version: VirtualBox
       Firmware Date: Fri 2006-12-01
        Firmware Age: 18y 1month 3w 3d
```

---

[8] Unless it's set by the DHCPD service at boot time.
[9] Use the command **man 8 nss-myhostname**.

CHAPTER 12   USING SYSTEMD-RESOLVED NAME SERVICE

That's a lot of interesting and important information. The little keyboard icon used on the "Chassis" line resolves visually a bit better here than in my terminal session. We've seen much of this information in somewhat less readable formats, but there is also information here that I've never seen displayed elsewhere, like the operating system support info.

Here's the data from my oldest PC, a Dell OptiPlex GX620 built in August of 2005.

```
# hostnamectl status
     Static hostname: intrepid.both.org
           Icon name: computer-desktop
             Chassis: desktop 🖥
          Machine ID: e28a5d4ba9cd4eb2a2f594f92c24edf9
             Boot ID: b79874ab2a10487eb7dc6f813dcf7846
        Product UUID: 44454c4c-5900-1051-8033-c3c04f423831
    Operating System: Fedora Linux 41 (Xfce)
         CPE OS Name: cpe:/o:fedoraproject:fedora:41
       OS Support End: Mon 2025-12-15
 OS Support Remaining: 10month 2w 5d
              Kernel: Linux 6.12.10-200.fc41.x86_64
        Architecture: x86-64
     Hardware Vendor: Dell Inc.
      Hardware Model: OptiPlex GX620
     Hardware Serial: CYQ3B81
    Firmware Version: A01
       Firmware Date: Tue 2005-05-24
        Firmware Age: 19y 8month 2d
```

This old computer has only an Intel Pentium 4 with two cores and 4G of RAM. It still runs 24x7 at full blast on the most recent releases of Fedora.[10] The desktop computer icon for the Chassis line is more realistic for a hardware system than a virtual one.

When used with no arguments, the **hostnamectl** utility displays the same status as above for the local host. Changing the hostname can be accomplished using this same utility. The new hostname should be the argument.

[root@testvm1 ~]# **hostnamectl hostname newhostname**

This name change is stored in the /etc/hostname file but does not take effect until the next boot. You could also just edit the /etc/hostname file and reboot because all the hostnamectl command does is to change the hostname in the /etc/hostname file.

The next entry in nsswitch.conf is mdns4_minimal. This tells nss-resolve to use the Avahi service daemon to use mDNS to locate the host. All of the hosts on the local network must be running the avahi-daemon.service in order to participate in mDNS.

The next thing we find in this list is [NOTFOUND=return] resolve. This bit of code instructs nss-resolve[11] to use systemd-resolved[12] for name resolution. This mode uses the /etc/resolv.conf file.

---

[10] For more details of this old system, see my website page, https://www.both.org/?p=7808

[11] Systemd Documentation, *nss-resolve,* https://systemd.network/nss-resolve.html#

[12] Systemd Documentation, *systemd-resolved.service,* https://systemd.network/systemd-resolved.service.html

Lastly, at least in Fedora, [!UNAVAIL=return] dns means that if the systemd-resolved is unavailable, then use the historical nss-DNS service for name resolution.

The man page for nsswitch.conf contains information about the other services that use name services, for example, the passwd database for user passwords.

Experiment 12-5 illustrates the complexity of the current name resolution strategy while also highlighting the flexibility available to the SysAdmin in aid of supporting local needs for name resolution.

systemd-resolved.service

We're finally up to the systemd-resolved.service. The systemd-resolved.service provides name resolution services for modern Fedora, Red Hat based, and other distributions. It works with and is a requirement for Multicast DNS (mDNS). We'll explore mDNS in this chapter, but for now let's just take a quick look at the service itself.

EXPERIMENT 12-6: SYSTEMD-RESOLVED.SERVICE

The systemd resolver can be started, restarted, and stopped, as well as having its status checked by using the **systemctl** command like the other systemd services. Check its current status; it should be running.

```
[root@testvm1 ~]# systemctl status systemd-resolved.service
● systemd-resolved.service - Network Name Resolution
Loaded: loaded (/usr/lib/systemd/system/systemd-resolved.service; enabled; preset: enabled)
Drop-In: /usr/lib/systemd/system/service.d
         └─10-timeout-abort.conf, 50-keep-warm.conf
```

```
Active: active (running) since Fri 2025-01-24 12:21:30
EST; 13h ago
Invocation: 349ff71eb299462996dbf59e1501501b
Docs: man:systemd-resolved.service(8)
      man:org.freedesktop.resolve1(5)
      https://systemd.io/WRITING_NETWORK_CONFIGURATION_MANAGERS
      https://systemd.io/WRITING_RESOLVER_CLIENTS
Main PID: 1012 (systemd-resolve)
Status: "Processing requests..."
Tasks: 1 (limit: 9472)
Memory: 9.7M (peak: 10.4M)
CPU: 1.272s
CGroup: /system.slice/systemd-resolved.service
        └─1012 /usr/lib/systemd/systemd-resolved

Jan 24 12:21:29 testvm1.both.org systemd[1]: Starting systemd-
resolved.service - Network Name Resolution...
Jan 24 12:21:29 testvm1.both.org systemd-resolved[1012]:
Positive Trust Anchors:
Jan 24 12:21:29 testvm1.both.org systemd-
resolved[1012]: . IN DS 20326 8 2
e06d44b80b8f1d39a95c0b0d7c65d08458e880409bbc6834571042>
Jan 24 12:21:29 testvm1.both.org systemd-resolved[1012]:
Negative trust anchors: home.arpa 10.in-addr.arpa 16.172.in-
addr.arpa 17>
Jan 24 12:21:29 testvm1.both.org systemd-resolved[1012]: Using
system hostname 'testvm1.both.org'.
Jan 24 12:21:30 testvm1.both.org systemd[1]: Started systemd-
resolved.service - Network Name Resolution.
Jan 24 12:21:33 testvm1.both.org systemd-resolved[1012]: enp0s3:
Bus client set search domain list to: both.org
Jan 24 12:21:33 testvm1.both.org systemd-resolved[1012]: enp0s3:
Bus client set default route setting: yes
```

CHAPTER 12   USING SYSTEMD-RESOLVED NAME SERVICE

```
Jan 24 12:21:33 testvm1.both.org systemd-resolved[1012]:
enp0s3: Bus client set DNS server list to: 192.168.0.52,
8.8.8.8, 8.8.4.4
Jan 24 12:21:33 testvm1.both.org systemd-resolved[1012]: enp0s8:
Bus client set default route setting: no
```

Other functionality for the systemd resolver is managed with the resolvectl command which we will look at later in this chapter.

Fedora Name Resolution Fails When Using systemd-resolved

When I first installed Fedora 33, one of the major changes, a switch from the nss resolver to systemd-resolved, caused me a significant amount of trouble and borked my entire network.

The change from the venerable nsswitch and NetworkManager to systemd-resolved damaged and slowed name services. The result of this resolver change was apparent in a number of symptoms. Inability to find the addresses of many remote servers resulting in timeouts was the most noticeable. When the connections were made, they were very slow to respond.

I hadn't realized how lengthy the delays in name resolution were until after resolving this problem. Web pages that took minutes to load—and some never did with all the external links they use to load pictures and advertisements—now take only a second or so. Tests using the **dig** command show name resolution times of around 100 milliseconds (msec) for sites that were not currently in the cache of my name server.

I run my own name server using BIND. I started this soon after I began learning Linux as a way to overcome the horrible name services provided by my series of ISPs. They were very slow and would fail intermittently, always at the most inopportune times for me. It was far less trouble for me to start my own name service, and that has been the case—until systemd-resolved forced its way onto my Fedora systems. All of them.

These problems still exist and still cause problems today.

Determining the Problem

A bit of problem determination showed that even connecting to name servers at Google DNS would time out:

```
# dig www.both.org
;; communications error to 8.8.8.8#53: timed out
;; communications error to 8.8.8.8#53: timed out
;; communications error to 8.8.8.8#53: timed out
;; communications error to 8.8.4.4#53: timed out
; <<>> DiG 9.18.28 <<>> www.both.org
;; global options: +cmd
;; no servers could be reached
```

I started with resolv.conf. The initial default configuration for resolv.conf is as a pointer to a stub as seen here:

```
lrwxrwxrwx. 1 root root 39 Apr 14 18:58 resolv.conf -> ../run/systemd/resolve/stub-resolv.conf
```

The /etc/resolv.conf file in Figure 12-2 defined the resolver as the localhost at 127.0.0.53. The comments in this file are enlightening. I had no idea that this had supplanted the previous resolver and resolv.conf managed by NetworkManager. This extracts the resolver function from NetworkManager but leaves it with the rest of its network management responsibilities.

CHAPTER 12   USING SYSTEMD-RESOLVED NAME SERVICE

```
# This is /run/systemd/resolve/stub-resolv.conf managed by man:systemd-resolved(8).
# Do not edit.
#
# This file might be symlinked as /etc/resolv.conf. If you're looking at
# /etc/resolv.conf and seeing this text, you have followed the symlink.
#
# This is a dynamic resolv.conf file for connecting local clients to the
# internal DNS stub resolver of systemd-resolved. This file lists all
# configured search domains.
#
# Run "resolvectl status" to see details about the uplink DNS servers
# currently in use.
#
# Third party programs should typically not access this file directly, but only
# through the symlink at /etc/resolv.conf. To manage man:resolv.conf(5) in a
# different way, replace this symlink by a static file or a different symlink.
#
# See man:systemd-resolved.service(8) for details about the supported modes of
# operation for /etc/resolv.conf.

nameserver 127.0.0.53
options edns0 trust-ad
search both.org
```

Figure 12-2. *The /run/systemd/resolve/stub-resolv.conf file points to the localhost as the name server*

The /etc/nsswitch.conf file is used to determine the order in which various resources are accessed for various services, including hostname resolution. This file has also changed and contains some weird logic in the hosts line. Based on my experiments, it's this logic that appears to slow things down, along with the use of mdns4_minimal and resolve sources. There's also this new thing called authselect which now generates the nsswitch.conf file.

The original file, seen in Figure 12-3, is found at the location, /etc/authselect/nsswitch.conf, and /etc/nsswitch.conf is a symlink to that file.

347

CHAPTER 12 USING SYSTEMD-RESOLVED NAME SERVICE

```
# Generated by authselect
# Do not modify this file manually, use authselect instead. Any user changes will be overwritten.
# You can stop authselect from managing your configuration by calling 'authselect opt-out'.
# See authselect(8) for more details.

# In order of likelihood of use to accelerate lookup.
passwd:     files systemd
shadow:     files
group:      files [SUCCESS=merge] systemd
hosts:      files mdns4_minimal [NOTFOUND=return] resolve [!UNAVAIL=return] myhostname dns
services:   files
netgroup:   files
automount:  files

aliases:    files
ethers:     files
gshadow:    files
networks:   files dns
protocols:  files
publickey:  files
rpc:        files
```

Figure 12-3. The original nsswitch.conf file has some interesting code for the hosts entry

I also found many named errors in the systemd journal. A small sample is shown in Figure 12-4.

```
Sep 15 01:41:27 yorktown.both.org named[1464]: SERVFAIL unexpected RCODE resolving 'dns-02.as49870.net/A/IN': 116.203.70.186#53
Sep 15 02:00:14 yorktown.both.org named[1464]: loop detected resolving 'ns6.pinterest.com/A'
Sep 15 02:00:14 yorktown.both.org named[1464]: loop detected resolving 'ns5.pinterest.com/A'
Sep 15 02:24:03 yorktown.both.org named[1464]: REFUSED unexpected RCODE resolving '218.67.58.103.in-addr.arpa/PTR/IN': 103.58.117.2#53
Sep 15 02:34:38 yorktown.both.org named[1464]:   validating in-addr.arpa/SOA: got insecure response; parent indicates it should be secure
Sep 15 02:34:53 yorktown.both.org named[1464]: REFUSED unexpected RCODE resolving '29.140.3.106.in-addr.arpa/PTR/IN': 101.251.253.10#53
Sep 15 02:34:54 yorktown.both.org named[1464]: REFUSED unexpected RCODE resolving '29.140.3.106.in-addr.arpa/PTR/IN': 221.228.99.114#53
Sep 15 02:34:54 yorktown.both.org named[1464]: REFUSED unexpected RCODE resolving '29.140.3.106.in-addr.arpa/PTR/IN': 38.83.110.66#53
```

Figure 12-4. A sampling of the name service errors from the systemd journal indicates resolver problems

Several online resources indicate that these errors are caused by configuration issues for the target domain's name services. The comments on these articles suggest that the domain admins should fix their problems, but the commenters recognize that's unlikely to happen. So we must implement our own changes to fix someone else's problem.

Resolving the Problem

It takes several steps to resolve this problem. This section describes each step and why it's needed as part of the complete solution.

1. **Stop and disable the Avahi service**

    The Avahi website describes Avahi better than I can.

    Avahi is a system which facilitates service discovery on a local network via the mDNS/DNS-SD protocol suite. This enables you to plug your laptop or computer into a network and instantly be able to view other people who you can chat with, find printers to print to or find files being shared. Compatible technology is found in Apple MacOS X (branded "Bonjour" and sometimes "Zeroconf").

    Avahi is the basis for many of the good things that end user simplification can support; however it's not going to be needed when we disable some of the other services that it supports.

    ```
    # systemctl disable --now avahi-daemon.service
    ```

2. **Stop and disable the Avahi daemon**

    The Avahi daemon socket is a part of the Avahi service. When a program requests Avahi services, it does so through the daemon rather than directly to the service itself. The socket then sends the request to the service. Other systemd services also work this way. This won't be required since we've disabled the Avahi service. A socket like this could also cause the service it belongs to to start even though the service is disabled. We don't want to allow that to happen.

    `# systemctl disable --now avahi-daemon.socket`

3. **Stop and disable the systemd-resolved service**

    The systemd-resolved service is the root cause of the problems we're having, so we disable it. The systemd-resolved man page states its purpose succinctly.

    systemd-resolved is a system service that provides network name resolution to local applications. It implements a caching and validating DNS/DNSSEC stub resolver, as well as an LLMNR and MulticastDNS resolver and responder.

    The man page then proceeds to describe the interfaces it exposes to programs and a high-level statement about how to access it as a resolver. This service is the root cause of the problem, and we disable it.

    `# systemctl disable --now systemd-resolved.service`

CHAPTER 12 USING SYSTEMD-RESOLVED NAME SERVICE

4. **Delete the /etc/resolv.conf link**

   The NetworkManager service examines the /etc/resolv.conf file to determine which servers to use for name resolution. Up to three servers are supported in a simple list format. This file also defines the name of the domain in which to search for hostnames if a simple hostname is provided, that is, host, rather than the FQDN (fully qualified domain name), that is, host.example.com.

   Only one name server is specified in this file, the local host. The systemd-resolved service and Avahi search the local network for other local hosts using systemd-resolved and can configure name resolution so that the hosts can talk among themselves. If there is a name server found, such as that provided on wired or wireless routers, it can use that to perform name resolution for external hosts such as www.both.org.

   If there's no locally accessible name server, external name resolution is not possible. This is what happened to me at the beach. The local name server at the hotel was intermittent, so no name resolution was possible. I could, however, still ping remote hosts such as www.both.org using the IP address. Yes—this is an edge case. But it clearly does happen.

   So we delete the existing /etc/resolve.conf link. We won't create a new resolv.conf file because once we get the rest of this mess sorted, NetworkManager will create a usable one. The NetworkManager service is responsible for creating the /etc/resolv.

conf file at boot time if it doesn't exist. If systemd-resolved is running, the default link is created, which is not the one we want.

`# rm -f /etc/resolv.conf`

5. **Delete the /etc/nsswitch.conf link**

   The man page for nsswitch.conf provides a brief description of the uses for this file.

   The Name Service Switch (NSS) configuration file, /etc/nsswitch.conf, is used by the GNU C Library and certain other applications to determine the sources from which to obtain name-service information in a range of categories, and in what order. Each category of information is identified by a database name.

   My testing determined that the /etc/nsswitch.conf file shown at the beginning of this chapter is directly responsible for the slow resolution speeds I encountered, whether at the beach or here in my home lab. If you look back at that file, the logic in the hosts line seems to be the cause.

   We don't need—or really want—to delete the actual nsswitch.conf file. We'll just delete the symbolic link (symlink) in /etc.

   `# rm -f /etc/nsswitch.conf`

6. **Create a revised nsswitch.conf**

   Since we deleted the symlink to this file in the previous step, we need to create a new version of this file, but it won't be a symlink. After the next step, it won't be changed or overwritten. I copied the original from /etc/authselect/nsswitch.conf to /etc so that it's not a symlink. I made my changes to this file, which are shown in bold in Figure 12-5. Note that some lines are wrapped.

```
# Do not modify this file manually, use authselect instead. Any user changes will be
overwritten.
# You can stop authselect from managing your configuration by calling 'authselect opt-
out'.
# See authselect(8) for more details.

# In order of likelihood of use to accelerate lookup.
passwd:     files sss systemd
shadow:     files
group:      files [SUCCESS=merge] sss [SUCCESS=merge] systemd
# hosts:      files mdns4_minimal [NOTFOUND=return] resolve [!UNAVAIL=return] myhostname
dns
hosts:      files myhostname dns
services:   files sss
netgroup:   files sss
automount:  files sss

aliases:    files
ethers:     files
gshadow:    files
networks:   files dns
protocols:  files
publickey:  files
rpc:        files
```

Figure 12-5. The revised nsswitch.conf file with the changes shown in bold

I commented out the original hosts line and added a new one with the desired changes. This leaves an easy option for returning to the original configuration.

7. **Opt out of authselect**

   In order to prevent authselect from changing /etc/nsswitch, we opt out.

   # **authselect opt-out**

You can safely ignore the first line of the nsswitch. conf file and make changes to it manually. I usually delete that first line or change it so I know I can modify this file.

8. **Restart NetworkManager**

    The last step is to restart the NetworkManager service. This will create a new /etc/resolv.conf and utilize the new nsswitch.conf file we created.

    # systemctl restart NetworkManager.service

Every time it's restarted, whether at Linux startup or a command-line restart, NetworkManager creates the new /etc/resolv.conf using the data provided by the DHCP server for the network or from NetworkManager Connection Files.[13] For many stand-alone systems in home and office, this DHCP server is usually the wired/wireless router.

The resolv.conf file for my VM is shown in Figure 12-6, and it contains the information obtained from my DHCP server.

```
# Generated by NetworkManager
search both.org
nameserver 192.168.0.52
nameserver 8.8.8.8
nameserver 8.8.4.4
```

Figure 12-6. The resolv.conf file generated by NetworkManager from the connection files I configured for this interface

---

[13] Both, David, *NetworkManager on Linux: #3 — How I migrated to NetworkManager Connection Files for configuration*, https://www.both.org/?p=4863

The server at 192.168.0.52 is my internal server. It handles name services for the local network with zone files and uses the top-level DNS servers for external network name resolution. If you want to override the network configuration provided by a DHCP server, you can explicitly configure the network interface using NetworkManager Connection Files.

At this point, name services are using NSSwitch with a decent and reliable resolv.conf file. I tested this using a few pings to internal and external hosts. I always use example.com for external testing like this.

Concluding Thoughts About nsswitch

Based on my experimentation, the nsswitch.conf file generated by authselect, and dependence on the Avahi daemon to locate services such as network configuration and other hosts on the local network, slows the entire process to the point of uselessness. I think aiming at Linux on the desktop is an admirable goal, and I'll be happy when Linux is on the majority of desktops. While this may work—once the problems are resolved—for minimally technical users, it can cause issues for those of us SysAdmins who've had things well configured and working for years.

In previous attempts about fixing the resolver problems, I was able to resolve the issues at hand, but after this last round of extreme symptoms, I finally realized the extent of the multiple root causes. Part of the issue is that various systemd name service tools have been added over a period of time rather than all at once. This section of the chapter considered all of the currently known root causes for name service resolution issues related to systemd-resolved and explained how to resolve them.

I suggest reading the man pages for each of the files mentioned in this article as there is additional important information about each that can be very helpful.

Summary

Name resolution is a critical service for hosts connected to the Internet, and systemd-resolved is the most current implementation of a resolver for many Linux distributions. Its intended use case is for small networks with no internal name service server, usually because no SysAdmin is available to create a DNS or DHCP server.

While it can work well in that limited use case, it has failed miserably in my use case in which I have both DNS and DHCP services on my internal server. Reverting to the nss-DNS resolver has resolved my name resolution problems.

Don't misunderstand me. I'm not suddenly saying I hate systemd. That's not it at all. What I am saying is that the unintended consequences of these decisions can cause SysAdmins pain as they try to determine what's changed and how to fix it. In this case, it's simply that what's good for one set of users is not necessarily good for other sets of users. The use case for some of my hosts is significantly different from that of nontechnical users.

Networks of any size with DHCP or static network configurations are much better suited to nss-DNS name resolution services.

Exercises

Complete the following exercises to finish this chapter:

1. What is the function of systemd-resolved?

2. What is its best use case?

3. Compare and contrast the functions of mDNS and nss-DNS. *I used to hate this type of question when I was in school.*

4. Describe the use case in which the nss-DNS resolver is a better choice than systemd-resolved.

CHAPTER 13

Replacing rc.local in systemd

Objectives

After reading this chapter, you will be able to

- Describe the function of rc.local
- State the reason that rc.local needs to be replaced with a systemd service unit
- Create a service unit that can launch one or more programs during Linux startup
- Test that service from the command line
- Enable the service to run during startup

Introduction

Have you been missing rc.local for adding commands to run on startup in a systemd system? Here's how to set up similar functionality with today's systemd.

© David Both 2025
D. Both, *systemd for Linux SysAdmins*, https://doi.org/10.1007/979-8-8688-1328-3_13

A few years ago, I encountered two different problems on two different Linux hosts. Each required a unique circumvention because I had not yet found a real solution. However, the method for delivering each circumvention was the same: run a command during or soon after Linux startup.

The rc.local file was—and in some cases still is—the place for Linux SysAdmins to put commands that need to be run at startup. Use of the rc.local file is not only deprecated but, after a couple of hours' worth of attempts, was not working in any event. This is despite the fact that the systemd documentation mentions the use of a "generator" that generates systemd services from an rc.local file if one exists. That seems to be a good way as any to enforce deprecation—make it not work.

The details of my specific problem are not particularly relevant to this discussion, so I will use a simple and easily tracked command as the content of our local startup file. We will add a date-stamped line to a local log file to verify that the Bash program we need to run at startup actually works.

Boot vs. Startup

Understanding the Linux boot and startup process is important for configuring Linux and resolving startup issues. In reality, there are two sequences of events that are required to boot a Linux computer and make it usable: boot and startup. The boot sequence starts when the computer is turned on and finishes when the kernel is initialized and `systemd` is launched. The startup process then takes over and finishes the task of getting the Linux computer into an operational state.

Overall, the Linux boot and startup process is fairly simple to understand. It is comprised of the following steps:

1. BIOS power-on self-test (POST)
2. Bootloader (GRUB2)
3. Kernel
4. systemd

For a much more detailed description of both the boot and startup sequences, refer to Chapter 2.

Local Startup

System administrators sometimes add commands to the startup sequence that are locally useful. These additions may aim to start or run local processes that are not part of the standard systemd startup. It is possible to add a new systemd service unit to launch each program needed at startup, but the old **rc.local** method provided a single executable Bash script for any and all local startup needs. We, too, can use this single file approach with systemd. The elegance of this solution is that it makes it easy to add more startup commands at a later time, without the need to add more service units to systemd unless there is a specific reason for doing so.

Our solution is to create a single systemd service unit and place any required Linux commands into the Bash script. There are two parts to this solution. One is obvious: we need an executable file. And two, we need to create a service unit for systemd that runs the executable.

Create the Executable File

This is a trivial exercise for any SysAdmin familiar with Bash programming. In fact, we will create a Bash program and place it in the Linux Filesystem Hierarchical Standard (FHS)[1] location for local executable files, /usr/local/bin. An argument could be made for placing this executable file in another location, but /usr/local/bin is the one that makes the most sense to me since this location makes it easy for the SysAdmin to run the script from the command line if necessary. The /usr/local/bin directory is always in every user's $PATH, including that of the root user.

---

[1] Both, David, The Linux Filesystem Hierarchical Standard, https://www.both.org/?p=6082

CHAPTER 13   REPLACING RC.LOCAL IN SYSTEMD

> **EXPERIMENT 13-1: CREATING AN EXECUTABLE FILE**

Create the mystartup.sh file shown here, and place it in /usr/local/bin and make it executable. I used 754 permissions. Be sure to use the location for Bash that is correct for your distribution in the shebang line. For example, Debian-based distributions locate Bash at /bin/bash, while Red Hat and related distributions such as Fedora place it in /usr/bin/bash.

```
#!/usr/bin/bash

################################################################
# mystartup.sh
#
# This shell program is for testing a startup like rc.local
# using systemd.
#
# By David Both
# Licensed under GPL V2 or later at your option.
#
################################################################
# This program should be placed in /usr/local/bin
################################################################
# This is a test entry
echo `date +%F" "%T` "Startup worked" >> /root/mystartup.log
```

This version of the mystartup.sh file is intended only to verify that our service and the executable file both work as expected.

Note The comments in the files tell you where they need to be located.

Be sure to test this executable by running it from the command line. The first time you run this shell script, you should see a new file, /root/mystartup.log, with a time and date along with the text, "Startup worked". We create this log file and add lines to it every time the script is run as a simple test to ensure that our script is working.

Run the script a couple more times. Your results should be similar to these:

```
# mystartup.sh
# cat mystartup.log
2025-01-25 15:17:52 Startup worked
2025-01-25 15:18:04 Startup worked
2025-01-25 15:18:05 Startup worked
```

That is all we need to do to create the file that may eventually contain our local startup commands. Just add anything that needs to run at startup to this file.

Create the systemd Service

The service unit we will now create is a standard `systemd` service unit file.

EXPERIMENT 13-2: CREATING THE SYSTEMD SERVICE

This simple file is used only to run the `mystartup.sh` script at startup. Create a new file, /usr/local/lib/systemd/system/mystartup.service. I had to create this directory as it isn't created by default during the installation.

```
# mkdir -p /usr/local/lib/systemd/system/
```

Add the following contents to the file:

```
###############################################################
# mystartup.service
#
# This service unit is for testing my systemd startup service.
# By David Both
# Licensed under GPL V2 or later
#
###############################################################
# This program should be placed in the
# /usr/local/lib/systemd/system/ directory.
# Create a symlink to it from the /etc/systemd/system directory.
###############################################################

[Unit]
Description=Runs /usr/local/bin/mystartup.sh

[Service]
ExecStart=/usr/local/bin/mystartup.sh

[Install]
WantedBy=multi-user.target
```

This file does not need to be executable. This file could also be located in /etc/systemd/system, but as a local file it is better placed in the /usr/local/lib/systemd/system/ directory to meet the Linux FHS standards.

We should test the final service unit file before rebooting the Linux host for the final test. First, let's verify that systemd sees the service:

systemctl status mystartup
• mystartup.service - Runs /usr/local/bin/mystartup.sh
Loaded: loaded (/usr/local/lib/systemd/system/mystartup.service; linked; vendor preset: disabled)
Active: inactive (dead)
[root@testvm1 ~]#

This result tells us that the service is recognized by systemd. Now, let's start the service. Doing so will run the script but will not configure the new service to run at boot time.

systemctl start mystartup

Check the log file's contents to verify the new line was added.

Enable the New Service

All that is left is to enable the service so that it runs on startup.

> **EXPERIMENT 13-3: ENABLE THE SERVICE**

This command enables the service so that it is activated during each startup sequence, as well as immediately.

[root@testvm1 ~]# systemctl enable --now mystartup
Created symlink /etc/systemd/system/multi-user.target.wants/mystartup.service ➤ /usr/local/lib/systemd/system/mystartup.service.
[root@testvm1 ~]#

Check the temporary log we created to verify that the service started.

CHAPTER 13   REPLACING RC.LOCAL IN SYSTEMD

Revise mystartup.sh

The initial version of the mystartup.sh executable file redirects the output of its final line to the file, /root/mystartup.log, so that we can easily verify its functioning at all stages of development. It's now time to finalize the executable file because we no longer need the temporary log file we've been using.

EXPERIMENT 13-4: FINALIZE THE EXECUTABLE FILE

Before making any changes, let's look at the systemd journal for the entries pertaining to our new service.

```
# journalctl -u mystartup
Jan 25 15:55:00 testvm1.both.org systemd[1]: Started mystartup.service - Runs /usr/local/bin/mystartup.sh.
Jan 25 15:55:00 testvm1.both.org systemd[1]: mystartup.service: Deactivated successfully.
Jan 26 07:58:16 testvm1.both.org systemd[1]: Started mystartup.service - Runs /usr/local/bin/mystartup.sh.
Jan 26 07:58:16 testvm1.both.org systemd[1]: mystartup.service: Deactivated successfully.
```

This shows that systemd is recording each time the service starts and completes in the journal. All we need to do is check the journal.

Change the last line of the mystartup.sh file by removing the redirection that adds a line to our test log file each time it runs. The revised line will still print the message, but it won't be redirected. Instead, it will appear in the journal. This is a good and easy way to add entries to the journal when needed.

The revised line looks like this:

```
echo `date +%F` "%T` "Startup worked"
```

Now start the service and verify that the journal contains the appropriate entries.

```
# journalctl -u mystartup
Jan 25 15:55:00 testvm1.both.org systemd[1]: Started mystartup.service - Runs /usr/local/bin/mystartup.sh.
Jan 25 15:55:00 testvm1.both.org systemd[1]: mystartup.service: Deactivated successfully.
Jan 26 07:58:16 testvm1.both.org systemd[1]: Started mystartup.service - Runs /usr/local/bin/mystartup.sh.
Jan 26 07:58:16 testvm1.both.org systemd[1]: mystartup.service: Deactivated successfully.
Jan 26 08:31:07 testvm1.both.org systemd[1]: Started mystartup.service - Runs /usr/local/bin/mystartup.sh.
Jan 26 08:31:07 testvm1.both.org mystartup.sh[8933]: 2025-01-26 08:31:07 Startup worked
Jan 26 08:31:07 testvm1.both.org systemd[1]: mystartup.service: Deactivated successfully.
```

Final Test

The final test for our new service is to reboot the host and verify the appropriate entries were added to the systemd journal.

EXPERIMENT 13-5: FINAL TESTING

Reboot the Linux host and check the journal to ensure that the appropriate entries were added.

```
# systemctl status mystartup
o mystartup.service - Runs /usr/local/bin/mystartup.sh
Loaded: loaded (/usr/local/lib/systemd/system/mystartup.service; enabled; preset: disabled)
```

CHAPTER 13   REPLACING RC.LOCAL IN SYSTEMD

Drop-In: /usr/lib/systemd/system/service.d
└─10-timeout-abort.conf, 50-keep-warm.conf
Active: inactive (dead) since Sun 2025-01-26 14:01:56
EST; 20s ago
Duration: 632ms
Invocation: e8c6bdee1b9043c68a21efd1345bef08
Process: 1050 ExecStart=/usr/local/bin/mystartup.sh
(code=exited, status=0/SUCCESS)
Main PID: 1050 (code=exited, status=0/SUCCESS)
Mem peak: 1.2M
CPU: 10ms

Jan 26 14:01:56 testvm1.both.org systemd[1]: Started
mystartup.service - Runs /usr/local/bin/mystartup.sh.
Jan 26 14:01:56 testvm1.both.org mystartup.sh[1050]:
2025-01-26 14:01:56 Startup worked
Jan 26 14:01:56 testvm1.both.org systemd[1]: mystartup.
service: Deactivated successfully.

journalctl -u mystartup
Jan 25 15:55:00 testvm1.both.org systemd[1]: Started
mystartup.service - Runs /usr/local/bin/mystartup.sh.
Jan 25 15:55:00 testvm1.both.org systemd[1]: mystartup.
service: Deactivated successfully.
Jan 26 07:58:16 testvm1.both.org systemd[1]: Started
mystartup.service - Runs /usr/local/bin/mystartup.sh.
Jan 26 07:58:16 testvm1.both.org systemd[1]: mystartup.
service: Deactivated successfully.
Jan 26 08:31:07 testvm1.both.org systemd[1]: Started
mystartup.service - Runs /usr/local/bin/mystartup.sh.
Jan 26 08:31:07 testvm1.both.org mystartup.sh[8933]:
2025-01-26 08:31:07 Startup worked

```
Jan 26 08:31:07 testvm1.both.org systemd[1]: mystartup.
service: Deactivated successfully.
-- Boot 1dafb37f3cfe468990a7a61e18573865 --
Jan 26 14:01:56 testvm1.both.org systemd[1]: Started
mystartup.service - Runs /usr/local/bin/mystartup.sh.
Jan 26 14:01:56 testvm1.both.org mystartup.sh[1050]:
2025-01-26 14:01:56 Startup worked
Jan 26 14:01:56 testvm1.both.org systemd[1]: mystartup.
service: Deactivated successfully.
```

Notice the entry indicating that a boot has taken place.

A Temporary Option

There is a `systemd` option for continuing to use rc.local for a little longer, the `rc-local` service. It is possible to continue support for the old rc.local file by enabling the service with the command **systemctl enable rc-local**. The commands in the rc.local file will run at the next boot. Of course, you can use **systemctl enable --now rc-local** to run rc.local immediately without performing a reboot.

However, it is still true that rc.local is obsolete. The man page for `systemd-rc-local-generator` states this explicitly:

> *Support for /etc/rc.local is provided for compatibility with specific System V systems only. However, it is strongly recommended to avoid making use of this script today, and instead provide proper unit files with appropriate dependencies for any scripts to run during the boot process.*

As a result, it is wise to use this option as a temporary solution while migrating the contents of your rc.local file to one or more systemd services.

CHAPTER 13   REPLACING RC.LOCAL IN SYSTEMD

Cleanup

Let's do just a bit of cleanup before moving on. It's not necessary to delete the new files you've created, so you can use them as templates. Just disable the service unit you created so it won't run every time you reboot the test system.

Summary

The rc.local file is obsolete, and all temporary support for it will soon be withdrawn completely. The Bash shell script and systemd service we have created for this runs once at startup and then exits. It does not remain in memory as a daemon because it was not designed to do so. The procedure we used to create our local startup service can also be used to create any new service for `systemd`. It's not that hard once we know how to do it.

We also saw that a service that is designed to run at startup can also be triggered at the command line using **systemctl**, which provides a less intrusive way to test it.

All support for rc.local will be removed in the relatively near future, so understanding how to replace it with systemd tools is important.

Exercises

Complete the following exercises to finish this chapter:

1. What are your use cases for running programs during system startup? It's OK if you don't have any now, but you might think of some later.

2. Describe and explain the content of the service unit file created in this chapter.

3. Why did we locate the service unit file in the directory we did?

4. Design and perform an experiment to determine whether the service unit you created in this chapter can execute two or more commands and other external executables such as locally created scripts.

CHAPTER 14

Getting More Out of the Journal

Objectives

After reading this chapter, you will be able to

- Narrow down the results of journal searches using various options of the journalctl command
- Extract relevant data from the systemd journal to use in solving problems

Introduction

We've already seen some uses of the journal in previous chapters. In this chapter, we'll explore the systemd journal and more ways to narrow down the results of the journalctl command to further help locate and identify problems—or just to satisfy your curiosity about what's going on in your Linux host.

CHAPTER 14   GETTING MORE OUT OF THE JOURNAL

Options to Narrow Search Results

The `journalctl(1)` man page lists all the options that can be used to narrow searches. Table 14-1 summarizes some of the options I use most frequently. Most of these options can be used in various combinations to further narrow a search. Refer to Chapter 7 for details on creating and testing timestamps, as well as important tips to help in narrowing down the results of a search.

Table 14-1. *Journal options that help narrow a search*

Option	Description
`--list-boots`	This displays a timestamped list of boots. The information can be used to show journal entries only for a particular boot.
`-b [offset| boot ID]`	Specifies which boot to display information for. It includes all journal entries from that boot through shutdown or reboot.
`--facility= [facility name]`	This specifies the facility names as they're known to syslog. Use `--facility=help` to list the valid facility names.
`-k, --dmesg`	These display only kernel messages and are equivalent to using the `dmesg` command.
`-S, --since [timestamp]`	These show all journal entries since (after) the specified time. They can be used with `--until` to display an arbitrary range of time. Fuzzy times such as "yesterday" and "2 hours ago"—with quotes—are also allowed.
`-u [unit name]`	The `-u` option allows you to select specific units to examine. You can use a unit name or a pattern for matching. This option can be used multiple times to match multiple units or patterns.
`-U, --until [timestamp]`	These show all journal entries until (prior to) the specified time. They can be used with `--since` to display an arbitrary range of time. Fuzzy times such as "yesterday" and "2 hours ago"—with quotes—are also allowed.

CHAPTER 14   GETTING MORE OUT OF THE JOURNAL

The **journalctl** command is designed to extract usable information from the systemd journals using powerful and flexible criteria for identifying the desired data.

It's not usually necessary or even desirable to list all the journal entries and manually search through them. Sometimes I look for entries related to a specific service, and in other instances I look for entries that happened at specific times. The **journalctl** command provides powerful options that allow you to see only the data you are interested in finding.

Let's explore a few more of these options, especially the ones that I find most helpful.

EXPERIMENT 14-1: NARROWING THE SEARCH

Start with the `--list-boots` option, which lists all the boots during the time period for which journal entries exist. Note that the `journalctl.conf` file may specify that journal entries are discarded after they reach a certain age or after the storage device (HDD/SSD) space taken by the journals reaches a specified maximum amount.

```
# journalctl --list-boots
IDX BOOT ID                              FIRST
ENTRY                 LAST ENTRY
-11 25efa06423ef47bbbe67a067c012e186 Wed 2025-01-29
05:22:09 EST Wed 2025-01-29 10:29:23 EST
-10 f171387baed24cceb96a29036ad58907 Wed 2025-01-29
05:30:30 EST Wed 2025-01-29 12:12:51 EST
 -9 de8d4f0972e348718efbcadcad795e1d Wed 2025-01-29
12:13:11 EST Wed 2025-01-29 21:14:12 EST
 -8 2faa4a8969884412b07d466d4a2a3c22 Wed 2025-01-29
21:14:32 EST Wed 2025-01-29 21:15:06 EST
 -7 75cdc4bc316147a1bc154a9fbfd358bf Wed 2025-01-29
16:16:19 EST Thu 2025-01-30 09:00:43 EST
```

373

```
-6 92a9a9e7872d4644aa3fc4cd0b4373b7 Thu 2025-01-30
09:00:59 EST Fri 2025-01-31 08:05:23 EST
-5 16d5be20d5974f81af174beb8e5936a3 Fri 2025-01-31
03:19:26 EST Fri 2025-01-31 10:04:41 EST
-4 1d43891f271c4310b0b63b17d7c9dc31 Fri 2025-01-31
10:05:01 EST Fri 2025-01-31 10:30:15 EST
-3 dcc5cd008dc64cbaa5a5ad414be7db1f Fri 2025-01-31
16:16:58 EST Fri 2025-01-31 21:21:35 EST
-2 0dc99b59d8e9467d97552d8e8451a12b Fri 2025-01-31
21:21:53 EST Fri 2025-01-31 21:30:06 EST
-1 638be7f2cd034ab998a79c23a866d9c9 Fri 2025-01-31
21:30:26 EST Fri 2025-01-31 21:31:45 EST
 0 51ddf40f75bd42bcb0d8631e6bdabf47 Fri 2025-01-31
16:33:10 EST Sat 2025-02-01 08:20:25 EST
```

The Index and ID for the most recent boot appears at the bottom of the list. The ID is the long, random hex number.

You can use this data to view the journals for a specific boot. This can also be specified using the boot offset number in the left-most column or the boot ID in the second column. This command displays the journal for the boot instance with the offset of -2—the second previous boot from the current one.

```
# journalctl -b -2
Jan 31 21:21:53 testvm1.both.org kernel: Linux version
6.12.11-200.fc41.x86_64 (mockbuild@8c05b49e2e66460390f7ce4
d04d4f464) (gcc (GCC) 14.2.1 20250110 (Red Hat>
Jan 31 21:21:53 testvm1.both.org kernel: Command line:
BOOT_IMAGE=(hd0,gpt2)/vmlinuz-6.12.11-200.fc41.x86_64
root=/dev/mapper/vg01-root ro rd.lvm.lv=vg01/root >
Jan 31 21:21:53 testvm1.both.org kernel: BIOS-provided
physical RAM map:
```

CHAPTER 14   GETTING MORE OUT OF THE JOURNAL

```
Jan 31 21:21:53 testvm1.both.org kernel: BIOS-e820: [mem
0x0000000000000000-0x000000000009fbff] usable
Jan 31 21:21:53 testvm1.both.org kernel: BIOS-e820: [mem
0x000000000009fc00-
<SNIP>
```

Or you could use the UUID for the desired boot. The offset numbers change after each boot, but the UUID does not.

journalctl -b   0dc99b59d8e9467d97552d8e8451a12b

The -u option allows you to select specific units to examine. You can use a unit name or a pattern for matching, and you can use this option multiple times to match multiple units or patterns. In this example, I used it in combination with -b to show chronyd journal entries for the current boot:

journalctl -u chronyd -b
```
Jan 31 16:33:23 testvm1.both.org systemd[1]: Starting
chronyd.service - NTP client/server...
Jan 31 21:33:25 testvm1.both.org chronyd[1166]: chronyd
version 4.6.1 starting (+CMDMON +NTP +REFCLOCK +RTC
+PRIVDROP +SCFILTER +SIGND +ASYNCDNS +NTS +SECHASH >
Jan 31 21:33:25 testvm1.both.org chronyd[1166]: Using
leap second list /usr/share/zoneinfo/leap-seconds.list
Jan 31 21:33:25 testvm1.both.org chronyd[1166]: Frequency
-0.417 +/- 0.545 ppm read from /var/lib/chrony/drift
Jan 31 21:33:25 testvm1.both.org chronyd[1166]: Loaded
seccomp filter (level 2)
Jan 31 21:33:25 testvm1.both.org systemd[1]: Started
chronyd.service - NTP client/server.
Jan 31 21:33:28 testvm1.both.org chronyd[1166]: Could not
add source 192.168.0.52 : Already in use
Jan 31 21:33:33 testvm1.both.org chronyd[1166]: Selected
source 192.168.0.52 (yorktown.both.org)
```

CHAPTER 14   GETTING MORE OUT OF THE JOURNAL

```
Jan 31 21:33:33 testvm1.both.org chronyd[1166]: System
clock TAI offset set to 37 seconds
Feb 01 08:07:25 testvm1.both.org chronyd[1166]: Could not
add source 192.168.0.52 : Already in use
```

Suppose you want to look at events that were recorded between two arbitrary times. You can also use -S or --since and -U or --until to specify the beginning and ending times. The following command displays journal entries starting at 15:36:00 on July 24, 2020, through the current time:

journalctl -S "2025-01-24 15:36:00"

And this command displays all journal entries starting at 15:36:00 on January 24, 2025, until 16:00:00 on January 25:

journalctl -S "2025-01-24 15:36:00" -U "2020-01-25 16:00:00"

This command combines -S, -U, and -u to give journal entries for the NetworkManager service unit starting at 15:36:00 on July 24, 2020, until 16:00:00 on July 25:

journalctl -S "2020-07-24 15:36:00" -U "2020-07-25 16:00:00" -u NetworkManager

Some syslog facilities, such as cron, auth, mail, daemon, user, and more, can be viewed with the --facility option. You can use --facility=help to list the available facilities. In this example, the mail facility is not the Sendmail service that would be used for an email service, but the local client used by Linux to send email to root as event notifications. Sendmail actually has two parts: the server, which (for Fedora and related distributions) is not installed by default, and the client, which is always installed so that it can be used to deliver system emails to local recipients, especially root:

journalctl --facility=mail

A Troubleshooting Example

I didn't originally consider systemd to be a troubleshooting tool, but when I encountered a problem on my web server, my growing knowledge of systemd and some of its features helped me locate and circumvent the problem.

Some of you will say that systemd itself is the cause of this problem, and, based on what I know now, I might agree with you. However, I had similar types of problems with SystemV. No software is perfect, and neither systemd nor SystemV is an exception, but systemd provides far more information for problem-solving than SystemV ever offered. I find that important and a major factor in why I find systemd to be superior to SystemV. So let's see how that works with a problem I encountered a few years ago.

Determining the Problem

The problem was that my server, yorktown, which provides DNS, DHCP, NTP, HTTPD, and Sendmail email services for my home office network, failed to start the Apache HTTPD daemon during normal startup. I had to start it manually after I realized that it was not running. The problem had been going on for some time, and I finally got around to trying to fix it.

The first step to finding the source of this problem was to determine the HTTPD service's status.

```
# systemctl status httpd
• httpd.service - The Apache HTTP Server
   Loaded: loaded (/usr/lib/systemd/system/httpd.service;
           enabled; vendor preset: disabled)
   Active: failed (Result: exit-code) since Thu 2020-04-16
           11:54:37 EDT; 15min ago
     Docs: man:httpd.service(8)
```

CHAPTER 14 GETTING MORE OUT OF THE JOURNAL

```
   Process: 1101 ExecStart=/usr/sbin/httpd $OPTIONS -DFOREGROUND
            (code=exited, status=1/FAILURE)
  Main PID: 1101 (code=exited, status=1/FAILURE)
    Status: "Reading configuration..."
       CPU: 60ms
```

Apr 16 11:54:35 yorktown.both.org systemd[1]: Starting The Apache HTTP Server...
Apr 16 11:54:37 yorktown.both.org httpd[1101]: (99)Cannot assign requested address: AH00072: make_sock: could not bind to address 192.168.0.52:80
Apr 16 11:54:37 yorktown.both.org httpd[1101]: no listening sockets available, shutting down
Apr 16 11:54:37 yorktown.both.org httpd[1101]: AH00015: Unable to open logs
Apr 16 11:54:37 yorktown.both.org systemd[1]: httpd.service: Main process exited, code=exited, status=1/FAILURE
Apr 16 11:54:37 yorktown.both.org systemd[1]: httpd.service: Failed with result 'exit-code'.
Apr 16 11:54:37 yorktown.both.org systemd[1]: Failed to start The Apache HTTP Server.

This status information is one of the systemd features that I find much more useful than anything SystemV offers. The amount of helpful information here leads me easily to a logical conclusion that takes me in the right direction. All I ever got from the old **chkconfig** command is whether or not the service is running and the process ID (PID) if it is. That is not very helpful.

The key entry in this status report shows that HTTPD cannot bind to the IP address, which means it cannot accept incoming requests. This indicates that the network is not starting fast enough to be ready for the HTTPD service to bind to the IP address because the IP address has not yet

CHAPTER 14   GETTING MORE OUT OF THE JOURNAL

been set. This is not supposed to happen, so I explored my network service systemd startup configuration files; all appeared to be correct with the right "after" and "requires" statements. Here is the **/lib/systemd/system/httpd.service** file from my server:

```
# Modifying this file in-place is not recommended, because changes
# will be overwritten during package upgrades. To customize the
# behaviour, run "systemctl edit httpd" to create an override unit.

# For example, to pass additional options (such as -D definitions) to
# the httpd binary at startup, create an override unit (as is done by
# systemctl edit) and enter the following:
#       [Service]
#       Environment=OPTIONS=-DMY_DEFINE
[Unit]
Description=The Apache HTTP Server
Wants=httpd-init.service
After=network.target remote-fs.target nss-lookup.target httpd-init.service
Documentation=man:httpd.service(8)

[Service]
Type=notify
Environment=LANG=C

ExecStart=/usr/sbin/httpd $OPTIONS -DFOREGROUND
ExecReload=/usr/sbin/httpd $OPTIONS -k graceful
# Send SIGWINCH for graceful stop
```

```
KillSignal=SIGWINCH
KillMode=mixed
PrivateTmp=true

[Install]
WantedBy=multi-user.target
```

The **httpd.service** unit file explicitly specifies that it should load after the **network.target** and the **httpd-init.service** (among others). I tried to find all of these services using the **systemctl list-units** command and searching for them in the resulting data stream. All were present and should have ensured that the HTTPD service did not load before the network IP address was set.

First Solution

A bit of searching on the Internet confirmed that others had encountered similar problems with HTTPD and other services. This appears to happen because one of the required services indicates to systemd that it has finished its startup—but it actually spins off a child process that has not finished. After a bit more searching, I came up with a circumvention.

I couldn't figure out why the IP address was taking so long to be assigned to the network interface card. So, I thought that if I could delay the start of the HTTPD service by a reasonable amount of time, the IP address would be assigned by that time.

Fortunately, the **/lib/systemd/system/httpd.service** file above provides some direction. Although it says not to alter it, it does indicate how to proceed: use the command **systemctl edit httpd**, which automatically creates a new file (**/etc/systemd/system/httpd.service.d/override.conf**) and opens the GNU Nano[1] editor. If you are not familiar with Nano, be sure to look at the hints at the bottom of the Nano interface.

---

[1] Nano Editor home page, https://www.nano-editor.org/

CHAPTER 14 GETTING MORE OUT OF THE JOURNAL

I added the following text to the new file and saved it:

```
# Trying to delay the startup of httpd so that the network is
# fully up and running so that httpd can bind to the correct
# IP address
#
# By David Both, 2020-04-16

[Service]
ExecStartPre=/bin/sleep 30
```

The **[Service]** section of this override file contains a single line that delays the start of the HTTPD service by 30 seconds. The following status command shows the service status during the wait time:

```
# systemctl status httpd
• httpd.service - The Apache HTTP Server
    Loaded: loaded (/usr/lib/systemd/system/httpd.service;
            enabled; vendor preset: disabled)
   Drop-In: /etc/systemd/system/httpd.service.d
            └─override.conf
            /usr/lib/systemd/system/httpd.service.d
            └─php-fpm.conf
    Active: activating (start-pre) since Thu 2020-04-16 12:14:29
            EDT; 28s ago
      Docs: man:httpd.service(8)
 Cntrl PID: 1102 (sleep)
     Tasks: 1 (limit: 38363)
    Memory: 260.0K
       CPU: 2ms
    CGroup: /system.slice/httpd.service
            └─1102 /bin/sleep 30
```

CHAPTER 14   GETTING MORE OUT OF THE JOURNAL

```
Apr 16 12:14:29 yorktown.both.org systemd[1]: Starting The
Apache HTTP Server...
Apr 16 12:15:01 yorktown.both.org systemd[1]: Started The
Apache HTTP Server.
[root@yorktown ~]#
```

And this command shows the status of the HTTPD service after the 30-second delay expires. The service is up and running correctly.

```
# systemctl status httpd
● httpd.service - The Apache HTTP Server
   Loaded: loaded (/usr/lib/systemd/system/httpd.service;
           enabled; vendor preset: disabled)
  Drop-In: /etc/systemd/system/httpd.service.d
           └─override.conf
           /usr/lib/systemd/system/httpd.service.d
           └─php-fpm.conf
   Active: active (running) since Thu 2020-04-16 12:15:01 EDT;
           1min 18s ago
     Docs: man:httpd.service(8)
  Process: 1102 ExecStartPre=/bin/sleep 30 (code=exited,
           status=0/SUCCESS)
 Main PID: 1567 (httpd)
   Status: "Total requests: 0; Idle/Busy workers
           100/0;Requests/sec: 0; Bytes served/sec:    0 B/sec"
    Tasks: 213 (limit: 38363)
   Memory: 21.8M
      CPU: 82ms
   CGroup: /system.slice/httpd.service
           ├─1567 /usr/sbin/httpd -DFOREGROUND
           ├─1569 /usr/sbin/httpd -DFOREGROUND
           ├─1570 /usr/sbin/httpd -DFOREGROUND
```

```
         ├─1571 /usr/sbin/httpd -DFOREGROUND
         └─1572 /usr/sbin/httpd -DFOREGROUND
Apr 16 12:14:29 yorktown.both.org systemd[1]: Starting The
Apache HTTP Server...
Apr 16 12:15:01 yorktown.both.org systemd[1]: Started The
Apache HTTP Server.
```

I could have experimented to see if a shorter delay would work as well, but my system is not that critical, so I decided not to. It works reliably as it is, so I am happy. Because I gathered all this information, I reported it to Red Hat Bugzilla as Bug 1825554. I believe that it is much more productive to report bugs than it is to complain about them. It's also a great way to contribute to open source.

The Better Solution

A couple days after reporting this as a bug, I received a response indicating that systemd is just the manager, and if HTTPD needs to be ordered after some requirements are met, it needs to be expressed in the unit file. The response pointed me to the **httpd.service** man page. I wish I had found this earlier because it is a better solution than the one I came up with. This solution is explicitly targeted to the prerequisite target unit rather than a somewhat random delay.

Here's the relevant excerpt from the **httpd.service** man page:[2]

> **Starting the service at boot time**
>
> The httpd.service and httpd.socket units are *disabled* by default. To start the httpd service at boot time, run: **systemctl enable httpd.service**. In the

---

[2] The httpd.service man page, `https://www.mankier.com/8/httpd.service#Description-Starting_the_service_at_boot_time`

default configuration, the httpd daemon will accept connections on port 80 (and, if mod_ssl is installed, TLS connections on port 443) for any configured IPv4 or IPv6 address.

If httpd is configured to depend on any specific IP address (for example, with a "Listen" directive) which may only become available during start-up, or if httpd depends on other services (such as a database daemon), the service *must* be configured to ensure correct start-up ordering.

For example, to ensure httpd is only running after all configured network interfaces are configured, create a drop-in file (as described above) with the following section:

```
[Unit]
After=network-online.target
Wants=network-online.target
```

I still think this is a bug because it is quite common—at least in my experience—to use a **Listen** directive in the **httpd.conf** configuration file. I have always used **Listen** directives, even on hosts with only a single IP address, and it is clearly necessary on hosts with multiple network interface cards (NICs) and Internet protocol (IP) addresses. Adding the lines above to the **httpd.service** default file would not cause problems for configurations that do not use a **Listen** directive and would prevent this problem for those that do.

In the meantime, I use the suggested solution.

Note Although the bug I reported was closed as "notabug," the problem appears to have been resolved.

Summary

In this chapter, we looked at using the `journalctl` command to extract various types of data from the systemd journal in different formats. It also explored managing journal files and how to add entries to the log from commands and scripts.

The systemd journal system provides a significant amount of metadata and context for entries compared to the old syslogd program. This additional data and the context available from the other journal entries around the time of an incident can help the SysAdmin locate and resolve problems much faster than having to search multiple syslog files.

The `journalctl` command meets the Unix philosophy that programs should do one thing and do it well. The only thing `journalctl` does is extract data from the journal and provide many options for selecting and formatting that data. At about 85K, it is not very big. Of course, that does not include shared libraries, but those are, by definition, shared with other programs.

We explored a problem I had with starting the Apache HTTPD service on my server. It leads you through the problem determination steps I took and shows how I used systemd to assist. I also covered the circumvention I implemented using systemd and the better solution that followed from my bug report.

You should now have enough information to use the systemd journal more effectively in problem determination. If you would like to know more than what I've covered here, look in the man pages for `journalctl` and `systemd-cat`.

Exercises

Complete the following exercises to finish this chapter:

1. What advantages do the systemd journals provide over the syslog log files?

2. Display the contents of the journal from the fourth previous boot.

3. What index number is the fourth previous boot?

4. View all NetworkManager journal entries in the current boot.

5. How long after boot did NetworkManager finish starting?

6. What network interface devices does NetworkManager see?

7. How many journal files are currently kept by the journal service?

8. If you're using a Linux host on which it's safe to do so—a non-production system—manually rotate the journal files.

CHAPTER 15

Analyzing systemd Startup and Configuration

Objectives

In this chapter, you will learn to

- Use systemd tools to analyze the Linux startup sequence
- Determine the length of time spent in BIOS boot before Linux startup
- Determine which services and systemd units are taking the most time during startup
- Create and interpret graphs to analyze the Linux boot and startup in detail
- Verify the correct syntax of systemd unit files
- Analyze the security status of systemd service unit files

CHAPTER 15   ANALYZING SYSTEMD STARTUP AND CONFIGURATION

Overview

One of our jobs as SysAdmins is to analyze the performance of the systems we support and to find and resolve problems that cause poor performance and long startup times. We also need to check other aspects of systemd configuration and usage.

The systemd system provides the **systemd-analyze** tool that can help us discover performance and other important systemd information. We have already used systemd-analyze earlier in this chapter to analyze timestamps and time spans for use in systemd timers, but it has other interesting and valuable uses as well. We will explore some of those uses in this section.

Linux Startup

The Linux startup sequence is a good place to begin our explorations because many of the functions provided by the systemd-analyze tool are targeted at startup. Before we begin, however, it is important to understand the difference between boot and startup, so I will say it again, here. The boot sequence starts with the BIOS power-on self-test (POST) and ends when the kernel is finished loading and takes control of the host system, which is the beginning of startup and the point at which the systemd journal begins.

The results in this section are all from my primary workstation which is much more interesting than those from a virtual machine. This workstation consists of an ASUS TUF X299 Mark 2 motherboard, an Intel i9-7960X CPU with 16 cores and 32 CPUs (threads), and 64GB of RAM.

There are several options we can use to examine the startup sequence. The simplest form of the **systemd-analyze** command displays a simple overview of the amount of time spent in each of the main sections of startup, the kernel startup, loading and running initrd which is a temporary system image that is used to initialize some hardware and mount the / (root) filesystem, and user space in which all of the programs and daemons required to bring the host up to a usable state are loaded. If no sub-command is passed to the command, **systemd-analyze time** is implied.

Basic Analysis

As mentioned above, I performed this experiment on my primary workstation which provides a more realistic view of a physical host. However, you should perform this experiment on your VM.

Unless otherwise noted, all commands in this chapter can be executed by a non-root user.

EXPERIMENT 15-1: USING SYSTEMD-ANALYZE

This command performs a very basic analysis that looks at the overall times for each stage of boot and startup. This can be done as a non-root user.

```
$ systemd-analyze
Startup finished in 53.951s (firmware) + 6.606s (loader) + 2.061s (kernel) + 5.956s (initrd) + 8.883s (userspace) = 1min 17.458s
graphical.target reached after 8.850s in userspace.
```

The most notable data in this output is the amount of time spent in firmware (UEFI BIOS) at almost 57 seconds. None of my other physical systems take anywhere near as long. My System76 Oryx Pro laptop only spends 7.216 seconds in BIOS, and all of my home-built systems take a bit less than 10 seconds. After some online searches, I found that this ASUS motherboard is known for its inordinately long BIOS boot time.

This is exactly the type of information that tools like this are intended to provide.

Be aware that the firmware data is not shown for all hosts. I have a 13-year-old Dell Optiplex 755 for which `systemd-analyze` does not display BIOS times. My unscientific experiments lead me to the hypothesis that BIOS data is shown for Intel processors only at gen 9 or above. But that could be incorrect. I have no AMD processors to check.

This overview of the boot startup process is interesting and provides good though limited information, but there is much more information available about startup itself.

The Blame Game

As a SysAdmin, I always want to determine the true culprit, the root cause, of a problem. That's the only way we can really be sure of preventing that same problem in the future.

EXPERIMENT 15-2: ASSIGNING BLAME

We can use **systemd-analyze blame** to discover which systemd units take the most time to initialize. This provides much more detail and enables us to see what portions of the startup process take the most time.

The results are displayed in order by the amount of time they took to initialize from highest to lowest. You can do this as a non-root user.

```
$ systemd-analyze blame
      2min 30.408s fstrim.service
     33.971s vboxdrv.service
      5.832s dev-disk-by\x2dpartuuid-4212eea1\x2d96d0\
      x2dc341\x2da698\x2d18a0752f034f.device
      5.832s dev-disk-by\x2ddiskseq-1\x2dpart1.device
      5.832s dev-sda1.device
<SNIP - removed lots of entries with increasingly
small times>
```

Because many of these services start in parallel, the numbers from this command may add up to equal significantly more than the total given by systemd-analyze time for everything that comes after the BIOS. The number of units that can truly start in parallel is determined by the number of CPUs in your host.

The data from this command can provide indicators of which services we might look at to improve boot times. Services that are not used can be disabled. The fstrim and vboxdrv services take a large amount of time during the startup sequence on my workstation. You will see different results for your VMs. If you have access to a physical host that runs a Linux distribution with systemd, try this to see what that looks like.

Critical Chain

Like the critical path in project management, the critical chain shows the time-critical chain of events that took place during startup. These are the systemd units you want to look at if the startup is slow—they are the ones that would be causing the delays. This tool does not display all units that started, only those in this critical chain of events.

Tip On a terminal that supports color—which most of today's terminal emulators do—the units that cause delays are highlighted in red.

EXPERIMENT 15-3: DETERMINE THE CRITICAL CHAIN

I have used this tool on two of my physical hosts and on my own StudentVM1 host, so we can compare them. The first is from my primary workstation.

```
$ systemd-analyze critical-chain
```
The time when unit became active or started is printed after the "@" character.
The time the unit took to start is printed after the "+" character.

```
graphical.target @8.850s
└─multi-user.target @8.849s
  └─vboxweb-service.service @8.798s +38ms
    └─network-online.target @8.776s
      └─NetworkManager-wait-online.service @4.932s +3.843s
        └─NetworkManager.service @4.868s +39ms
          └─network-pre.target @4.850s
            └─dkms.service @3.438s +1.411s
              └─basic.target @3.409s
                └─dbus-broker.service @3.348s +55ms
                  └─dbus.socket @3.309s
                    └─sysinit.target @3.267s
                      └─systemd-binfmt.service
                         @2.814s +452ms
```

CHAPTER 15   ANALYZING SYSTEMD STARTUP AND CONFIGURATION

```
      └─proc-sys-fs-binfmt_misc.mount
        @3.232s +21ms
         └─proc-sys-fs-binfmt_misc.
           automount @967ms
```

The numbers with "@" preceding them show the absolute number of seconds since startup began at which the unit becomes active. The numbers preceded by "+" show the amount of time it takes for the unit to start.

Among others, the vboxweb-service.service was highlighted as a blockage on my workstation. If it were not needed, I could disable it and speed up the overall start time. However, that doesn't mean that another service won't take its place with a startup that is only slightly faster. I live with it because I need VirtualBox so I can run the VMs I use to create the experiments for this course and other testing.

Here are the results from my System76 Oryx Pro laptop:

$ **systemd-analyze critical-chain**
```
The time when unit became active or started is printed after
the "@" character.
The time the unit took to start is printed after the "+"
character.

graphical.target @36.899s
└─multi-user.target @36.899s
  └─vboxweb-service.service @36.859s +38ms
    └─vboxdrv.service @2.865s +33.971s
      └─basic.target @2.647s
        └─dbus-broker.service @2.584s +60ms
          └─dbus.socket @2.564s
            └─sysinit.target @2.544s
              └─systemd-resolved.service @2.384s +158ms
                └─systemd-tmpfiles-setup.service
                  @2.290s +51ms
```

393

CHAPTER 15   ANALYZING SYSTEMD STARTUP AND CONFIGURATION

```
            └─systemd-journal-flush.service
              @2.071s +193ms
              └─var.mount @1.960s +52ms
                └─systemd-fsck@dev-mapper-vg01\x2dvar.
                  service @1.680s +171ms
                  └─dev-mapper-vg01\x2dvar.
                    device @1.645s
```

In this example, the vboxdrv.service and vboxweb-service.service both take a good bit of startup time.

This next example is for another VM host. Compare this output to your VM and see how much it differs.

$ **systemd-analyze critical-chain**
The time when unit became active or started is printed after the "@" character.
The time the unit took to start is printed after the "+" character.

```
graphical.target @56.173s
└─multi-user.target @56.173s
  └─plymouth-quit-wait.service @51.543s +4.628s
    └─systemd-user-sessions.service @51.364s +93ms
      └─remote-fs.target @51.347s
        └─remote-fs-pre.target @51.347s
          └─nfs-client.target @42.954s
            └─gssproxy.service @41.430s +1.522s
              └─network.target @41.414s
                └─NetworkManager.service @40.803s +609ms
                  └─network-pre.target @40.793s
                    └─firewalld.service @24.867s +15.925s
                      └─polkit.service @19.081s +5.568s
                        └─basic.target @18.909s
```

CHAPTER 15   ANALYZING SYSTEMD STARTUP AND CONFIGURATION

```
└─dbus-broker.service
  @17.886s +1.015s
  └─dbus.socket @17.871s
    └─sysinit.target @17.852s
      └─systemd-resolved.service
        @16.872s +978ms
        └─systemd-tmpfiles-setup.
          service @16.265s +272ms
          └─systemd-journal-
            flush.service
            @13.764s +2.493s
            └─var.mount
              @13.013s +593ms
              └─systemd-fsck@dev-
                mapper-fedora_
                studentvm1\
                x2dvar.service
                @11.077s +1.885s
                └─local-fs-pre.
                  target @11.056s
                  └─lvm2-monitor.
                    service
                    @5.803s
                    +5.252s
                    └─dm-event.
                      socket
                      @5.749s
                      └─system.slice
                        └─-.slice
```

I was surprised at the long chain here, but it's probably because there was no single service that took up a lot of time, like VirtualBox, and which hid the others, thus removing them from the critical chain.

CHAPTER 15   ANALYZING SYSTEMD STARTUP AND CONFIGURATION

System State

You may sometimes need to determine the current state of the system. The **systemd-analyze dump** command dumps a massive amount of data about the current system state.

EXPERIMENT 15-4: ANALYZE THE STATE OF THE SYSTEM

This starts with a list of the primary boot timestamps and a list of each systemd unit and a complete description of the state of each.

```
$ systemd-analyze dump
Manager: systemd 253 (253.2-1.fc38)
Features: +PAM +AUDIT +SELINUX -APPARMOR +IMA +SMACK +SECCOMP
-GCRYPT +GNUTLS +OPENSSL +ACL +BLKID +CURL +ELFUTILS +FIDO2
+IDN2 -IDN ->
Timestamp firmware: 1min 557.292ms
Timestamp loader: 6.606226s
Timestamp kernel: Sun 2023-04-30 17:09:49 EDT
Timestamp initrd: Sun 2023-04-30 17:09:51 EDT
Timestamp userspace: Sun 2023-04-30 17:09:57 EDT
Timestamp finish: Sun 2023-04-30 21:10:06 EDT
Timestamp security-start: Sun 2023-04-30 17:09:57 EDT
Timestamp security-finish: Sun 2023-04-30 17:09:57 EDT
Timestamp generators-start: Sun 2023-04-30 21:09:57 EDT
Timestamp generators-finish: Sun 2023-04-30 21:09:57 EDT
Timestamp units-load-start: Sun 2023-04-30 21:09:57 EDT
Timestamp units-load-finish: Sun 2023-04-30 21:09:58 EDT
Timestamp units-load: Tue 2023-05-02 13:30:41 EDT
Timestamp initrd-security-start: Sun 2023-04-30 17:09:51 EDT
Timestamp initrd-security-finish: Sun 2023-04-30 17:09:51 EDT
Timestamp initrd-generators-start: Sun 2023-04-30
```

CHAPTER 15   ANALYZING SYSTEMD STARTUP AND CONFIGURATION

```
17:09:51 EDT
Timestamp initrd-generators-finish: Sun 2023-04-30
17:09:51 EDT
Timestamp initrd-units-load-start: Sun 2023-04-30
17:09:51 EDT
Timestamp initrd-units-load-finish: Sun 2023-04-30
17:09:51 EDT
-> Unit logwatch.service:
        Description: Log analyzer and reporter
        Instance: n/a
        Unit Load State: loaded
        Unit Active State: inactive
        State Change Timestamp: Wed 2023-05-03 00:00:20 EDT
        Inactive Exit Timestamp: Wed 2023-05-03 00:00:05 EDT
        Active Enter Timestamp: n/a
        Active Exit Timestamp: n/a
<SNIP - Deleted a bazillion lines of output>
```

On my main workstation, this command generated a stream of 59,859 lines and about 1.75MB. This command is very fast, so you don't need to wait for the results. It does call the default pager, so you can page through the data. I do like the wealth of detail provided for the various connected devices such as storage. Each systemd unit has a section with details such as modes for various runtime, cache, and log directories, the command line used to start the unit, the PID, and the start timestamp, as well as memory and file limits.

There's another option, systemd-analyze --user dump, that displays information about the internal state of the user manager. systemd user instances are instances of systemd that are used to manage and control the resources for the hierarchy of processes belonging to each user. The processes for each user are part of a control group.

CHAPTER 15   ANALYZING SYSTEMD STARTUP AND CONFIGURATION

$ **systemd-analyze --user dump**
Manager: systemd 256.12 (256.12-1.fc41)
Features: +PAM +AUDIT +SELINUX -APPARMOR +IMA +SMACK +SECCOMP
-GCRYPT +GNUTLS +OPENSSL +ACL +BLKID +CURL +ELFUTILS +FIDO>
Timestamp userspace: Fri 2025-03-14 09:48:17 EDT
Timestamp finish: Fri 2025-03-14 09:48:17 EDT
Timestamp generators-start: Fri 2025-03-14 09:48:17 EDT
Timestamp generators-finish: Fri 2025-03-14 09:48:17 EDT
Timestamp units-load-start: Fri 2025-03-14 09:48:17 EDT
Timestamp units-load-finish: Fri 2025-03-14 09:48:17 EDT
Timestamp units-load: Sat 2025-03-15 14:37:50 EDT
Subscribed: :1.206
Subscribed: :1.2
→ Unit blockdev@dev-mapper-vg01\x2dusr.target:
Description: blockdev@dev-mapper-vg01\x2dusr.target
Instance: dev-mapper-vg01\x2dusr
Unit Load State: not-found
Unit Active State: inactive
State Change Timestamp: Fri 2025-03-14 09:48:22 EDT
Inactive Exit Timestamp: n/a
Active Enter Timestamp: n/a
Active Exit Timestamp: n/a
Inactive Enter Timestamp: n/a
May GC: yes
Need Daemon Reload: no
Transient: no
Perpetual: no
Garbage Collection Mode: inactive
Before: usr.mount (destination-mountinfo)
ReferencedBy: usr.mount (destination-mountinfo)
→ Unit background.slice:

CHAPTER 15   ANALYZING SYSTEMD STARTUP AND CONFIGURATION

```
Description: User Background Tasks Slice
Instance: n/a
Unit Load State: loaded
Unit Active State: active
State Change Timestamp: Fri 2025-03-14 09:48:22 EDT
Inactive Exit Timestamp: Fri 2025-03-14 09:48:22 EDT
Active Enter Timestamp: Fri 2025-03-14 09:48:22 EDT
Active Exit Timestamp: n/a
Inactive Enter Timestamp: n/a
<SNIP>
```

Take some time to explore the data provided by these commands. I found a lot of interesting information here.

Analytic Graphs

Most pointy-haired bosses (PHBs)—and many good managers—find pretty graphs easy to read and easier to understand than the text-based system performance data I usually prefer to work with. Sometimes even I like a good graph, and **systemd-analyze** provides the capability to display boot and startup data in an *.svg vector graphics chart.

EXPERIMENT 15-5: CREATING ANALYTIC GRAPHS

The command below generates a vector graphics file that displays the events that take place during boot and startup. It takes a few seconds to generate this file.

$ **systemd-analyze plot > /tmp/bootup.svg**

CHAPTER 15 ANALYZING SYSTEMD STARTUP AND CONFIGURATION

The svg file created by the preceding command is a text file that defines a series of graphic vectors that are used by a number of applications to generate a graph. The svg files created by this command can be processed to create an image by a number of svg-capable applications such as Image Viewer, Ristretto, Okular, Eye of Mate, LibreOffice Draw, and others.

I used LibreOffice Draw to render the graph. The graph is huge, and you need to zoom in considerably to make out any detail. Figure 15-1 shows a small portion of the resulting graph.

Figure 15-1. The bootup.svg file displayed in LibreOffice Draw

The bootup sequence is to the left of the zero (0) point on the time line in the graph, and the startup sequence is to the right of zero. This small portion shows the kernel and initrd and the processes started by initrd.

This graph shows at a glance what started when, how long it took to start up, and the major dependencies. The critical path is highlighted in red.

CHAPTER 15   ANALYZING SYSTEMD STARTUP AND CONFIGURATION

Another command that generates graphical output is the systemd-analyze plot which generates textual dependency graph descriptions in dot format. The resulting data stream is then piped through the **dot** utility which is part of a family of programs that can be used to generate vector graphic files from various types of data. The resulting svg file can be viewed by same svg tools listed previously.

First, generate the file. This took almost nine minutes on my primary workstation.

```
$ time systemd-analyze dot | dot -Tsvg > /tmp/test.svg
    Color legend: black     = Requires
                  dark blue = Requisite
                  dark grey = Wants
                  red       = Conflicts
                  green     = After
real    8m37.544s
user    8m35.375s
sys     0m0.070s
[root@david ~]#
```

I won't reproduce the resulting graph here because it's pretty much spaghetti. But you should definitely try this and view the result yourself to see what I mean.

Conditionals

One of the more interesting yet somewhat generic capabilities I discovered while reading the man page for systemd-analyze(1) is the **condition** sub-command. This condition sub-command can be used to test the various conditions and asserts that can be used in systemd unit files.

EXPERIMENT 15-6: USING CONDITIONALS TO TEST SYSTEMD UNIT FILES

This command can also be used in scripts to evaluate one or more conditions and return a zero (0) if all are met or a 1 if any condition is not met. In either case, it also spews text indicating its findings.

The example in the man page is a bit complex, but the one I have concocted for this experiment is less so. It is testing for a kernel version greater than 5.1 and that the host is running on AC power. I have added the echo $? statement to print the return code.

```
$ systemd-analyze condition 'ConditionACPower=|true'
'ConditionKernelVersion = >=5.1' ; echo $?
test.service: ConditionKernelVersion=>=5.1 succeeded.
test.service: ConditionACPower=|true succeeded.
Conditions succeeded.
0
```

The return code of zero (0) indicates that all conditions that were tested for were met. The list of conditions and asserts can be found starting on about line 600 on the systemd.unit(5) man page.

Listing Configuration Files

I frequently find it useful to examine the content of systemd unit and other configuration files. The systemd-analyze tool provides us with a means of sending the contents of various configuration files to STDOUT.

CHAPTER 15   ANALYZING SYSTEMD STARTUP AND CONFIGURATION

EXPERIMENT 15-7: EXAMINING SYSTEMD CONFIGURATION FILES

Let's start by looking at the display manager service. The **cat-config** sub-command is used for this. The base directory for this command is /etc/.

```
[root@david ~]# systemd-analyze cat-config systemd/system/
display-manager.service
# /etc/systemd/system/display-manager.service
[Unit]
Description=LXDM (Lightweight X11 Display Manager)
#Documentation=man:lxdm(8)
Conflicts=getty@tty1.service
After=systemd-user-sessions.service getty@tty1.service
plymouth-quit.service livesys-late.service
#Conflicts=plymouth-quit.service

[Service]
ExecStart=/usr/sbin/lxdm
Restart=always
IgnoreSIGPIPE=no
#BusName=org.freedesktop.lxdm

[Install]
Alias=display-manager.service
[root@david ~]#
```

I find that to be a lot of typing to do little more than a standard cat command. It does, however, render the data stream with syntax colors that make the files easier to read. The cat command doesn't do that.

The syntax I do find a bit helpful is this next one. It can at least search out all of the files with the specified pattern within the standard systemd locations.

```
$ systemctl cat basic*
# /usr/lib/systemd/system/basic.target
#   SPDX-License-Identifier: LGPL-2.1-or-later
#
#  This file is part of systemd.
#
#  systemd is free software; you can redistribute it and/or
   modify it
#  under the terms of the GNU Lesser General Public License
   as published by
#  the Free Software Foundation; either version 2.1 of the
   License, or
#  (at your option) any later version.

[Unit]
Description=Basic System
Documentation=man:systemd.special(7)
Requires=sysinit.target
Wants=sockets.target timers.target paths.target slices.target
After=sysinit.target sockets.target paths.target slices.target tmp.mount

# We support /var, /tmp, /var/tmp, being on NFS, but we don't pull in
# remote-fs.target by default, hence pull them in explicitly here. Note that we
# require /var and /var/tmp, but only add a Wants= type dependency on /tmp, as
# we support that unit being masked, and this should not be considered an error.
RequiresMountsFor=/var /var/tmp
Wants=tmp.mount
```

Both of these commands preface the contents of each file with a comment line containing the full path and name of the file.

Unit File Verification

After creating a new unit file, it can be helpful to verify that it is at least syntactically correct. That is what the verify sub-command does. It can list directives that are spelled incorrectly and call out missing service units.

> **EXPERIMENT 15-8: VERIFYING SYSTEMD UNIT FILES**
>
> The backup.service unit is one that I created, so it won't be present on your systems. For now, just know that this command works as it is supposed to.
>
> `# systemd-analyze verify /etc/systemd/system/backup.service`
>
> Adhering to the Linux philosophy tenet, "silence is golden," a lack of output messages means that there are no errors in the scanned file.

Security

The security sub-command checks the security level of specified services. It only works on service units and not on other types of unit files. So let's check the NetworkManager service unit.

CHAPTER 15　ANALYZING SYSTEMD STARTUP AND CONFIGURATION

EXPERIMENT 15-9: SECURITY CHECKS

[root@david ~]# **systemd-analyze security NetworkManager.service**

NAME DESCRIPTION	..
✕ RootDirectory=/RootImage= Service runs within the host's root directory	0.1
SupplementaryGroups= Service runs as root, option does not matter	
RemoveIPC= Service runs as root, option does not apply	
✕ User=/DynamicUser= Service runs as root user	0.4
✓ NoNewPrivileges= Service processes may acquire new privileges	0.2
✓ CapabilityBoundingSet=~CAP_SYS_TIME Service processes cannot change the system clock	
✓ AmbientCapabilities= Service process does not receive ambient capabilities	
✕ PrivateDevices= Service potentially has access to hardware devices	0.2
✕ ProtectClock= Service may write to the hardware clock or system clock	0.2
✕ CapabilityBoundingSet=~CAP_KILL Service may send UNIX signals to arbitrary processes	0.1
✕ ProtectKernelLogs= Service may read from or write to the kernel log ring buffer	0.2

<SNIP>

→ Overall exposure level for NetworkManager.service: 7.8 EXPOSED 🙀

lines 40-83/83 (END)

Yes, the emoji is part of the output. I ran this program against several services, including my own backup service, and the results may differ, but the bottom line seems to be mostly the same—EXPOSED or UNSAFE. But, of course, most services need pretty much complete access to everything in order to perform their work.

This tool would be very useful for checking and fixing user space service units in security-critical environments. Developers will find it useful in identifying the areas that they should concentrate on when securing services as much as possible. I don't think it has much to offer for most of us who work as SysAdmins.

Summary

This chapter explored the use of various tools that we can use to analyze systemd startup. We learned how to analyze the boot and startup and to determine which services were taking the longest to start.

We looked at using the critical chain and analytic graphics to determine which services were the ones to be concerned with when tuning startup performance. The **systemd-analyze verify** tool can be used to ensure that unit files we create at least conform to syntactical and functional constructs correct for systemd.

Security is always a concern, and we learned how to check the security stance of systemd service unit files. This is an interesting exercise because so many system services need to run as root or with elevated levels of access.

CHAPTER 15 ANALYZING SYSTEMD STARTUP AND CONFIGURATION

Exercises

Complete the following exercises to finish this chapter:

1. How long does your host take to get through BIOS boot?

2. What two services take the longest to start?

3. Display any kernel messages that are Warning or Info class.

4. Are there any Error class messages at all in the journals?

CHAPTER 16

Why I Support the systemd Plan to Take Over the World

Introduction

Over the last 15 years or so, I've read many articles and posts about how systemd is trying to replace everything and take over everything in Linux. I agree; it is taking over pretty much everything.

But not really "everything-everything." Just "everything" in that middle ground of services that lies between the kernel and things like the GNU core utilities, graphical user interface desktops, and user applications.

Examining Linux's structure is a way to explore this. Figure 16-1 shows the three basic software layers found in the operating system. The bottom is the Linux kernel; the middle layer consists of services that may perform startup tasks, such as launching various other services like Network Time Protocol (NTP), Dynamic Host Configuration Protocol (DHCP), Domain Name System (DNS), secure shell (SSH), device management, login services, gettys, NetworkManager, journal and log management, logical volume management, printing, kernel module management, local and remote filesystems, sound and video, display management, swap space, system statistics collection, and much more. There are also tens of thousands of new and powerful applications at the top layer.

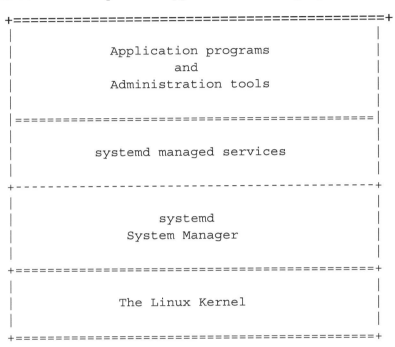

Figure 16-1. *systemd and the services it manages with respect to the kernel and application programs, including SysAdmin tools (David Both, CC BY-SA 4.0)*

This diagram, as well as the collective experience of many SysAdmins over the last several years, makes it clear that systemd is indeed intended to completely replace the old SystemV init system. But I also know that it significantly extends the capabilities of the init system.

It is also important to recognize that, although Linus Torvalds rewrote the Unix kernel as an exercise, he did nothing to change the middle layer

CHAPTER 16   WHY I SUPPORT THE SYSTEMD PLAN TO TAKE OVER THE WORLD

of system services. He simply recompiled SystemV init to work with his completely new kernel. SystemV is much older than Linux and has needed a complete change to something totally new for decades.

So the kernel is new and is refreshed frequently through the leadership of Torvalds and the work of thousands of programmers around the planet. But until recently, there have been no significant enhancements to the init system and management of system services.

In authoring systemd, Lennart Poettering[1] has done for system services what Linus Torvalds did for the kernel. Like Torvalds and the Linux kernel, Poettering has become the leader and arbiter of what happens inside this middle system services layer. And I like what I see.

More Data for the Admin

The new capabilities of systemd include far more status information about services, whether they're running or not. I like having more information about the services I am trying to monitor. For example, look at the DHCPD service. Were I to use the SystemV command, `service dhcpd status`, I would get a simple message that the service is running or stopped. Using the systemd command, `systemctl status dhcpd`, I get much more useful information.

This data is from the server on my personal network.

```
[root@yorktown ~]# systemctl status dhcpd
● dhcpd.service - DHCPv4 Server Daemon
    Loaded: loaded (/usr/lib/systemd/system/dhcpd.service;
            enabled; vendor preset: disabled)
    Active: active (running) since Fri 2021-04-09 21:43:41
            EDT; 4 days ago
```

---
[1] Wikipedia, "Lennart Poettering," https://en.wikipedia.org/wiki/Lennart_Poettering

CHAPTER 16 WHY I SUPPORT THE SYSTEMD PLAN TO TAKE OVER THE WORLD

```
     Docs: man:dhcpd(8)
           man:dhcpd.conf(5)
 Main PID: 1385 (dhcpd)
   Status: "Dispatching packets..."
    Tasks: 1 (limit: 9382)
   Memory: 3.6M
      CPU: 240ms
   CGroup: /system.slice/dhcpd.service
           └─1385 /usr/sbin/dhcpd -f -cf /etc/dhcp/dhcpd.
           conf -user dhcpd -group dhcpd --no-pid

Apr 14 20:51:01 yorktown.both.org dhcpd[1385]: DHCPREQUEST for
192.168.0.7 from e0:d5:5e:a2:de:a4 via eno1
Apr 14 20:51:01 yorktown.both.org dhcpd[1385]: DHCPACK on
192.168.0.7 to e0:d5:5e:a2:de:a4 via eno1
Apr 14 20:51:14 yorktown.both.org dhcpd[1385]: DHCPREQUEST for
192.168.0.8 from e8:40:f2:3d:0e:a8 via eno1
Apr 14 20:51:14 yorktown.both.org dhcpd[1385]: DHCPACK on
192.168.0.8 to e8:40:f2:3d:0e:a8 via eno1
Apr 14 20:51:14 yorktown.both.org dhcpd[1385]: DHCPREQUEST for
192.168.0.201 from 80:fa:5b:63:37:88 via eno1
Apr 14 20:51:14 yorktown.both.org dhcpd[1385]: DHCPACK on
192.168.0.201 to 80:fa:5b:63:37:88 via eno1
Apr 14 20:51:24 yorktown.both.org dhcpd[1385]: DHCPREQUEST for
192.168.0.6 from e0:69:95:45:c4:cd via eno1
Apr 14 20:51:24 yorktown.both.org dhcpd[1385]: DHCPACK on
192.168.0.6 to e0:69:95:45:c4:cd via eno1
Apr 14 20:52:41 yorktown.both.org dhcpd[1385]: DHCPREQUEST for
192.168.0.5 from 00:1e:4f:df:3a:d7 via eno1
Apr 14 20:52:41 yorktown.both.org dhcpd[1385]: DHCPACK on
192.168.0.5 to 00:1e:4f:df:3a:d7 via eno1
[root@yorktown ~]#
```

CHAPTER 16   WHY I SUPPORT THE SYSTEMD PLAN TO TAKE OVER THE WORLD

Having all this information available in a single command is empowering and simplifies problem determination for me. I get more information right at the start. I not only see that the service is up and running but also some of the most recent log entries.

Here is another example that uses a non-operating-system tool. BOINC,[2] the Berkeley Open Infrastructure Network Computing Client, is used to create ad hoc supercomputers out of millions of home computers around the world that are signed up to participate in the computational stages of many types of scientific studies. I am signed up with the World Community Grid[3] and participate in studies about COVID-19, mapping cancer markers, rainfall in Africa, and more.

The information from this command gives me a more complete picture of how this service is faring.

```
[root@yorktown ~]# systemctl status boinc-client.service
● boinc-client.service - Berkeley Open Infrastructure Network
Computing Client
     Loaded: loaded (/usr/lib/systemd/system/boinc-client.
             service; enabled; vendor preset: disabled)
     Active: active (running) since Fri 2021-04-09 21:43:41
             EDT; 4 days ago
       Docs: man:boinc(1)
   Main PID: 1389 (boinc)
      Tasks: 18 (limit: 9382)
     Memory: 1.1G
        CPU: 1month 1w 2d 3h 42min 47.398s
```

---

[2] UC Berkeley, BOINC, https://boinc.berkeley.edu/
[3] World Community Grid, https://www.worldcommunitygrid.org/

CHAPTER 16   WHY I SUPPORT THE SYSTEMD PLAN TO TAKE OVER THE WORLD

```
     CGroup: /system.slice/boinc-client.service
             ├─ 1389 /usr/bin/boinc
             ├─712591 ../../projects/www.worldcommunitygrid.
org/wcgrid_mcm1_map_7.43_x86_64-pc-linux-gnu -SettingsFile
MCM1_0174482_7101.txt -DatabaseFile dataset>
             ├─712614 ../../projects/www.worldcommunitygrid.
org/wcgrid_mcm1_map_7.43_x86_64-pc-linux-gnu -SettingsFile
MCM1_0174448_7280.txt -DatabaseFile dataset>
             ├─713275 ../../projects/www.worldcommunitygrid.
org/wcgrid_opn1_autodock_7.17_x86_64-pc-linux-gnu -jobs
OPN1_0040707_05092.job -input OPN1_0040707_050>
             ├─713447 ../../projects/www.worldcommunitygrid.
org/wcgrid_mcm1_map_7.43_x86_64-pc-linux-gnu -SettingsFile
MCM1_0174448_2270.txt -DatabaseFile dataset>
             ├─713517 ../../projects/www.worldcommunitygrid.
org/wcgrid_opn1_autodock_7.17_x86_64-pc-linux-gnu -jobs
OPN1_0040871_00826.job -input OPN1_0040871_008>
             ├─713657 ../../projects/www.worldcommunitygrid.
org/wcgrid_mcm1_map_7.43_x86_64-pc-linux-gnu -SettingsFile
MCM1_0174525_7317.txt -DatabaseFile dataset>
             ├─713672 ../../projects/www.worldcommunitygrid.
org/wcgrid_mcm1_map_7.43_x86_64-pc-linux-gnu -SettingsFile
MCM1_0174529_1537.txt -DatabaseFile dataset>
             └─714586 ../../projects/www.worldcommunitygrid.
org/wcgrid_opn1_autodock_7.17_x86_64-pc-linux-gnu -jobs
OPN1_0040864_01640.job -input OPN1_0040864_016>

Apr 14 19:57:16 yorktown.both.org boinc[1389]: 14-
Apr-2021 19:57:16 [World Community Grid] Finished upload of
OPN1_0040707_05063_0_r181439640_0
```

CHAPTER 16   WHY I SUPPORT THE SYSTEMD PLAN TO TAKE OVER THE WORLD

```
Apr 14 20:57:36 yorktown.both.org boinc[1389]: 14-Apr-2021
20:57:36 [World Community Grid] Sending scheduler request: To
report completed tasks.
Apr 14 20:57:36 yorktown.both.org boinc[1389]: 14-Apr-2021
20:57:36 [World Community Grid] Reporting 1 completed tasks
Apr 14 20:57:36 yorktown.both.org boinc[1389]: 14-Apr-2021
20:57:36 [World Community Grid] Not requesting tasks: don't
need (job cache full)
Apr 14 20:57:38 yorktown.both.org boinc[1389]: 14-Apr-2021
20:57:38 [World Community Grid] Scheduler request completed
Apr 14 20:57:38 yorktown.both.org boinc[1389]: 14-Apr-2021
20:57:38 [World Community Grid] Project requested delay of
121 seconds
Apr 14 21:38:03 yorktown.both.org boinc[1389]: 14-Apr-2021
21:38:03 [World Community Grid] Computation for task
MCM1_0174482_7657_1 finished
Apr 14 21:38:03 yorktown.both.org boinc[1389]: 14-
Apr-2021 21:38:03 [World Community Grid] Starting task
OPN1_0040864_01640_0
Apr 14 21:38:05 yorktown.both.org boinc[1389]: 14-
Apr-2021 21:38:05 [World Community Grid] Started upload of
MCM1_0174482_7657_1_r1768267288_0
Apr 14 21:38:09 yorktown.both.org boinc[1389]: 14-
Apr-2021 21:38:09 [World Community Grid] Finished upload of
MCM1_0174482_7657_1_r1768267288_0
[root@yorktown ~]#
```

The key is that the BOINC client runs as a daemon and should be managed by the init system. All software that runs as a daemon should be managed by systemd. In fact, even software that still provides SystemV start scripts is managed by systemd.

CHAPTER 16   WHY I SUPPORT THE SYSTEMD PLAN TO TAKE OVER THE WORLD

systemd Standardizes Configuration

One of the problems I have had over the years is that, even though "Linux is Linux", not all distributions store their configuration files in the same places or use the same names or even formats. With the huge numbers of Linux hosts in the world, that lack of standardization is a problem. I have also encountered horrible config files and SystemV startup files created by developers trying to jump on the Linux bandwagon and who have no idea how to create software for Linux—and especially services that must be included in the Linux startup sequence.

The systemd unit files standardize configuration and enforce a startup methodology and organization that provides a level of safety from poorly written SystemV start scripts. They also provide tools that the SysAdmin can use to monitor and manage services.

In April 2011, Lennart Poettering wrote a short blog post describing standard names and locations[4] for common critical systemd configuration files. This standardization makes the SysAdmin's job easier. It also makes it easier to automate administrative tasks in environments with multiple Linux distributions. Developers also benefit from this standardization.

Sometimes, the Pain

Any undertaking as massive as replacing and extending an entire init system will cause some level of pain during the transition. I don't mind learning the new commands and how to create configuration files of various types, such as targets, timers, and so on. It does take some work, but I think the results are well worth the effort.

---

[4] Poettering, Lennart, Blog entry, *The New Configuration Files*, http://0pointer.de/blog/projects/the-new-configuration-files

New configuration files and changes in the subsystems that own and manage them can also seem daunting at first. Not to mention that sometimes new tools such as systemd-resolved can break the way things have worked for a long time, as I point out in my article, *"Resolve systemd-resolved name-service failures with Ansible."*[5]

Tools like scripts and Ansible can mitigate the pain while we wait for changes that resolve the pain.

Five Reasons SysAdmins Love systemd

> **Author's Note** This section was originally published as an article on Opensource.com,[6] by Seth Kenlon, my technical reviewer for this book. It makes a great finale to this book, and it's included here with his permission.

systemd's speed and ease make it a popular way to manage modern Linux systems.

As systems administrators know, there's a lot happening on modern computers. Applications run in the background, automated events wait to be triggered at a certain time, log files are written, and status reports are delivered. Traditionally, these disparate processes have been managed and monitored with a collection of Unix tools to great effect and with great efficiency. However, modern computers are diverse, with local services running alongside containerized applications, easy access to clouds and the clusters they run on, real-time processes, and more data to process than ever.

---

[5] Both, David, "Resolve systemd-resolved name-service failures with Ansible," https://www.both.org/?p=3889

[6] Opensource.com is no longer active and no new articles have been published there since Red Hat abandoned it in early 2023.

Having a unified method of managing them is an expectation for users and a useful luxury for busy SysAdmins. For this nontrivial task, the system daemon, or **systemd**, was developed and quickly adopted by all major Linux distributions.

Of course, systemd isn't the only way to manage a Linux system. There are many alternative init systems, including sysvinit, OpenRC, runit, s6, and even BusyBox, but systemd treats Linux as a unified dataset, meant to be manipulated and queried consistently with robust tools. For a busy systems administrator and many users, the speed and ease of systemd is an important feature. Here are five reasons why.

Boot Management

Booting a Linux computer can be a surprisingly rare event, if you want it to be. Certainly in the server world, uptimes are often counted in *years* rather than months or weeks. Laptops and desktops tend to be shut down and booted pretty frequently, although even these are as likely to be suspended or hibernated as they are to be shut down. Either way, the time since the most recent boot event can serve as a sort of session manager for a computer health check. It's a useful way to limit what data you look at when monitoring your system or diagnosing problems.

In the likely event that you can't remember the last time you booted your computer, you can list boot sessions with systemd's logging tool, journalctl:

```
$ journalctl --list-boots
-42 7fe7c3... Fri 2020-12-04 05:13:59 - Wed 2020-12-16 16:01:23
-41 332e99... Wed 2020-12-16 20:07:39 - Fri 2020-12-18 22:08:13
[...]
 -1 e0fe5f... Mon 2021-03-29 20:47:46 - Mon 2021-03-29 21:59:29
  0 37fbe4... Tue 2021-03-30 04:46:13 - Tue 2021-03-30 10:42:08
```

CHAPTER 16   WHY I SUPPORT THE SYSTEMD PLAN TO TAKE OVER THE WORLD

The latest boot sessions appear at the bottom of the list, so you can pipe the output to `tail` for just the latest boots.

The numbers on the left (42, 41, 1, and 0 in this example) are index numbers for each boot session. In other words, to view logs for only a specific boot session, you can use its index number as reference.

Log Reviews

Looking at logs is an important method of extrapolating information about your system. Logs provide a history of much of the activity your computer engages in without your direct supervision. You can see when services launched, when timed jobs ran, what services are running in the background, which activities failed, and more. One of the most common initial troubleshooting steps is to review logs, which is easy to do with `journalctl`:

```
$ journalctl --pager-end
```

The `--pager-end` (or `-e` for short) option starts your view of the logs at the end of the `journalctl` output, so you must scroll up to see events that happened earlier.

systemd maintains a "catalog" of errors and messages filled with records of errors, possible solutions, pointers to support forums, and developer documentation. This can provide important context to a log event, which can otherwise be a confusing blip in a sea of messages or, worse, could go entirely unnoticed. To integrate error messages with explanatory text, you can use the `--catalog` (or `-x` for short) option:

```
$ journalctl --pager-end --catalog
```

To further limit the log output you need to wade through, you can specify which boot session you want to see logs for. Because each boot session is indexed, you can specify certain sessions with the `--boot` option and view only the logs that apply to it:

```
$ journalctl --pager-end --catalog --boot 42
```

You can also see logs for a specific systemd unit. For instance, to troubleshoot an issue with your secure shell (SSH) service, you can specify `--unit sshd` to see only the logs that apply to the `sshd` daemon:

```
$ journalctl --pager-end \
--catalog --boot 42 \
--unit sshd
```

Service Management

The first task for systemd is to boot your computer, and it generally does that promptly, efficiently, and effectively. But the task that's never finished is service management. By design, systemd ensures that the services you want to run do indeed start and continue running during your session. This is nicely robust, because in theory even a crashed service can be restarted without your intervention.

Your interface to help systemd manage services is the `systemctl` command. With it, you can view the unit files that define a service:

```
$ systemctl cat sshd
# /usr/lib/systemd/system/sshd.service
[Unit]
Description=OpenSSH server daemon
Documentation=man:sshd(8) man:sshd_config(5)
After=network.target sshd-keygen.target
Wants=sshd-keygen.target
```

CHAPTER 16   WHY I SUPPORT THE SYSTEMD PLAN TO TAKE OVER THE WORLD

```
[Service]
Type=notify
EnvironmentFile=-/etc/crypto-policies/back-ends/
opensshserver.config
EnvironmentFile=-/etc/sysconfig/sshd
ExecStart=/usr/sbin/sshd -D $OPTIONS $CRYPTO_POLICY
ExecReload=/bin/kill -HUP $MAINPID
KillMode=process
Restart=on-failure
RestartSec=42s

[Install]
WantedBy=multi-user.target
```

Most unit files exist in `/usr/lib/systemd/system/`, but, as with many important configurations, you're encouraged to modify them with local changes. There's an interface for that, too:

```
$ systemctl edit sshd
```

You can see whether a service is currently active:

```
$ systemctl is-active sshd
active
$ systemctl is-active foo
inactive
```

Similarly, you can see whether a service has failed with `is-failed`. Starting and stopping services are nicely intuitive:

```
$ systemctl stop sshd
$ systemctl start sshd
```

421

And enabling a service to start at boot time is simple:

```
$ systemctl enable sshd
```

Add the `--now` option to enable a service to start at boot time or to start it for your current session.

Timers

Long ago, when you wanted to automate a task on Linux, the canonical tool for the job was `cron`. There's still a place for the cron command, but there are also some compelling alternatives. For instance, the `anacron`[7] command is a versatile, cron-like system capable of running tasks that otherwise would have been missed during downtime.

Scheduled events are little more than services activated at a specific time, so systemd manages a cron-like function called timers.[8] You can list active timers:

```
$ systemctl list-timers
NEXT                            LEFT
Tue 2021-03-30 12:37:54 NZDT    16min left [...]
Wed 2021-03-31 00:00:00 NZDT    11h left [...]
Wed 2021-03-31 06:42:02 NZDT    18h left [...]

3 timers listed.
Pass --all to see loaded but inactive timers, too.
```

You can enable a timer the same way you enable a service:

```
$ systemctl enable myMonitor.timer
```

---

[7] Both, David, *How I use cron in Linux*, https://www.both.org/?p=3685
[8] Both, David, *systemd — #7: Use systemd timers instead of cronjobs*, https://www.both.org/?p=3862

Targets

Targets are the final major component of the systemd matrix. A target is defined by a unit file, the same as services and timers. Targets can also be started and enabled in the same way. What makes targets unique is that they group other unit files in an arbitrarily significant way. For instance, you might want to boot to a text console instead of a graphical desktop, so the `multi-user` target exists. However, the `multi-user` target is only the `graphical` target without the desktop unit files as dependencies.

In short, targets are an easy way for you to collect services, timers, and even other targets together to represent an intended state for your machine.

In fact, within systemd, a reboot, a power-off, or a shutdown action is just another target.

You can list all available targets using the `list-unit-files` option, constraining it with the `--type` option set to `target`:

```
$ systemctl list-unit-files --type target
```

Taking Control with systemd

Modern Linux uses systemd for service management and log introspection. It provides everything from personal Linux systems to enterprise servers with a modern mechanism for monitoring and easy maintenance. The more you use it, the more systemd becomes comfortably predictable and intuitive, and the more you discover how disparate parts of your system are interconnected.

To get better acquainted with systemd, you must use it. And to get comfortable with using it, download our cheat sheet[9] and refer to it often.

---

[9] Kenlon, Seth, *Linux systemd cheat sheet*, https://opensource.com/downloads/linux-systemd-cheat-sheet

CHAPTER 16   WHY I SUPPORT THE SYSTEMD PLAN TO TAKE OVER THE WORLD

Final Exercise

This is the last exercise in this book, and it's a bit different because there's no list of tasks or questions. It's a simple suggestion that you spend time exploring systemd and its many facets and learn as much more about it as you can.

Follow your curiosity wherever it leads. Create your own experiments and use them to guide your explorations.

APPENDIX A

systemd Resources

There is a great deal of information about systemd available on the Internet, but much is terse, obtuse, or even misleading. The following web pages offer detailed and reliable information about systemd startup:

- The systemd.unit(5) manual page contains a nice list of unit file sections and their configuration options, along with concise descriptions of each.
  - https://man7.org/linux/man-pages/man5/systemd.unit.5.html
- Fedora Magazine has a good description of the unit file structure as well as other important information.
  - https://fedoramagazine.org/systemd-getting-a-grip-on-units/
- For detailed technical information about systemd and the reasons for creating it, check out Freedesktop.org's description of systemd. This page is one of the best I have found because it contains many links to other important and accurate documentation.
  - https://www.freedesktop.org/wiki/Software/systemd/

APPENDIX A   SYSTEMD RESOURCES

- Linux.com's "More systemd fun" offers more advanced systemd information and tips.
    - `https://www.linux.com/training-tutorials/more-systemd-fun-blame-game-and-stopping-services-prejudice/`
- The Fedora Project has a good, practical guide to systemd. It has pretty much everything you need to know in order to configure, manage, and maintain a Fedora computer using systemd.
    - `https://docs.fedoraproject.org/en-US/quick-docs/systemd-understanding-and-administering/`
- For detailed technical information about systemd and the reasons for creating it, check out systemd.io's description of systemd.
    - `https://systemd.io/`

There is also a series of deeply technical articles for Linux SysAdmins by Lennart Poettering, the designer and primary developer of systemd. These articles were written between April 2010 and September 2011, but they are just as relevant now as they were then.

- Rethinking PID 1
    - `http://0pointer.de/blog/projects/systemd.html`
- systemd for Administrators, Part I
    - `http://0pointer.de/blog/projects/systemd-for-admins-1.html`

- systemd for Administrators, Part II

  - http://0pointer.de/blog/projects/systemd-for-admins-2.html

- systemd for Administrators, Part III

  - http://0pointer.de/blog/projects/systemd-for-admins-3.html

- systemd for Administrators, Part IV

  - http://0pointer.de/blog/projects/systemd-for-admins-4.html

- systemd for Administrators, Part V

  - http://0pointer.de/blog/projects/three-levels-of-off.html

- systemd for Administrators, Part VI

  - http://0pointer.de/blog/projects/changing-roots

- systemd for Administrators, Part VII

  - http://0pointer.de/blog/projects/blame-game.html

- systemd for Administrators, Part VIII

  - http://0pointer.de/blog/projects/the-new-configuration-files.html

- systemd for Administrators, Part IX

  - http://0pointer.de/blog/projects/on-etc-sysinit.html

APPENDIX A   SYSTEMD RESOURCES

- systemd for Administrators, Part X
  - `http://0pointer.de/blog/projects/instances.html`
- systemd for Administrators, Part XI
  - `http://0pointer.de/blog/projects/inetd.html`

Index

A

ASCII
    ASCII file, 5, 289
    ASCII plain text, 119, 323, 326, 337
    ASCII text, 5, 226, 228, 253, 289
Automation
    automate everything, 6
    Bash scripts, 146
    scripts, 6, 146, 267

B

Backup
    remote, 327
    shell script, 216
Bash
    configuration files
        /.bash_logout, 64
    program, 195, 244, 358, 359
    shell scripts, 368
BIOS
    POST, 25, 29, 358, 388
    UEFI, 3, 25–27, 29
Books
    "The Art of Unix Programming", 226
    "The Unix Philosophy", 226

Boot, 2–3, 25–26, 28, 70, 358–359, 418–419
Boot record, 2, 29

C

Chrony, 150, 151, 154, 156, 164, 176
Chronyc, 150, 154, 155, 162–164
Chronyd, 149, 150, 154, 165, 169
Code
    source, 4, 21
Command line
    interface, 16, 38, 63–64, 74, 79, 150
    recall and editing, 164
Command prompt, 61, 163
Comments, 48, 49, 170, 299, 346, 349, 360
Common Unix Printing System (CUPS)
Console
    virtual, 45, 57, 59–61, 63, 316
CPU
    usage, 306
cron
    crond, 120
    crontab, 182, 183, 212
Curiosity, 371, 424

INDEX

D

D-bus, 8, 91, 92
Directory
    home, 121, 243
    listing, 42, 43, 80, 81, 249
DNF, 33
Domain
    domain name, 162, 319, 323, 326, 351
    FQDN, 159, 323, 332, 351
Domain Name System/Domain Name Services (DNS), 9, 162, 262, 293, 320, 324, 327, 329, 337, 346, 350, 355, 377, 409
Drive
    hard, 33, 119, 123, 246, 306
    SSD, 25, 26, 201, 215, 306, 373
    USB, 25, 26, 76, 224, 256, 285
Dynamic Host Configuration Protocol (DHCP)
    client configuration, 151

E

example.com, 258, 292, 327, 355

F

Fail2Ban, 255, 298–302
Fedora, 6, 17, 39, 47, 57, 70, 118, 128, 139, 151–153, 155, 164, 196, 261, 263, 330, 343, 345–346, 360, 426

Firewall
    firewalld, 256, 259–266, 279, 283, 287–289, 295–298, 300, 303
    iptables, 259, 261–263, 285, 287, 298, 301
    netfilter, 260, 261, 266
    rules
        adding, 259
        managing, 261
Fully qualified domain name (FQDN), 159, 323, 332, 351

G

GRUB, 27–29, 33, 46, 59, 65, 69–73
GRUB2, 24, 28, 29, 32, 33, 358
GUID, 26, 29–30, 32
GUID Partition Table (GPT), 26, 29–30

H

Help
    facility, 238, 239, 372, 376
HTTP, 257, 258, 293
HTTPD, 377, 378, 380–383, 385

I

IPTables, 120, 259–263, 283, 285, 287, 289, 298, 300, 301

INDEX

J

Journal
  EXT4 filesystem, 134
  systemd, 68, 71, 72, 88, 89, 154, 180, 181, 183, 186, 187, 220-222, 224-226, 348, 364, 365, 371, 373
journalctl, 68, 71, 72, 187, 191, 204, 220, 228-238, 247, 371, 373, 385, 419

K

Kenlon, S., 417, 423

L

Linux
  boot, 2-3, 24, 25, 28, 59, 221, 222, 358
Log files
  /var/log/messages, 71, 221
  /var/log/secure, 301
Logrotate, 215
Logwatch, 302

M

Man page, 17, 19, 20, 39-71, 73, 77, 91, 119, 120, 124, 128, 150, 180, 208, 210, 224-226, 352, 372, 383, 401, 402
Master boot record (MBR), 25-30, 32

Motherboard, 25, 148, 388, 390
Mount point, 91, 119, 123, 125, 133-135, 139

N

Name server
  caching, 262, 350
  root servers, 321
  top level, 321, 322
Name services
  BIND, 329, 345
  DNS database, 324
  Domain Name System (DNS), 320
  forwarder, 321
  named, 50
  name search, 319-322
  record types, 98
  resolver, 319-321, 329, 337, 345, 348
  root server, 321
  zone, 355
  zone file, 355
Network
  adapter, 285
  interface, 255, 264, 268, 270-272, 296, 304, 355
  interface card (NIC), 36, 123, 272-274, 380, 384
  NIC, 272-274
  port, 256
  startup, 17, 39, 111, 112, 172, 354

431

INDEX

NetworkManager, 9, 112, 120, 237, 238, 323, 336, 345, 346, 351, 354, 355, 386, 405, 409
Network Time Protocol (NTP)
 Chrony, 145, 147-165, 176, 375
 configuring, 151-153
 implementation choices, 150
 protocol, 9, 146, 148-153, 156-159, 162, 164, 165, 170, 172, 175-177, 293, 377, 409
 reference source, 162
 server, 146, 148-151, 153, 157-160, 164, 172, 176
 server hierarchy, 149
 sources, 158, 162
 stratum, 149, 157, 177
NFS
 filesystem, 16, 38
 mounting, 16, 38

O

Opensource.com, 417
Opensource.org, 320

P, Q

Philosophy
 Linux, 4, 94, 95, 140, 214, 405
 Unix, 226, 385
 Unix and Linux, 172, 226

Pipe, 121, 226, 227, 243, 419
Pointy-haired boss (PHB), 399
Power-on self-test (POST), 25, 29, 358, 388
Present working directory (PWD), 43, 82, 121, 126, 226, 243, 247, 270, 289, 298
proc filesystem
 proc, 126
Protocols
 DHC, 9, 151, 153, 293, 354-356, 409
 DNS, 330
 FTP, 257
 HTTP, 257, 258, 293
 HTTPS, 257
 IMAP, 293
 IP, 153, 162, 260, 298, 301, 302, 320-323, 326, 329, 330, 337, 351, 378, 380, 384
 NFS, 16, 38, 74
 NTP, 9, 146, 148-153, 156-159, 162, 164, 165, 170, 172, 175-177, 293, 377, 409
 SMTP, 293
 SSH, 9, 259, 278, 279, 409
 TCP, 260, 278, 279
 TCP/IP, 291
 Telnet, 279
Public/Private Keypairs (PPKP)
Python, 267

R

Raymond, E.S. (RMS), 226
Reboot, 45, 55, 68, 84, 85, 98,
    104–107, 112, 130, 138, 203,
    239, 263, 266, 272, 274, 293,
    298, 328, 365, 367, 368,
    372, 423
Recovery
    mode, 58, 65
Redirection, 70, 364
Repository
    Fedora, 151
Requirements, 17, 39, 45, 82, 83,
    208, 230, 303, 343, 383
Ritchie, D., 57, 58
Route
    default, 332
    gateway, 266
    router, 76, 158, 265, 266, 275,
        282, 293, 351, 354
Router, 76, 158, 265, 266, 275, 282,
    293, 351, 354

S

Secure shell (SSH)
    connection, 76, 257, 274
Security
    firewall, 256, 263, 302
    password, 26, 61, 300, 301, 343
    rootkit, 225
    SELinux, 88, 114
SELinux, 88, 114
SendMail, 238, 376, 377

Server
    BIND, 329, 345
    DHCPD, 340, 411
    email, 297
    name services, 293, 355, 356
    NTP, 146, 148–151, 153,
        157–160, 164, 172, 176
    SendMail, 238, 376, 377
    SSH, 257, 260, 262, 293
    web, 258, 260, 377
Sets, 175, 230, 259, 262, 266, 284,
    292, 296, 307, 356
Shebang, 360
Shell
    Bash, 315, 368
Sockets, 8, 20, 40, 91, 120, 132,
    279, 350
Software
    open source, 298
    proprietary, 262
State of North Carolina, 147
STDIO
    STDOUT, 70, 204, 207, 227,
        243, 402
Storage media
    disk drive, 26
    hard drive, 33, 119, 123, 246, 306
    HDD, 25, 26, 234, 373
    RAM, 19, 25, 32–34, 40, 225, 245,
        305–307, 388
    solid state drive (SSD), 25, 26,
        201, 215, 234, 306, 373
    USB external drive, 26
    USB thumb drive, 26

Stream
    data, 8, 34, 70, 72, 101, 103, 105, 130, 189, 227–229, 240, 338, 380, 401, 403
    text, 226
System Activity Report (SAR), 118, 123
System Administrator (SysAdmin), 4, 10, 58–60, 151, 202, 220, 224, 316, 326, 359, 390, 410
systemctl, 11, 20, 68, 92, 107, 117, 121–128, 264, 309, 343, 368, 420
systemd
    controversy, 3
    default target, 15, 16, 36, 37, 45, 73, 74, 110
    mounts, 15, 36, 117, 142
    services, 51, 63, 92, 121–128, 204, 343, 350, 358, 359, 361–363, 407
    targets, 15–17, 37, 38, 73, 74, 91
    timers, 8, 118, 147, 154, 181, 186, 191, 195–197, 208, 210–212, 215, 388
SystemV, 4, 6–7, 12, 16, 36–39, 73–76, 88, 131, 279, 306, 309, 377, 410, 411, 415, 416

T

Tab completion, 123
TCP, 72, 220, 231, 260, 276–279, 281, 282, 291, 300, 301
TCP/IP, 291
Terminal, 54, 57–63, 66, 69, 70, 109, 113, 114, 121, 123, 154, 164, 207, 229, 247, 258, 294, 316, 341, 392
Testing
    final, 362, 365
Time
    at, 8
    chrony, 154
    chronyc, 154
    chronyd, 154
    cron, 422
    date, 145–177
    hardware, 172
    NTP, 146, 148, 149, 153, 157, 160, 163, 167, 170
    servers
        public, 159
    system, 401
    zones, 148, 166–168, 172, 173, 175, 176, 184, 230, 274
Torvalds, L., 6, 10, 11, 410, 411

U

udev
    rule, 151
UDP, 276–279
Unified Extensible Firmware Interface (UEFI), 2, 3, 25, 27, 29
URL, 234, 258, 321
User

account, 63, 300
home directory, 121, 243
login, 61–63, 311
non-root, 19, 118, 183, 184, 197, 222, 223, 389, 390
password, 300, 343
student, 54
Utilities
core, 9, 409
GNU, 9, 337, 409

V, W, X, Y, Z

Variables
$?, 402
environment, 131, 339
$HOSTNAME, 339
$PATH, 359
unset, 131
Virtual
network, 324
network computing, 413
VirtualBox
Network Manager, 121
Volume
logical, 9, 32, 120, 133, 134, 143, 410
physical, 32
volume group, 133, 134